Supervising the Reflective Practitioner

...velopment as a reflective practitioner has become an essential quality for ...actitioners in the fields of health, education and social care. *Supervising the flective Practitioner* provides guidance for supervisors, focusing on what ...ey can do to facilitate the development of reflective practice in supervisees. This book contains a wide range of practical examples including personal ...counts and illustrations. Topics covered include:

what is reflective practice and why is it important now?
how reflective practice connects with personal and professional development
key issues in supervising reflective practice
methods that can be used in supervision.

...is accessible book will be of great interest to both supervisors and supervi-...es who practise clinically in a range of professions, including applied ...ychology, counselling, psychotherapy, psychiatry and nursing. It will also ...useful for professionals working in education, health, and social care who ...int to support supervisees in the development of reflective practice.

...yce Scaife, former Director of Clinical Practice for the Doctor of Clinical ...sychology training course at the University of Sheffield, is a clinical psych-...ogist with a career-long interest in supervision.

Supervising the Reflective Practitioner

An essential guide to theory and practice

Joyce Scaife

Routledge
Taylor & Francis Group

LONDON AND NEW YORK

First published 2010
by Routledge
27 Church Road, Hove, East Sussex, BN3 2FA

Simultaneously published in the USA and Canada
by Routledge
270 Madison Avenue, New York, NY 10016

*Routledge is an imprint of the Taylor & Francis Group,
an Informa business*

Typeset in Times by
RefineCatch Limited, Bungay, Suffolk
Printed and bound in Great Britain by
TJ International Ltd, Padstow, Cornwall

Paperback cover design by Andrew Ward

British Library Cataloguing in Publication Data
A catalogue record for this book is available
from the British Library

Library of Congress Cataloging-in-Publication Data
Scaife, Joyce, 1950–
    Supervising the reflective practitioner / Joyce Scaife.—1st ed.
       p. cm.
    1. Mental health personnel—Supervision of.   2. Reflection
    (Philosophy).   I. Title.
    RC459.S23 2010
    616.89′023—dc22   2010001976

ISBN: 978-0-415-47957-8 (hbk)
ISBN: 978-0-415-47958-5 (pbk)

Contents

Illustrations

Figures

Table

Preface

The Mexican Sierra has 'XVII-15-IX' spines in the dorsal fin. These can easily be counted, but if the sierra strikes hard on the line so that our hands are burned, if the fish sounds and nearly escapes and finally comes in over the rail, his colors pulsing and his tail beating the air, a whole new relational externality had come into being – an entity which is more than the sum of the fish plus the fisherman. The only way to count the spines of the sierra unaffected by this second relational reality is to sit in a laboratory, open an evil-smelling jar, remove a stiff colorless fish from the formalin solution, count the spines and write the truth . . . There you have recorded a reality that cannot be assailed – probably the least important reality concerning the fish or yourself.

It is good to know what you are doing. The man with this pickled fish has set down one truth and recorded in his experience many lies. The fish is not that color, that texture, that dead, nor does he smell that way.

(Steinbeck 2000: 2)

Steinbeck's passage speaks to me about the complexity of professional practice, of Donald Schön's murky swamp in which we flounder with greater or lesser success. It is tempting to imagine that professionally we know what we are doing, like the man with the pickled fish, and sometimes we probably do. This book is about living with uncertainty; about unpicking our experiences at work with a view to improving practice; about openness to questioning and challenge of our values, beliefs, ideas and practices at work. Voltaire's maxim 'doubt is an uncomfortable condition, but certainty is a ridiculous one' seems relevant. Guy Claxton (1998: 195) advocates that we walk a narrow line between 'the twin perils of rigid dogmatism and paralysing indecision' and I think that reflection on our practice can help us to do this at work.

In the writing I have read a lot and found myself agreeing and disagreeing with the authors more vehemently than I would have done earlier in my career. I no longer think that there is just one truth, the one to be sought through the scientific investigative process to which pickled specimens are so

Illustrations

Figures

Table

Preface

The Mexican Sierra has 'XVII-15-IX' spines in the dorsal fin. These can easily be counted, but if the sierra strikes hard on the line so that our hands are burned, if the fish sounds and nearly escapes and finally comes in over the rail, his colors pulsing and his tail beating the air, a whole new relational externality had come into being – an entity which is more than the sum of the fish plus the fisherman. The only way to count the spines of the sierra unaffected by this second relational reality is to sit in a laboratory, open an evil-smelling jar, remove a stiff colorless fish from the formalin solution, count the spines and write the truth . . . There you have recorded a reality that cannot be assailed – probably the least important reality concerning the fish or yourself.

It is good to know what you are doing. The man with this pickled fish has set down one truth and recorded in his experience many lies. The fish is not that color, that texture, that dead, nor does he smell that way.

(Steinbeck 2000: 2)

Steinbeck's passage speaks to me about the complexity of professional practice, of Donald Schön's murky swamp in which we flounder with greater or lesser success. It is tempting to imagine that professionally we know what we are doing, like the man with the pickled fish, and sometimes we probably do. This book is about living with uncertainty; about unpicking our experiences at work with a view to improving practice; about openness to questioning and challenge of our values, beliefs, ideas and practices at work. Voltaire's maxim 'doubt is an uncomfortable condition, but certainty is a ridiculous one' seems relevant. Guy Claxton (1998: 195) advocates that we walk a narrow line between 'the twin perils of rigid dogmatism and paralysing indecision' and I think that reflection on our practice can help us to do this at work.

In the writing I have read a lot and found myself agreeing and disagreeing with the authors more vehemently than I would have done earlier in my career. I no longer think that there is just one truth, the one to be sought through the scientific investigative process to which pickled specimens are so much more amenable than are living things. Too often I think we locate our investigations where it is easy to search and not where it matters:

> One night Nasrudin was on his hands and knees in the road outside his house. Seeing him, a passing stranger crossed over to ask what was wrong and whether he might help. Nasrudin replied that he was searching for a lost key. Falling to his own knees beside Nasrudin, the stranger asked him whether he could remember exactly where he had been when he had last held the key. Nasrudin turned and, pointing vaguely towards the shadow near his house, said, 'Over there'.
>
> 'But why, then', asked the stranger in puzzlement, 'are you searching for it out here?'
>
> 'Obviously', replied a tight-lipped Nasrudin, exasperated by the naiveté of the question, 'because that is where the light is!'
>
> (Hunt 2001: 280)

In this book I have felt a greater right than previously to assert a view of my own. For the first time in an academic text I have experimented with writing in the first person. I've found it both freeing and also frightening. I have liked taking the opportunity to say what I think while at the same time it feels exposing. To write in this way runs counter to the practice that I have developed over the rest of my career and I am not the only one to find it so:

> it's the style that is so different because M [practice learning tutor] wants 'I want, I think, I feel, I felt' whereas [applied social science tutor] is looking at writing in the third person . . . Well, you write that to your Auntie Jane, you don't write it for a course, I've never written it for a course . . . In this course you are going to be asked to write about yourself **big style**. You have got to be **king**. You have got to be in the centre. (Student 'Patricia')
>
> (Rai 2006: 792)

'I' is in the centre of this book.

You will find many quotes from authors whose work means something to me. Their practical examples help me to understand. I have reproduced material that I have found particularly enlightening or challenging within the domain of reflective practice. I hope that you will draw on your own reading and experiences but I also hope that you like my selection.

One of the crucial reasons in my view for the importance of reflective practice is the interpersonal nature of work in health, education and social care. Patricia Benner (2001: 216) states, 'if the nurse does not care – the patient's chances for recovery, or for dignity and comfort in dying, are slim.' These professions – health care, teaching and social work – demand that we are involved as people who mind about what happens to other people. I don't hear this vocabulary (caring and minding) used very much today. The language we use does not only serve to represent things but also 'the public space between us is founded on and shaped by our language' (C. Taylor 1985: 270). I hope that as you read there will be opportunities to reflect on the culture in which we follow our chosen professions and to challenge the premises which lie beneath the language of expression.

I wish to have found a balance in this book between theory and practice. My heart lies in practice and I prefer to work outwards from my experiences to locate them in explanatory frameworks rather than force my experiences into conceptual straitjackets. Theoretical frameworks are the maps that help me to sort out the complexities of my journeys at work and to plan routes to further destinations. They are not meant to constrain me from interesting detours and sightseeing tours.

I am writing this preface after completing, in final draft, the rest of the book and I shall be sad to see it go. A state of mind where we are so engaged in an activity that our worries evaporate and we lose track of time has been referred to as 'flow' (Csikszentmihalyi 1990). My family will testify to the way that this writing has so focused my mind. I hope that at times the reading of it may have this effect on you.

Acknowledgements

This book owes its gestation to the many people who have generously shared their ideas and experiences with me both in my personal and professional life. It arose out of an invitation to lead a workshop on reflective practice for the University of Glasgow clinical psychology department. My thanks are due to Ruth Sumpter and Alice Reay for the initial invitation. It could not have been written without the unerring support of Jon Scaife. Too many of his original ideas are included to be given individual acknowledgement. His challenging questions and editorial comments have helped enormously to shape the contents and his ready availability for a hug has prevented me from becoming too downhearted when I have stalled. Neither could I have managed without the technical support of the two Jons in my life so thank you both for being available at a moment's notice to fix my computer when it has had a mind of its own, and to Hannah for her invariably positive attitude to whatever I do. Joanne Forshaw, my commissioning editor, and Jane Harris, her assistant, have provided their invaluable encouragement, sound advice and practical support throughout.

For constructive and timely feedback on my writing I would like particularly to thank Mike Pomerantz, whose enthusiasm and encouragement have been hugely uplifting, and Robin Waller and Gill Wallis, who took time from their busy schedules to give me really valuable feedback. I would also like to express many thanks to Robin for his permission to reprint two of his poems – *The birth of humility* and *A view from the trenches*. I am very grateful to people, some of whom I have never met, who have responded to my email requests for help and shared their ideas. They include Jayne Dalley for clarification of guidelines and email discussion of assessment, Karen Anderton who gave permission for me to reproduce one of her coursework assignments, Guy Claxton for clarifying the copyright for a cartoon from *Hare brain, tortoise mind*, John Oates for providing a copy of his excellent Open University teaching materials, Derek Milne for material on DVD and our discussions about constructivism, Mantz Yorke, Gillie Bolton, Sarah Beglin, Judy Nokes, Siobhan Breen, Jan Hughes, Sue McCarthy, Steph Fretwell, Sam Willerton and the clinical psychology supervisors who attended a workshop at Trinity

College in April 2009 for their contribution to clarification of the definition of reflective practice. Many thanks are due to Paul Livock, a multi-talented colleague who very kindly drew the cartoon on page 67 and to Brigid Proctor and Francesca Inskipp for their enthusiastic encouragement and permission to reproduce Figure 8.1 'Overall map for running group supervision'.

Acknowledgement is also due for permissions as follows: Karen Anderton for permission to use the essay that she wrote as a first year student nurse at Northumbria University in 2004; the lines from F.R. Scott's poem *Examiner* are reproduced with the kind permission of William Toye, literary executor for the estate of F.R. Scott; Quay Books for Figure 2.3, 'Interrelated reflective cycles', which was published in *Learning Journals and Critical Incidents* by Tony Ghaye and Sue Lillyman in 1997; Egmont UK Ltd for the excerpt from *The velveteen rabbit* by Margery Williams in 1998, originally published by Heinemann; an advertisement of General Mills' appliances from 1951 courtesy of the General Mills Archives; Guy Claxton for clarifying the source of the cartoon Figure 7 on page 111 of *Hare brain, tortoise mind* published in 1998 by Fourth Estate; Taylor and Francis Books (UK) for Figure 4.3, 'A cyclical model of supervision', which was published as Figure 3.1 on page 36 of *Supervising the counsellor: a cyclical model* by Steve Page and Val Wosket in 2001 and for Figure 6.3, 'An architectural metaphor and hovering attentiveness', which was published as Figure 2.1 on page 33 of *Dramatherapy: theory and practice 2* by Sue Jennings in 1992; the Office of Public Sector Information for cartoons from the *Children's Learning in Science Project: Interactive Teaching in Science: Workshops for Training Courses: Workshop 1* by Kate Johnston, Richard Needham and Angela Brook in 1990; Jessica Kingsley (www.jkp.com) for Figure 7.1, 'Spectrogram: talking with the duke and the shepherd', which was published as Figure 7.1 on page 87 of *Creative supervision: the use of expressive arts methods in supervision and self-supervision* by Mooli Lahad in 2000; Dr Sarah Beglin for Figure 7.2, 'Diagrammatic formulation', which was published online at www.bps.org.uk/downloadfile. cfm?file_uuid=26D76984-1143-DFD0-7E8B-80F0BD2968EF&ext=ppt in 2007; the British Psychological Society for the extract from 'An awareness-raising tool addressing lesbian and gay lives', which was published in *Clinical Psychology* in 2004; John Wiley and Sons Inc. for Figure 7.3, 'Concept map', by Kathy Edmundson which was published in the *Journal of Research in Science Teaching* in 1995; Jon Oates and the Open University for the transcripts from *Terry* (DVD 00128) and *Susan* (DVD 00127); Olivia Hunt at United Agents for Figure 9.1, 'Bittersweets', by Posy Simmonds which was published in the *Guardian*; and John Bransford for the figure in Appendix 2 which was published in the *Journal of Verbal Learning and Verbal Behaviour* in 1972.

Chapter 1

Introduction and context

Reflective practice; I hate it.
I don't know what it is.
I passed it last year though.
(Radiography student)

Why do some people?

When I was thinking about writing this book, I was asked to consider, 'Why do some people find reflective practice more difficult than others? Is it about their learning style or personal philosophy?' I have not sought or found a definitive answer. But just as with any other skill such as dancing, cooking, listening, carpentry, bagpipe playing, swimming or golf, a limited level of current attainment tells us nothing about the impact that learning may have on future accomplishment. What I hope to do in this book is to make the idea of reflective practice accessible, and provide material with which supervisors can help supervisees to find out about and develop their skills in reflective practice.

The demonstration of reflective practice has become a pre-registration requirement across a wide and diverse range of professions during the period since the publication of Donald Schön's seminal 1983 and 1987 texts *The reflective practitioner* and *Educating the reflective practitioner*. My search of article titles for the term 'reflective practice' on the electronic database PsycINFO produced one reference in total for the years 1960–1989 and 145 for the years 1990–2008. The growth of interest is also reflected in the emergence in 2000 of a journal entitled *Reflective Practice* devoted entirely to this topic across professional groups. This book is similarly addressed to a wide professional audience, drawing on diverse illustrative examples from practice settings in health, education and social care. Later in this chapter I explore the factors that may account for the surge in interest in reflective practice at the present time.

In this introduction I want to clarify and simplify the concept of reflective practice by reviewing various definitions and approaches and exploring the relationships between reflective practice (Dewey 1933), reflexivity (Burnham 1993; Von Foerster 1981, 1991), critical thinking (Brookfield 1987, 2005; Paul 1993), experiential learning (Kolb 1984) and transformative learning (Mezirow and associates 1990).

What is reflective practice?

From among the many definitions of reflection and reflective practice that I have met in the literature, I have tried to distil a personal view with the aim of clarifying for myself and for you how I am using the term 'reflective practice' in this book. I see it as an instance of thoughtful practice. For many purposes, neither thoughtful practice nor reflective practice are necessary and may even be positively dangerous. Take the example of crossing the road. If you reflect too deeply on something while crossing the road, you increase your chances of being run over. Safely crossing the road relies on the development of a routine (look right, look left, look right again . . .) that has been learned in childhood and is produced automatically. While learning this routine you probably recited to yourself the words that you had been taught to guide your action. This self-talk usually disappears once the behaviour has become a habit.

But when visiting a place which involves driving on the opposite side of the road from your home country, the routine does not work and it is necessary to give more conscious thought than usual to the action. Let's imagine that you look right, and seeing nothing coming, take a step into the road before looking left, whereupon you experience a near miss when a car swerves to avoid you. You decide to be more cautious when next crossing the road and make sure that you look in each direction several times before stepping out. I would call this thoughtful practice. If, however, you not only think about but also analyse the incident, you might say to yourself that because the traffic drives on the other side of the road it is necessary to reverse the sequence of your normal looking before crossing the road. You have created a hypothesis or possible explanation for the experience. You might even decide to train yourself to recite the reverse sequence when next faced with crossing the road. You have undergone a conversation with yourself about the incident in which you have considered your normal behaviour, thought about why it did not work on this occasion and decided to make a conscious change in what you will do on the next occasion. This becomes reflective *practice* when the critical reflection shapes future action. This may be changed action but could equally well result in unchanged practice if the conclusion of the reflection is that all is well. From this perspective, reflective practice does not have to be associated with a need for change. In the case of crossing the road the reflection has involved creating an explanation of the experience, reviewing your usual practice, thinking of possible ways to approach the matter in the future and making a decision about your own future action.

It would have been possible to reflect on the incident without engaging in reflective practice. For example you could have said to yourself: 'That was a near miss.' 'I could have been knocked over.' 'I might have been badly hurt.' 'Stupid driver.' If the reflection goes no further it would not count as reflective practice because it has closed down at the level of description; it has no implications for your future action.

The term reflective practice carries the implication that the consequences of reflecting will impact upon and possibly bear fruit in one's own practice but whether this is the case will be determined not only by the process and outcomes of reflection but also by the potentially competing demands of well-established habits and feelings. Many people reflect on their smoking behaviour and conclude that they should change their practice but for various reasons fail to carry this through.

Reflective practice involves thinking from a bird's-eye view about an event and/or aspects of my practice. The perspective includes myself, encompassing my behaviour, thoughts and/or feelings in relation to my practice, with the implication that the reflection will impact on, although not necessarily alter, my practice. Gillie Bolton (2005) refers to this orientation as 'the hawk in your mind'. Such a distanced perspective may also include an analysis of social, ethical and cultural issues. This dimension arises particularly in health, social care and education settings because the worker is discharging a moral responsibility to care about the feelings of the student, client or patient. The practical actions of these professionals have wider and potentially more enduring consequences than is likely to be the case in occupations that deal with inanimate material although contemplation of value positions is still relevant.

Reflective practice can involve becoming aware of how underlying taken-for-granted cultural or personal assumptions influence our judgements. Developing awareness can lead to experimentation with other ways of seeing which might lead to more desirable courses of action. In the crossing the road example, it would be possible to question the organisation of transport into systems which allow pedestrians and traffic to intermingle with the risk of fatality. Broader reflection might question the need or desirability for citizens to engage in rapid movements between destinations in individual motorised vehicles run on fossil fuels.

To take this reflection even further, or deeper, it is possible to see concealed in this example the underlying issue of time as a commodity. Reductions in the time taken to get from A to B have featured in adverts for public transport in the UK. In the traditional society of Ladakh a rapid lifestyle change occurred after the introduction of new tools, crops and livestock (Norberg-Hodge 1991). Yak were replaced by cows, which provide about ten times the amount of milk, thereby creating a surplus which could be turned into cheese and sold. This newly created wealth gave the Ladhakis a different view of time, as something in short supply. Ladhakis have become busy creating wealth and saving time. Leisure time has been reduced by the introduction of time-saving technology. Their wedding celebrations now last just half a day instead of a fortnight. Guy Claxton (1998) suggests that within the Western mindset time is a commodity with an accompanying imperative to think faster, to solve problems and make decisions as rapidly as possible.

If we were to reflect so widely or deeply on all of our professional actions I imagine that we wouldn't get much done. Not only is reflective practice impractical and potentially dangerous in situations where judgements need to be made in an instant and on the basis of well-established routines, but also it is unsuited to learning that takes place through 'osmosis' unconsciously in what Claxton (1998) calls 'the undermind'. He cites much evidence to suggest that some everyday predicaments are better and more effectively approached with a slow 'tortoise' mind which cannot be rushed. The non-conscious mind extracts patterns from rich perceptual data, a process which can be hindered by attempts to express this in language before the learner has had time to build up a solid body of first-hand experience. Later, attempting to bring this to consciousness with the purpose of thinking critically about it may be helpful to learning and this is where reflective practice comes in. Claxton, referring to some experiments with children carried out by Annette Karmiloff-Smith, states:

> It is as if, when faced with a challenge, children use whatever is at hand to respond to it, like someone after a shipwreck constructing an emergency raft out of all kinds of flotsam in order to keep them afloat. But later, when they have a little more leisure, after the storm has passed, they move into a more reflective mode in which they experiment with taking this lash-up to bits again to see what happens, and where it might fruitfully draw on pre-existing pockets of know-how developed to cope with different situations, to make their know-how as a whole more elegant, integrated and powerful.
>
> (Claxton 1998: 45)

Reflection that involves analysis and/or synthesis is sometimes called critical reflection in the literature. The term implies that the reflection involves making discriminations, evaluating, judging, assessing, and weighing up options. This is the kind of reflection that I think is involved in reflective practice and which can result in more elegant, integrated and useful know-how.

Reflective practice is the process of thinking analytically about what we are doing, thinking and/or feeling, both as we are doing it and later in review from an observer perspective that allows us to include ourselves and the wider value-laden context in the frame, and which may lead to changes in or consolidation of our practice. It is a process which can be engaged without the need for the stimulation of particular incidents, but rather involves an attitude of open-minded curiosity oriented towards ongoing learning based on any of our experiences that are capable of informing professional practice:

> very often we find that we have reached some kind of a conclusion in our thinking without having recorded or noted any actual instances: they have occurred, but the separate incidents have disappeared into a general sense of knowing ... we often find that we are acting from a value position which is not actually based upon the facts. We then need to examine our practice for data that will confirm, modify or challenge our existing value position.
>
> (Tripp 1993: 39)

Schön referred to these processes as 'reflection-in-action' and 'reflection-on-action'. The additional concept of 'anticipatory reflection' is discussed by Conway (2001) and Van Manen (1990), highlighting the circularity of the reflective process when it informs subsequent practice. Meaning-making follows an original experience but when reflecting-in-action the timescales are very short. Reflection-on-action can take place minutes, hours, weeks, months or years after the original interaction. I think that there is great skill in being able simultaneously to participate in a process and take an observer perspective, particularly when it involves interpersonal processes. This is the case in many of the professions that aspire to produce reflective practitioners.

I find reflection-in-action to be particularly challenging when strong emotions are involved and when interactions are taking place in intimate relationships. Take the example of my having a disagreement with my spouse. We have a history of managing our disagreements and long-standing habits that direct the process. If I feel unheard or misunderstood, I might raise my voice and/or use an accusatory tone. I might go silent. I might (although this is less likely) adopt a position of curiosity about my spouse's position in relation to the issue. My prior mood is likely to influence my reactions. If I can manage my feelings and mentally step back, I might be able to rein in my habitual repertoire of responses and think about alternatives that may lead to more constructive outcomes. In my relationship with my spouse I might prefer to allow myself free rein.

In professional contexts my role is different. The well-being of others is the focus and purpose of my work. I need to keep this in mind at all times. My personal reactions are important and useful. I need to engage with the issues with energy and resourcefulness. In this context my feelings and thoughts are information and my task is to monitor these and generate ideas from among which I choose in deciding what next to do and say. I might jot down some of my ideas and return to these later if the direction of the work does not seem optimally useful. Successful analytical reflection on practice should lead to learning and skill development because it involves maintaining a stance of curiosity and questioning automatic responses. Instead of doing things in the way that they have habitually been done or according to a manual or technical prescription, the worker feels, thinks and modifies what he or she is doing responsively to the ongoing process. No wonder Schön referred to this as professional artistry. The creative element is forefront.

This is not to deny the importance of theory and technique in skilful practice. It is from a consolidated theoretical and practical base that workers develop the capacity to adapt and improvise according to the demands of the situation. Here is an account by a clinical nurse specialist for nutrition who modified her approach to a patient through reflection-in-action. She was consciously attempting to develop her skills in reflective practice and used the Burford model (Johns 2000) to guide her actions:

> The reflective cues – 'How is this person feeling?' and 'How do I feel about this person?' – keep popping into my head. I had a situation with a patient, Kim, it changed the whole way the experience went. She is 26 with Crohn's disease. She has a nasty fistula pouring fluid. She is on total parenteral nutrition (TPN). I visited her on the ward. Her dressing had been done. The 'Hickman line' should have been fixed in . . . she had sat on it and it pulled out. The doctor said he would sort another out but she had said, 'no!' I went in. I knew she would not get better without a new line. My intention was to be forceful just like the doctors. And then I stopped myself. I asked myself, 'why am I acting like this?' I noted my feelings – that I was anxious she was not safe without the TPN. I asked her how she was feeling. She was reacting against having the TPN forced on her. She has been like this for two years now. Her life has been turned upside down with no feeling of control – her only control was to say 'no!' I confronted her with this, 'Is this how you are feeling?' She said, 'yes! That's exactly how I am feeling. I am not having it!' I sat and talked it through with her. In the end we negotiated a compromise; that she could go home for the weekend to spend it with her children without the line and return on Monday to have the line resited. We agreed!
>
> (Johns 2004: 105)

In this example the worker was able to 'freeze frame' the interaction between herself and the patient. She made space to question herself and as a result consciously stopped her automatic reaction. Often, the action seems to take place at such a pace that stopping to think in the middle of it while simultaneously continuing to participate presents a serious challenge.

Characteristics of reflective practice

In my view reflective practice is characterised by the following:

• It is an active process implying an element of purposeful intention to explore (coming up with an insight immediately upon waking would not count as reflective practice, although reflection on this insight and subsequent application in practice would count).

- It goes beyond the description of an experience; beyond replaying a remembered episode.
- It is exploratory, not necessarily oriented towards a predetermined end.
- It involves reflectors in responding to questions about their experiences (these can be asked of oneself and/or by others).
- It requires reflectors critically to examine and evaluate their experiences, to create possible explanations for their experiences, and to stay open to alternative possibilities even if fundamental beliefs and values are brought into question.
- It requires a 'bird's-eye view' or 'observer perspective' in which reflectors include themselves and the wider social and cultural context in the frame.
- It is focused on and necessarily involves practice. It may result in a different or better understanding of practice and/or changes to practice. Such changes may involve giving up old ways, sometimes called un-learning, and trying out new ways of feeling, thinking or doing. It may also result in unchanged practice.
- It involves making links between current and previous experiences, ideas from different domains, theories, literature and research.
- It is personal; it involves things that are meaningful to the reflector. This implies a degree of independence from a 'teacher' in the determination of what is to be learned.
- It may lead to more conscious awareness of 'tacit' knowledge.
- It can include any or all of people's behaviour, thoughts, feelings, values, attitudes, skills and the social and cultural context.

I think that these characteristics are consistent with John Dewey's vision when he described reflective open-mindedness as:

> active desire to listen to more sides than one; to give heed to facts from whatever source they come; to give full attention to alternative possibilities; to recognise the possibility of error even in the beliefs that are dearest to us.
>
> (Dewey 1933: 29)

The characteristics of reflective practice also connect with David Tripp's descriptions of diagnostic, critical and reflective judgement. He described four types of judgement (Tripp 1993: 140). *Practical judgement* is non-reflective and involves instant responses on the basis of professional knowledge-in-action. *Diagnostic judgement* involves recognising, describing, understanding and explaining. *Reflective judgement* concerns more personal and moral judgements involving the identification, description, exploration and justification of the judgements made and values implicit and espoused in practical decisions and their explanations. *Critical judgement* involves challenge to and evaluation of the judgements and values revealed by reflection.

Reflective practice and reflexivity

In the context of professional practice I understand the term reflexivity to describe any process that includes itself within its own imperative. 'Writing is good' is reflexive; 'Stamp out violence' is non-reflexive; 'It is essential to be flexible in your thinking' is non-reflexive. Most statements are non-reflexive (e.g. 'It is sunny today'). It is when non-reflexivity results in contradiction that a difficulty arises.

If, as a teacher or supervisor, I prevail upon students and supervisees to adopt a curious and questioning attitude, and I exemplify this in my own teaching and supervisory practice then I am adopting a reflexive stance. Reflexivity in teaching has been described as the creation of 'coherence between the educational approach used to teach and the subject taught' (Neden and Burnham 2007: 359). It is a 'do as I do' approach where actions are consistent with espoused theory. Paulo Friere (1972) propagated this attitude towards education which he saw as a powerful liberating force. He argued that the relationship between student and teacher should involve a co-investigative dialogue in which 'the problem-posing educator constantly re-forms his reflections in the reflection of the students' (Freire 1972: 54, cited in Redmond 2006: 19). From a reflexive perspective we include ourselves in our thinking about our work because the accounts that we give cannot be given independently of the observer. In the words of Heinz von Foerster (1991: 65), 'without the observer's ability to observe and describe, there wouldn't be any descriptions in the first place'. And our observations and descriptions are created from our experiences that are set within our own times and places.

A distinction that I find useful in understanding the concept of reflexivity is that between what I say I do (espoused theory) and what I end up doing (theory-in-use) (Argyris and Schön 1974). Espoused theories are our conscious beliefs about what we think and believe. They can be changed with relative ease in response to new information. 'Traditional models of education generally presume that espoused theories guide our actions, but this is often not the case' (Osterman and Kottkamp 2004: 9). They argue that it is our tacit beliefs and assumptions that guide behaviour. These tacit schemas are our theories-in-use. Theories-in-use are shaped by our experiences within our culture of origin through daily processes of living. They are thought to account for apparent resistance to change in professional and organisational behaviour (Senge et al. 2000).

A recent example of incongruity between these two positions in my own practice was when I found myself preparing a PowerPoint presentation espousing the view that there is a low probability of meaningful learning resulting from being told something. Argyris and Schön (1974) argued that espoused theories and theories-in-use may be incompatible and that further-more, the practitioner may be unaware of this incompatibility. Empirical evidence for this incompatibility has been provided by Pawel Lewicki et al. (1992). Their findings suggested that most of the work of the mind is being carried out at a level to which our consciousness has no access. Asking people to describe their espoused theories may give little information about what drives their behaviours in practice. I think this has serious implications for the methods by which fitness to practice is assessed.

Argyris (1976) argued that in order to increase effectiveness it was neces-sary to bring together espoused theories and theories-in-use. This he termed 'double loop learning' which 'involves reflection on values and norms and by implication the social structures which were instrumental in their develop-ment and which render them meaningful' (Greenwood 1998: 1049). He later developed these ideas into what he called 'action science'.

As a practitioner I aspire to consistency between my beliefs and my actions. Keeping reflexivity in mind allows me to check that an opportunity for con-gruence between my beliefs and my actions has not been missed. This seems to me to be an ethical stance requiring me to subject my values, beliefs and practice to critical review. It is at this point that reflexivity and reflective practice coincide. It is all too easy for me to *say* that I attend to issues of diversity and difference in my practice, for example, but to do so requires that I continually scrutinise my behaviour for evidence of racist, sexist and homo-phobic attitudes associated with my upbringing in a society that has failed to tolerate or celebrate such differences in the past. If I engage in reflective practice, subjecting my own beliefs and attitudes to critical examination, I can carry out a checking process that compares my espoused theory and theory-in-use. The hawk's-eye view reminds me that I am the person who is creating narratives about a professional system to which I belong, and this system is set within a social and cultural context by which I am bound. Sheila McNamee argues that such self-reflexivity leads to moments of 'entertaining doubt about our own positions and pausing to ask, "How else could it be?", "What else could I do now?"' (Guanaes and Rasera 2006: 133). John Burnham (2005) discusses the notion of 'relational reflexivity', emphasising the contri-bution of conversation to the construction of meaning and the importance of asking questions such as, 'How is this process going?' and 'How are *we* doing?'

Reflective practice and critical thinking

In the twenty-first century the gain in popularity of the critical thinker as a desirable outcome of education has become enshrined in tertiary education in Britain through the introduction of taught courses and formal examin-ations. Stephen Brookfield (1986) suggested that 'educators should assist adults to speculate creatively on possible alternative ways of organising their personal worlds', 'developing in adults a sense of their personal power and self-worth ... and fostering a willingness to consider alternative ways of living' (Brookfield 1986: 233, 283). He identified four characteristics of critical thinking (Brookfield 1987: 7):

- It involves the identification and challenge of underlying assumptions in order to examine their validity.
- It requires a questioning approach that includes the importance of context and cultural setting in understanding actions.
- It involves a process of imagining and exploring alternative ways of thinking and behaving.
- It is based on an attitude of scepticism in which beliefs, habitual behaviours and the social context are all subject to questioning.

I would argue that these factors also characterise reflective practice although I do discern contrasts in the vocabularies used to describe the two processes. Some of the critical thinking literature (Fisher 2001; Paul and Elder 2006) discusses evaluation of the 'truth' of a claim and the degree of confidence with which a claim may be accepted or rejected. Quality of argument is subjected to evaluation criteria such as credibility, accuracy, precision, relevance and fairness. Knowledge of formal methods of logical inquiry and reasoning are invoked. To me, some of this vocabulary fits within an objectivist frame, whereas the language of reflective practice sits more comfortably with constructivist accounts.

Brookfield (1987, 1995, 2005) argues that critical thinking needs to be grounded firmly in the description of concrete events. Reflective practice emphasises 'experiences'. As his work has developed, Brookfield has used the term 'critically reflective practice' because in his view the term 'reflective practice' has widened to the point where it is in danger of becoming meaningless (Brookfield 1995: 7). Critically reflective practice is what this book is about.

Reflective practice and experiential learning

In experiential learning theory (Kolb 1984) learning is defined in terms of a continuous process grounded in experience rather than being regarded as an outcome. David Kolb (1984: 28) stated, 'the education process begins by bringing out learners' beliefs and theories, examining and testing them, and then integrating the new more refined ideas into the person's belief systems.' He described a cycle of learning in which there are four stages, namely 'concrete experience', 'reflective observation', 'abstract conceptualisation' and 'active experimentation'. The cycle repeats and may be entered by the learner at any of the four stages but the stages follow in sequence.

Depending on your stance towards theories of learning, you might argue that all learning involves experience. If an organism did not experience anything I find it difficult to see how it would learn. Experiential learning appears to emphasise the learner's conscious and active exploration both during and following some experience in a context which may have been designed by a tutor with the aim of bringing about learning. In the next stage of the process the experiencer thinks about the experience and this has the potential to lead to changes in knowledge at an abstract or cognitive level that may later be applied experimentally in practice.

Susan Weil (personal communication, 1995) identifies the key features of experiential learning as follows:

- Learners are involved in active exploration of experience. Experience is used to test out ideas and assumptions rather than passively to obtain practice. Practice can be very important but it is greatly enhanced by reflection.
- Learners must selectively reflect on their experience in a critical way, rather than take experience for granted and assume that the experience on its own is sufficient.
- The experience must matter to the learner. Learners must be committed to the process of exploring and learning.
- There must be scope for the learner to exercise some independence from the teacher. Teachers have an important role in devising appropriate experiences and facilitating reflection. However, the transmission of information is but a minor element and the teacher cannot experience what the learner experiences or reflect for the learner.
- Experiential learning is not the same as 'discovery' learning. Learning by doing is not simply a matter of letting learners loose and hoping that they discover things for themselves in a haphazard way through sudden bursts of inspiration. The nature of the activity may be carefully designed by the teacher and the experience may need to be carefully reviewed and analysed afterwards for learning to take place. A crucial feature of experiential learning is the structure devised by the teacher within which learning takes place.
- Openness to experience is necessary for learners to have the evidence upon which to reflect. It is therefore crucial to establish an appropriate emotional tone for learners: one which is safe and supportive, and which encourages learners to value their own experience and to trust themselves to draw conclusions from it. This openness may not exist at the outset but may be fostered through successive experiences of the experiential learning cycle.

Added to this list might be the emphasis placed by authors such as David Boud on the influence of the learner's social environment and culture (Boud et al. 1993).

I suggest that there are many characteristics in common between reflective practice and experiential learning as defined by the features listed above. Experiential learning can involve topics that do not focus on the learner as a practitioner. I also think that there may be an implication that experiential learning takes place in an environment purposefully designed by a teacher with the aim of bringing about learning from experience. For a review of the different definitions of experiential learning you may wish to consult Moon (2004: 103–116).

Reflective practice and transformative learning

Transformative learning is described in the literature on adult learning. In this literature, adults are regarded as equipped with the skills to reflect on and manage their own learning. This capacity for self-educating encourages a perspective in which learner and educator engage with each other as peers. It is argued that this involves a conscious effort on behalf of the educator to reduce the influence of prestige, counter the right–wrong dialogue commonly found in schools, and encourage critical reflection in a context of openness towards alternative perspectives (Mezirow 1997: 13).

Jack Mezirow regards the adult learner as capable of transformative learning which is a process of becoming changed by what is learned in a highly meaningful way. 'We transform frames of references – our own and those of others – by becoming critically reflective of their assumptions and aware of their context – the source, nature, and consequences of taken-for-granted beliefs' (Mezirow 2000: 19). He proposed that transformative learning can result from a 'disorienting dilemma' (Mezirow 2000: 22) which may be triggered by a major life transition (e.g. a natural disaster, job loss, divorce, war, or retirement). Such an event may lead to a complete loss of bearings because the experience does not fit with established habits of mind and ways of understanding. For example, Sue McGregor (2004) describes how critical feedback about her teaching, the closure of her department and transfer to a different department ultimately led to a radical revision of her views of herself and how she fitted into her world. She experienced a shattering breach of trust and lost friendships, blaming herself for what had taken place. She gradually came to the view that 'much larger issues were at play and that self-blaming was wrong' (McGregor 2004). It has been suggested that teachers are able to promote transformational learning in the context of less dramatic predicaments (Torosyan 2001).

Although I have earlier said that reflective practice is exploratory and not oriented towards a predetermined end, I regard changes in knowledge to be the likely outcome of successful reflective practice. I take learning to be a change process which cannot be observed directly but the outcomes of which are modifications in knowledge. I am using 'knowledge' with an inclusive definition that includes 'knowing that' (declarative knowledge: Anderson 1980), understanding, skills or 'knowing how', interpersonal interactions, values and attitudes.

For me, reflective practice, because it challenges underlying attitudes, assumptions and beliefs, stands a good chance of bringing about transformative learning and what might be regarded as significant changes in knowledge.

Here is an excerpt from an example offered by Jenny Moon (2004) as showing deep reflection. It demonstrates the author's (Annie's) inclusion of herself in the reflective frame. Annie questions the beliefs and values on which her behaviour was based. Annie had been on her way to a shop and had passed a group of children in a park, noticing that one child looked hot and unfit. On the following day a scathing article appeared in the newspaper reporting that the child was very seriously ill in hospital but passers-by in the park had taken no action to help at the time.

That was an easy way of excusing myself – to say that I had to get to the shop. Then I began to go through all of the agonizing as to whether I could have mis-read the situation and really thought that the boy was over-dressed and perhaps play-acting or trying to gain sympathy from me or the others. Could I have believed that the situation was all right? All of that thinking, I now notice, would also have let me off the hook – made it not my fault that I did not act at the time.

I talked with Tom about my reflections on the event – on the incident, on my thinking about it at the time and then immediately after. He observed that my sense of myself as a 'good person who always lends a hand when others need help' was put in jeopardy by it all. At the time and immediately after, it might have been easier to avoid shaking my view of myself than to admit that I had avoided facing up to the situation and admitting that I had not acted as a 'good person'. With this hindsight, I notice that I can probably find it easier to admit that I am not always 'a good person' and that I made a mistake in retrospect rather than immediately after the event. I suspect that this may apply to other situations.

As I think about the situation now, I recall some more of the thoughts – or were they feelings mixed up with thoughts? I remember a sense at the time that this boy looked quite scruffy and reminded me of a child who used to play with Charlie. We did not feel happy during the brief period of their friendship because this boy was known as a bully and we were uneasy either that Charlie would end up being bullied, or that Charlie would learn to bully. Funnily enough, we were talking about this boy – I now remember – at the dinner table the night before. The conversation had reminded me of all the agonizing about the children's friends at the time. The fleeting thought/feeling was possibly something like this – if this boy is like one I did not feel comfortable with – then maybe he deserves to get left in this way . . . I remember social psychology research along the lines of attributing blame to victims to justify their plight . . .

The significance of this whole event is chilling when I realize that my lack of action nearly resulted in his death – and it might have been because of an attitude that was formed years ago in relation to a different situation.

(Moon 2004: 199)

In summary

In summary, my notion of reflective practice is that it belongs to a class of ideas about learning in work. It is not an exclusive idea; its defining characteristics link and overlap with other ideas about how learning to practise takes place. I believe that reflective practice is compatible in particular with constructivist accounts of learning which assert that knowledge is subjectively constructed and intersubjectively tested, something built up from what the learner already knows, rather than poured or written in. In this view experiences do not arrive with labels already attached (Edelman and Tononi 2000: 81). The experiencer builds and rebuilds personal meaning. Learning to practise may be enhanced through a process of active reflection. Although we cannot step outside our own personal world, reflective practice requires that we at least attempt to take an observer perspective and imagine what other worlds and meanings are inhabited by our fellow humans in order to subject our own constructions to critical review.

Because this text focuses on reflective practice, it would be easy to get carried away with the idea that it is the panacea for all ills within professional worlds. I don't think that we could get by in the absence of a profusion of unthinking routines that are as effortless to us as keeping breathing.

> The mind operates most efficiently by relegating a good deal of high-level, sophisticated thinking to the unconscious, just as a modern jetliner is able to fly on automatic pilot with little or no input from the human, 'conscious' pilot. The adaptive unconscious does an excellent job of sizing up the world, warning people of danger, setting goals, and initiating action in a sophisticated and efficient manner.
>
> (Wilson 2002: 6)

Reflective practice can be out of place and even a liability when it fails to fit with the task in hand, as Mrs Edmund Craster describes:

> A centipede was happy quite
> Until a frog in fun
> Said, 'Pray, which leg comes after which?'
> This raised her mind to such a pitch,
> She lay distracted in a ditch
> Considering how to run.
>
> (Craster 1975)

One of the troubles that I perceive with the 'mindless' option is that there are limits to the fit that can be achieved when dealing with human interactions. The frustrations of automated responses can be experienced in miniature when listening to a menu-driven answering service in which none of the options offered address my query. The choice of 'menus' is limited in an atomistic approach to task specification.

> In the beginning, I was writing down all the times that blood pressures were to be taken, and then I thought, 'Hey, wait a minute, let me think about this and decide whether I need to take them or not. After all it's not just something I'm supposed to do to make *me* feel better.' So I stop and think, what if I know what someone's blood pressure is? What does that tell me? Do I really need to know it? Especially with some of the postoperative eye patients who have been postop for a couple of days.
>
> (Benner 2001: 141)

Compared with non-reflective or automatic practice, reflective practice is often slow, tentative and doubting and it may undermine, for a period of time, previously fluent performance. It is these very qualities that may take the reflective practitioner on otherwise inaccessible and potentially highly fruitful learning journeys.

Supervisors might usefully ask themselves questions about the suitability of this approach to particular intended learning as part of their own reflective practice.

The context of the development of reflective practice

How might the growth of interest across disciplines in reflective practice during the latter part of the twentieth century be accounted for? In my own discipline of clinical psychology we spent many years advocating the 'scientist-practitioner' model and it is only relatively recently that we have supplemented (and not replaced) this with the idea of the 'reflective-practitioner'. I think that there are a number of factors that may have contributed to its ascendancy. I also think that it sits in a position of potential and actual conflict with other dominant themes and orientations that are present in our professional worlds. These can make it hard to be a reflective practitioner with its associated critical questioning approach. What follows is a personal analysis based on my own experiences of working in the public sector in Britain from the 1960s to the present day.

Changes in the physical sciences and in societies

My understanding as a schoolgirl of the aims of science was that its theories and accounts of observed phenomena aspired to approximate further and further to 'the truth' or universals. The notion of 'the' truth was dealt a blow when it was observed that light could behave either as waves or particles. This led to the emergence of a 'both and' position which was a development from the previous 'either or' approach. At the same time, world travel became accessible to many, travel became faster, pictures and films could be broadcast instantly across the globe and population movements led to the creation of some increasingly diverse and pluralistic societies. In the UK there is no longer one dominant religious faith but many, no single set of overriding values to which the majority of the population subscribe. Maybe there never was, but now, in my experience, the opportunity openly to hold a wider range of views and to engage in a more diverse range of behaviours is not only possible but also sustained in law. More and more statutes make it illegal to discriminate against people on the basis of different beliefs, values and characteristics.

When there is no one commonly held 'truth', individuals have greater freedom to make up their own minds. Rather than being indoctrinated into a dominant ideology, children grow up among a multiplicity of ideas through which they need to navigate an adaptive course. For this, I think that they are likely to benefit from an education which encourages them to examine their experiences, question them and take personal responsibility for engaging in a process through which they construct 'useful' (to them) knowledge. There is no longer an established canon of knowledge which is held to be 'the right' way to think and act and which is poured in through schooling.

This move away from 'the truth' and 'the right way' is manifest in the view that 'there are profound, long term and altogether fundamental disagreements around the topic of "health", which reflect deeper value conflicts and political dilemmas' (Beattie 1987: 25). Advocates of this view argue that educators have a moral imperative to create awareness of the relationships in society between knowledge and power and that a contradiction would arise if knowledge were presented as a set of subject matter. Education becomes a process in which dilemma and debate are central, where the curriculum is open-ended and there are no clear enduring correct answers.

Economic drivers

I see economics as one of the defining characteristics of our era. We live in a marketplace economy with a prevailing motivation to make a financial profit. How does this fit with education? In the context of the industrial revolution, profit-making required a large unskilled workforce to carry out manual labour which became increasingly mechanised as the twentieth century progressed.

This workforce needed little in the way of education to be actors in the process of profit creation. The end of the Second World War in Britain heralded the vision of a welfare state where education, health and social care would be provided for all. Workers in these settings would need a different and extended period of education in order to fit them for the tasks required. Grammar schooling allowed a proportion of the population from economically poor homes to join the ranks of white collar workers and the professions. The capability to demonstrate declarative knowledge – the 'rational knowledge' traditionally valued in universities – was held to be key as an indicator of competence to fulfil these roles.

This kind of knowledge is no longer the exclusive possession of the 'high priests' of education. It is accessible to anyone who can read and has access to the Internet. Mass education has spread across continents and employers can out-source work to locations in which a capable workforce costs a great deal less than in traditional Western contexts.

If cheap labour is now available to carry out work that was previously done by the inhabitants of wealthy countries, what work will the latter now carry out? The National Center on Education and the Economy in the USA has argued strongly for a radical change to the education system whereby the most capable graduates are encouraged through financial incentives to join the teaching profession. This body has stated that competence requires 'a deep vein of creativity that is constantly renewing itself' (National Center on Education and the Economy 2006: 6). Their report asserted that the American education system currently 'rewards students who will be good at routine work, while not providing opportunities for students to display creative and innovative thinking and analysis' and argued that the standards movement has reached a point where it is no longer leading to educational gains that will fit students to be members of the twenty-first century workforce.

In their analysis, the capability to engage in reflective practice is central to the production of a workforce suited to the tasks and activities required to produce profit in the future. They suggest that education in the USA is lagging behind in responding to social changes and the global economy. I am in any case doubtful about the viability of profit motive as a means of organising society in the long term, a topic I sometimes find myself subjecting to critical reflection.

The information explosion and communication revolution

I have experienced massive changes during my career in my capability to access information, to turn it into digital formats and to produce and distribute it in the form of documents, books, papers and electronically to far-flung corners of the globe. This capability seems to have fostered an acceleration in changes to what is regarded as the core knowledge of my profession as members exchange views and ideas in an instant across vast distances. The canon of knowledge that defines my profession now is hugely different from that which was extant when I joined it. In light of a vastly expanding knowledge base in psychology, it has been argued that 'half of the facts' in psychology are replaced within the span of a typical graduate school stint (Flannery-Schroeder 2005: 389).

If 'the facts' that define a professional knowledge base change at such a rate, I can see little mileage in students committing the majority of them to long-term memory. What else, then, would assist them in their practice? Would it not be the capability to reflect critically on experiences stimulated by material that they had read, practices that they had observed, and information from any source that might be relevant to their practice? Falender and Shafranske (2007) drew attention to the notion of metacompetence; the use of available skills and knowledge to solve problems or tasks and to determine which skills or knowledge are missing, how to acquire these, and whether they are essential to success. Weinert (2001) regarded metacompetence as being dependent on self-reflection and self-awareness. The reflective practitioner would stand a good chance of bringing to work the thinking skills that would support them in tackling novel and complex problems; those of the kind referred to classically by Schön (1987: 1) as inhabiting the 'swampy lowland of messy and confusing problems that defy technical solution'.

In the context of a constantly changing canon of professional knowledge the notion of lifelong learning would be useful or even essential. I doubt that the state could afford to be responsible for the provision of lifelong education although the period of compulsory formal education in the UK has been extended more than once in my lifetime. In the absence of state provision the responsibility shifts to individual learners. This is compatible with the characteristic of reflective practice (and adult learning in general) that learners exercise a degree of independence from the educator with an element of freedom to determine their own curriculum.

Challenges to the reflective practitioner

Persistence of traditional values

I perceive a number of contextual obstacles to aspiring reflective practitioners which need to be overcome if they are going to be able to conduct their work within this frame. Traditional transmission views of teaching and learning have not disappeared overnight and are unlikely to do so given the habits and vested interests that work to maintain them. Johns (2004: 10) stated: 'Despite the rhetoric of developing the practitioner as a critical thinker, the weight of tradition and authority continues to suppress her emergence.' This weight has led Visintainer (1986) to the view that even when nurses govern their own practice, they succumb to the belief that the 'soft stuff', such as feelings and beliefs and support, are not quite as substantive as the hard data from laboratory reports and sophisticated monitoring.

(Visintainer 1986: 37)

In some cases, the capability to practise reflectively has been incorporated into pre-existing lists of competency statements and intended learning outcomes:

as more of the work of health and social service practitioners is starting to come under some form of outcome evaluation and measurement, the appearance of 'ability to reflect' as an assessable category on a competency checklist can only be regarded as a retrograde step, lacking any basic comprehension of the concept.

(Redmond 2006: xiii)

I agree with Bairbre Redmond and suggest that this type of approach promulgates the hierarchical nature of traditional approaches to teaching and learning, failing to acknowledge the centrality of the learner in reflective practice. Students and practitioners prevailed upon to engage in reflective practice would, in my view, be able to produce traditional types of coursework assignment and obtain a pass mark, without having fully engaged with the process. Examples of such assignments can readily be found on the Internet using a search engine.

I am not arguing against assessment of skills in reflective practice, rather that the approach to assessment benefits from a fresh look since traditional approaches were designed to assess a different kind of knowledge. This is discussed further in Chapter 10.

The organisational culture

The very process of reflecting on practice encourages workers to question the underlying assumptions and beliefs inherent in their profession and in the organisations in which they work. Such questioning is not always welcome.

The ethos and functions of the employing organisation and the motivation of individual employees can be at cross-purposes. Employers may have priorities to make a profit, to cut costs, to improve the league table position, to reduce waiting lists, to increase bed occupancy and the like. In 'scientific management' (F.W. Taylor [1911] 1998), the worker is regarded as an 'economic cog' and reduced to mindlessly executing management thinking. Not much room for reflective practice there! In the context of social work, Patrick Kidner (2000: 201) argues that 'the struggle for high quality reflective practice is not widely understood or supported in the realms of senior management or the political arena'. The incompatibility of the purposes of the individual and of the organisation can produce a sense of misery, helplessness, outrage and alienation (Obholzer 1994).

This incompatibility is noted by Kidner (2000), who discusses the difficulties for social work managers that have arisen as purchaser and provider roles have been separated, as there has been increased reliance on market forces as a means of coordinating services, and as responsibility for resource allocation has been passed down the line. He states:

> A new managerial culture has emerged in response to these developments, valuing competition between managers and teams in achieving specified targets, and offering the rewards (and sanctions) of performance related pay. For many team managers and practice supervisors it has been difficult to reconcile the values implicit in these changes with their existing commitments to the notion of 'needs led' services. If they over-identify with practitioners, they risk becoming collusive in their rejection of the agency's values; conversely, they may become persecutory in the eyes of practitioners if they adopt the new culture with too much enthusiasm – 'suckers or bastards' as earlier commentators have described them (Mattinson and Sinclair 1979).
>
> (Kidner 2000: 208)

He cites a study of three social work teams which found that staff members were preoccupied with top-down information, and that there was an absence of structures and policies to support practice (Kearney and Rosen 1999).

It can even be argued that the demand for reflective practice as an item on the curriculum is a manifestation of the commodification (the process whereby a human quality or relationship becomes regarded as a product, good or commodity to be bought and sold on the open market: Brookfield 2001: 9) of education. Some authors (Cotton 2001; T. Gilbert 2001; Rolfe and Gardner 2006) have questioned whether reflective practice is being employed, possibly unwittingly, as a management tool to facilitate the governance of the workforce by establishing conditions whereby so-called reflective practitioners monitor and regulate their own practice in an essentially self-repressive way. The organisation specifies not only what, but also how staff are allowed to think.

It seems to me that there is a fundamental question to address. What do we want of our workforce? Thinking and artful practitioners or automatons who faithfully but mindlessly reproduce methods and techniques with a view to reducing risk? I do not think it possible to live without risk. To be a safe practitioner these risks need to be acknowledged, calculated, evaluated and a course steered that balances them against the potential usefulness of an intervention. This needs a critically reflecting practitioner supported by a work culture that values thinking and learning. If reflective practice takes place in a 'watch your back' culture (Hawkins and Shohet 2006: 198) then it is likely to become an exercise in which painful or difficult issues are never discussed in case they are held against me. I have encountered practitioners who do all of their reflective thinking with their friends outside the work context for fear of being punished for their mistakes by managers who are in thrall to a punitive organisational culture. In a learning culture, failures and difficult feelings are seen as experiences from which learning can emerge, not as evidence for attributing blame to individuals.

The impossibility of standing outside context

Johns (1999: 242) argues that nurses are coerced into conforming to the dominant work culture and find it difficult if not impossible to stand outside or distance themselves from it. He suggests that they need help in the form of support and challenge from a colleague who acts as a guide in peeling away the masks of self-distortion and habitual unreflective practice. It may be difficult to see how this guide could help with the process if he or she were similarly constrained by the work context. While someone employed in a different organisation, profession or from a different cultural background than the worker might bring a different perspective to the matter under consideration, no one can take a context- or culture-free perspective. But we can work with awareness of this.

The responsibility for whether or not the process of *guided* reflection leads to new perspectives that help workers in their efforts to provide a good quality service lies with the workers themselves. As Gillie Bolton (2005) puts it:

> No tutor (facilitator or supervisor) can guide anyone else towards their own emancipation, no one can have this wisdom or power. People cannot be 'empowered' or 'given a voice' by a more powerful other; they can only give it to themselves: take it, that is.
>
> (Bolton 2005: 84)

In other words the responsibility for change and development lies with the person doing the reflecting. Gary Rolfe and Lyn Gardner (2006) state:

> the 'enlightened guide' is, in fact, no more enlightened than the practitioner who is being guided. It is therefore folly to believe that, while the practitioner is not able to stand outside of the oppressive organizational culture to see it for what it is, the guide somehow can. Like it or not, there is no transcendental position; we are all in it together.
>
> (Rolfe and Gardner 2006: 596)

I think that it is as well to keep in mind the aims of reflective practice: learning and skill development. For this, the guide may not have to be 'enlightened' but rather genuinely attempting to aid colleagues in their quest to make use of their experiences in improving practice. An attitude of alertness to different perspectives, active questioning of the status quo and the hovering hawk in the mind could help guard against subjugation of the reflective process to management imperatives of 'vigilance, inspection and correction': the production of a docile workforce, as feared by authors such as Cotton (2001).

Fear of appearing incompetent

At its heart, reflective practice involves questioning; taking nothing for granted and often exposing our uncertainties and vulnerabilities not only to ourselves but also to our supervisors or mentors. Even long-in-the-tooth practitioners may find themselves fearing to be 'found out' in their lack of competence. Michael Mahoney (1986) expresses it thus:

> I eventually came to recognise that I was naively (and unconsciously) assuming that there was actually an 'underground' handbook of how to be helpful that was secretly circulated among professional counsellors after their graduate rites of passage . . . I slowly began to appreciate that my expert clinical mentors were themselves operating according to abstract and tacit 'rules' rather than concrete and explicit guidelines.
>
> (Mahoney 1986: 169)

These fears are sometimes regenerated when experienced practitioners return to further their training after a few years in a qualified post (Dumas 2000). Approaches to training may have moved on. I recall a nurse colleague in such a situation who told me that in her initial training she had been taught to be the doctor's handmaiden. Learning to act with the authority of a 'modern' nurse beggared her belief.

This desire to prove oneself is perhaps most potent at the point of qualification as a registered practitioner. This is described by Sally Ballard (2000):

> I had a fairly healthy level of anxiety about this admission! I was at a stage in my training at which I wanted to demonstrate to myself and to my mentor that I could act as an autonomous practitioner. I wanted to do everything for the patient and be able to answer every question that arose. This might have been an unrealistic goal to set myself, given my relative inexperience, but I wanted to feel confident that I could act alone. I felt that I wanted to manage the overall situation and therefore prove to myself that – yes – I was good enough to qualify as a nurse in a month's time! In this way the worries I had were exaggerated because I

was putting pressure on myself. I felt that there was a clear distinction between the unqualified and qualified nurse, and I was trying to leap the gap between the two.

(Ballard 2000: 96)

Fear of opening oneself to scrutiny and of emotional connectedness

For me, compassion and caring are at the heart of health and social care professions. 'The client-therapist relationship provides a special context for vital experiments in living . . . One clear and crystalline moment of understanding and caring can ripple across endless lives and generations' (Mahoney 2003: 15). It is this potential so positively to impact on other lives that carries with it the rewards of working in these professions.

As soon as the worker cares, the whole spectrum of feelings including elation, anger, uselessness, sexual arousal, confusion, depression, amusement, disgust and the like can be generated in relationships with clients. These can be very difficult to handle since feelings of warmth and empathy are espoused. Those clients who eat away at us in our waking (and sometimes sleeping) hours present us with challenges that can approach resolution if we make meaning of the feelings that they arouse and use them to inform the work. I contend that maintaining too great a distance from clients and failing to work on such feelings can significantly impair the work, constrain the possibilities for positive outcomes, and is not an ethical option. If these feelings can be consciously recognised, there is a greater possibility that they can be used constructively in the work (Falender and Shafranske 2004: 84).

Here is a moving description from Johns (2004) by a nurse about her relationship with Sally, a woman suffering from T-cell lymphoma. Sally's skin is 'burnt all over'. The nurse writes:

> Standing at the doorway my eyes transfix onto the small wispy figure covered only by a thin linen sheet. Her face, peaceful in sleep, is disfigured by ferocious, sore red patches which connect and weave their way into every crease and feature of beauty. The main attack centres on her eyes producing a monstrous appearance of two cracked shivering starfish oozing from tentacles. Small mounds of decaying skin cling desperately all around her head reluctant to completely give up and let go. Goose pimples emerge on my arms; my body shudders coldly ending the momentary glance . . . Disgust and horror overwhelm my mind.
>
> (Johns 2004: 127)

Jill, the nurse, reflects on these feelings and calms herself in conversation with another patient. Sally calls for assistance and requests that Jill cream a very sensitive sore area on her back. As she attempts to soothe Sally's skin, Jill's feelings of sadness and hesitation are replaced with pleasure as the moist warmth infuses the dryness of her own hands. Sally offers her appreciation, commenting that although she is not contagious the other nurses have worn gloves because her skin is so revolting. The following day Sally tells Jill the story of her illness, and expresses her bewilderment about her history and prognosis. Jill is very moved. She says:

> The simplicity of Sally's needs brings tears to my eyes. Lowering my hand a spontaneous kiss reaches her erupting cheek; fragments of her scabby skin adhere to my lips but I only feel love.
>
> (Johns 2004: 128)

Reflective practice requires practitioners to include themselves in the frame within which they view their work. I don't think that this is easy, particularly when feeling vulnerable at work. It is much less threatening to seek explanations that locate any problems and difficulties in fellow workers or in the system. However, in order to bring about change, the process needs to begin with me. If I act differently, then others around me will struggle to maintain their usual behavioural routines in relation to me. When I examine my practice, there are times when I adopt a secret self-congratulatory stance. My cultural history tells me not to 'brag' openly about these matters, but I hide even from myself some of the things that I have thought or done that put me in a bad light with myself.

Consider then the task for the supervisor who seeks to facilitate the development of the reflective practitioner. The chances of supervisees revealing their insecurities, their successes, and their innermost thoughts and feelings in order critically to review how these are impacting on their work are slim unless the conditions have been created in which mutual respect and trust pertain. At the heart of the supervisory enterprise is a strong supervisory alliance, and I will return to this in Chapter 4.

I began this chapter with the aim of trying to make the notion of reflective practice clear and simple. I have ended it by highlighting some of the challenges faced by supervisors who wish to facilitate reflective practice. As a supervisor continuing to try and learn more about myself as well as trying to create conditions in which reflective practice can flourish, I find it helpful to keep in mind the aim of critical reflection: to expand practitioners' ways of seeing ourselves in relation to our work, the results bearing fruit in practice.

Chapter 2

Frameworks supporting reflective practice

I have encountered moving examples of deeply reflective practice that have made no reference to models or frameworks as structural supports for the thinking that has taken place. Maybe this is because the structures that help us to organise our thinking are of particular use when learning a new skill and may lose their importance as competence develops. One of the dangers of using a framework to guide thinking and reflection is that the subject of the reflection can become distorted to fit the structure. I have come across this in case studies submitted as coursework requirements. The personhood of the client has been lost in the attempt to fit them into a technical prescription by which the author attempts to show her or his mastery of the theory, thinking that this is what the university requires. There is also the danger that reliance on a particular structure can constrain rather than expand opportunities for thinking. To paraphrase Lev Vygotsky (1962: 115), if someone is taught to operate within a system without coming to understand that it is one among other possible ones then he has not *mastered* the system but is *bound* by it.

On the other hand, I find that frameworks are essential in helping me to structure my thinking and make sense of the material brought by clients in conversations that might otherwise meander randomly and unhelpfully along well-worn pathways that merely consolidate the very stories that have maintained the client's difficulties. I have preferred different models at different stages of my career, based on changes in my beliefs and values over time.

In this chapter I describe some structures that can support the process of reflective practice. Following other authors I have organised them under the headings of 'cyclical', 'structured', 'hierarchical' and 'holistic'. The selection reflects my own interests and is by no means comprehensive. The decision to facilitate reflection with the aid of a structure is probably of greater importance than the specific choice of framework. In the context of reflective practice I tend to think of these aids to thinking as structures or frameworks rather than models because they are primarily descriptive rather than theoretical. In other words they attempt to describe rather than explain the process of reflection and its manifestation in practice. As you read the descriptions that follow you may wish to ask yourself about what kind of structure would suit you as a support to reflective practice.

Cyclical models

Kolb's experiential learning cycle

David Kolb's (1984) cycle of experiential learning (illustrated in Figure 2.1) is widely reported in the literature about learning. It draws on the work of his predecessors, Kurt Lewin and Jean Piaget. In Kolb's cycle, 'concrete experience' is followed by 'reflective observation'. The learner is necessarily the person who has the concrete experience although this may be in response to an attempt by a teacher or supervisor to design or shape the experience with particular learning in mind. The learner may have little or no guidance in deciding how to frame the experience, how to choose what is figure and what is ground, and how to select what is relevant. It has been suggested that anyone trying to design an intended learning experience needs to bear in mind the 'architecture of variation': the need to take into account the range of ways in which material provided as a basis for a learning experience will be perceived by different learners (Marton and Booth 1997).

When used as a framework to support reflective practice, the second stage of 'reflective observation' represents the phase in which practitioners are attempting to view their experiences from a position of the 'hawk in the mind', including themselves in the frame and examining feelings, thoughts, actions, values, and beliefs. This is followed by a phase of 'abstract conceptualisation' in which the learner attempts to identify patterns, understand relationships, apply theories and knowledge and develop hypotheses. In this

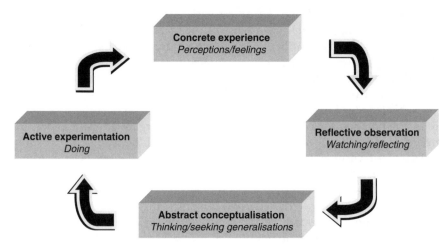

Figure 2.1 Kolb's experiential learning cycle.

phase learners may be asking themselves questions such as, 'What does this experience mean?', 'What sense do I make of it?', 'How does this experience fit with my current understandings?', 'How might my neighbour have interpreted this experience?'

The final stage of 'active experimentation' involves making decisions to act in particular ways. This is the point at which reflection is translated into practice. I like the term 'experimentation' because it suggests that despite all the thinking that goes into the subsequent action, the outcomes are indeterminate; this fits with my experience. In the first three stages of Kolb's cycle the result of reflecting remains untested and therefore lacks affirmation. The fourth part of the cycle is application, in which provisional knowledge from the first three stages may be consolidated. The fourth stage results in learning *from*, which differs from learning *about*. The fourth stage also implies that while learning facilitators may design what they hope will be useful learning experiences, it is the learners who determine whether the aim is achieved.

Kolb's cycle has been criticised for its simplicity (Moon 2001; Rowland 2000) but this is the very reason why I like it. It has face validity; it fits with my ideas about how I learn, and I can keep it in mind without it dominating my thinking. His cycle has been developed by subsequent authors. John Cowan (1998), for example, redrew the cycle as an overstretched spring. Graham Gibbs' (1988) model, described below, appears to be based on the experiential learning cycle with the provision of more detailed and prescriptive guidance on how a practitioner might operationalise the different stages.

Gibbs' reflective cycle

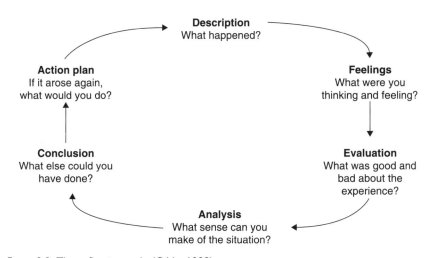

Figure 2.2 The reflective cycle (Gibbs 1988).

Gibbs' (1988) structure for reflection follows Kolb's in proposing a cyclical process specifically addressed to reflection about practice. Deepening awareness and learning are viewed as arising from repeated 'clockwise' movements around the cycle and practitioners are encouraged to examine their experiences through a series of specific questions.

Below is an extract from an unpublished coursework assignment submitted by a student nurse in which her reflections are carried out within the structure of Gibbs' cycle.

> The first stage of Gibbs (1988) model of reflection requires a description of events. I was asked to administer a drug to a patient via IM [intramuscular] injection. I had observed this clinical skill on a variety of occasions and had previously administered an IM injection under supervision. On this occasion I was being observed by two qualified nurses, one of which was my mentor. The drug had been drawn up and was ready to be administered and the patient consented to have a student administer the injection. My mentor was talking me through the procedure step by step and informed me that I should use an alcohol wipe to cleanse the injection site, when the other nurse interrupted and said that this was not necessary. This was in front of the patient, who then requested that the alcohol wipe was omitted as on previous occasions this had caused a stinging sensation. My mentor said that this was acceptable and I continued to administer the injection, omitting the use of the alcohol wipe. On the previous occasions when I had administered IM injections I had not cleansed the site and had never been instructed to adopt this practice.
>
> I am now going to enter into the second stage of Gibbs (1988) model of reflection, which is a discussion about my thoughts and feelings. I was aware of being under the supervision of two qualified nurses and this made me feel very nervous and self conscious. Once my mentor questioned my practice, concerning skin cleansing, I became even more aware of feeling nervous and under pressure. The patient was present and I did not want the patient to feel that I did not know what I was doing. I thought that as I had been observed carrying out this clinical procedure on many other occasions then my practice must have been seen to be correct. I was now feeling very confused about the use of alcohol wipes in the administration of IM injection. I was also concerned that the practice of the qualified nurses was so inconsistent, which led me to evaluate the whole process.
>
> Evaluation is the third stage of Gibbs (1988) model of reflection and requires the reflector to state what was good and bad about the event. I was aware that research by Workman (1999) suggests that the use of skin cleansing wipes is inconsistent and not necessary in IM injections if the patient appears to be physically clean and an aseptic technique is adopted, along with stringent hand washing by the nurse. It has also been noted

that the use of cleansing with an alcohol wipe can cause skin hardening (Mallet & Dougherty 2000). The trust policy was to follow guidelines published by the Royal Marsden Hospital (Mallet & Dougherty 2000). The Royal Marsden (Mallet & Dougherty 2000) advocate the use of skin cleansing wipes, however it is stated within their guidelines that they adopt this because their patients are often immunocompromised, and give evidence of previous studies which indicate that skin cleansing is not normally necessary. Therefore my practice was within the trust protocol. This experience made me think about my attitude towards literature and how it is applied in practice. Burnard (2002) suggests that a learner is a passive recipient of received knowledge, and that learning through activity engages all of our senses.

The site used in the IM injection was the gluteus maximus, this the most commonly used site for the administration of IM injections (Greenway 2004, Workman 1999). The gluteus maximus area is both thick and fleshy with a good blood supply (Watson 2000). It is located in the hip area and forms the buttock (Watson 2000). It has been noted by Watson (2000) that the gluteus maximus is near the sciatic nerve and Greenway (2004) suggests that this presents a risk of threat of injury in the administration of IM injections. When I administered the IM injection to the patient, I injected into the gluteus maximus muscle, as the evidence stipulates this is best practice.

Stage four of Gibbs (1988) is an analysis of the event, where Gibbs encourages the reflector to make sense of the situation. I will do this by exploring the skill and looking at the evidence underpinning it. An IM injection is the administration of medication into the muscle; there are many reasons why drugs are given via the IM route (Workman 1999). These include a rapid absorption rate, the conscious state of the patient, and the drug effect being altered by ingestion (Mallet & Dougherty 2000, Workman 1999). Workman (1999) suggests there are four considerations in giving an injection, the site of injection, the technique, the equipment and the route. On my clinical placement, an orthopaedic outpatient centre, IM injections were administered on an almost daily basis. However Hemsworth (2000) comments that IM injections are rarely used in certain specialities and suggests that, in this case, nurses current practice in IM injections may not be up to date with recent research findings.

Through evaluation of the event in question I have become more aware of different practices concerning the use of alcohol wipes in skin cleansing. I am aware that both practices have been researched, but as I develop professionally I am developing my own skills and will not cleanse the skin in future unless the trust policy dictates so or the patient requests me to do so. There is no clear evidence in this area but I will use the literature which is available to justify my actions, and therefore give evidence based care. The reason my mentor suggested using the alcohol wipe could be that she has been qualified for a long time, and practices have changed. In this scenario I have learnt from experience and through experience (Burnard 2002). Following this incident in practice I will now be more prepared to challenge the views of others in relation to my clinical practice.

In conclusion, stage five of the Gibbs (1988) model, I am aware that all nurses do not use evidence in the same way and may use different methods but as long as my practice is safe and evidence based then I can practise safely. My future practice will depend on the area in which I am working and I aim to find out the trust protocol concerning clinical procedures before I commence any procedure.

Within my action plan my aim is to research further into the theory of using alcohol wipes in the administration of IM injections. I am also planning to have a discussion with the qualified nurses on the subject of skin cleansing.

In conclusion my reflection skills have developed through the production of this essay. Using a model of reflection has helped me to structure my thoughts and feelings appropriately. My level of awareness concerning evidence based practice, and its importance, has been enhanced with the use of critical reflection. My competence, within this clinical skill, has been further developed and I now feel that my personal and professional development is progressing. Using this reflective model has helped me to realise that my learning is something which I must be proactive in. Furthermore as a student nurse I have recognised that reflection is an important learning tool in practice.

(Karen Anderton, RN, 2004)

I found this assignment interesting, not only because it is so stringently carried out within Gibbs' structure, but also because it deals with what might be seen as a relatively 'trivial' issue about whether or not to use alcohol wipes to clean skin prior to an injection. It raised issues to do with the student nurse's confidence, sense of shame at being taught in front of a patient, consistency of approach between experienced nurses, and the 'evidence based' justification for the practice which may say something about organisational imperatives. It raises questions about how the assessor of the work might respond to the assignment; this is explored in more detail in Chapter 10.

You might like to ask yourself how you judge the use of the framework in terms of the balance between its enabling and/or constraining properties? In its absence to what extent might the author have been left floundering without direction? How did the framework assist the writer in determining what was figure and what was ground in the experience described? To what extent has the structure skewed the writer's attention towards or away from useful issues? To what extent has the writer taken risks or played safe in response to a requirement to follow a structure?

Tony Ghaye and Sue Lillyman (1997: 26) refer to cyclical models as 'iterative', suggesting an ongoing process of reflection and learning in which the actions in the final stage lead on to further experiences which begin the cycle over again. Boud et al.'s (1985) model of reflection follows a similar cycle, guiding the learner through the process of reflection. Atkins and Murphy (1994) also proposed a cyclical model beginning with the experience of uncomfortable thoughts and feelings. These three models – Gibbs (1988) Boud et al. (1985) and Atkins and Muphy (1994) – specifically highlight the relevance of feelings as information on which reflections can usefully be based.

Structured models of reflective practice

There are a number of structured models of reflective practice, defined by sets of pre-specified questions that aim to support workers in thinking about their practice. Barbara Carper (1978) was one of the first authors to offer what she referred to as a set of cues to help practitioners access, make sense of and learn though experience.

Carper's set of cues, which can be viewed in full in Appendix 1, was developed in the context of nursing, informed by traditional ideas of science. The *aesthetic* way of knowing is described as 'grasping, interpreting, envisioning what is to be achieved, and responding to the unfolding moment'. She saw this as the art of nursing which was expressed in the bearing, conduct, attitudes and interactions of nurses with their patients. The *personal* way of knowing is responding to the situation in terms of the practitioner's own mental models, vision, attitudes, feelings, concerns and ignorance. She suggested that this involves being open to others, centred or focused on the other person (patient), and 'realising' (developing understanding of others through our own personal experience). The *ethical* way of knowing is responding to the situation in terms of what is judged to be the best or right action or non-action. It involves making moment-to-moment judgements about what should be done and what is 'right'. This may mean confronting conflicting values, norms, interests or principles in different situations. The *empiric* way of knowing is responding to the situation in terms of what is accessible through the senses that can be observed and measured in some kind of way (e.g. physiological measures of heart rate, descriptions of anatomical structures, pharmacology).

A structured model developed from the work of Carper (1978) which has been subject to repeated modifications is that of Johns (2004). The original purpose of Johns' framework was to create a strategy for learning based on assessment of current knowledge and identification of points for development. Johns states that the structure consists of cues arranged in logical order. The cues are said to be 'merely cues' and the structure is not intended to be prescriptive. The first cue, 'bringing the mind home' is described as a preparatory cue inspired by Sogyal Rinpoche (1992) in *The Tibetan book of living and dying*. Rinpoche states, 'So many contradictory voices, dictates, and feelings fight for control over our inner lives that we find ourselves scattered everywhere, in all directions leaving no one at home. Reflection then helps to bring the mind home' (Rinpoche 1992: 59). Johns regards reflection as a meditative activity in which workers give time to reflecting on themselves in the context of their work.

Johns (2004) developed Carper's (1978) taxonomy of 'ways of knowing' by adding the category *reflexivity*, which he described as being about responding to the situation in terms of a tacit way of knowing made conscious by reflection on past experiences. Each cue, other than the first and last, has been constructed to represent one of the five 'ways of knowing'. The fourteenth version is reproduced below.

Johns' model for structured reflection (MSR) (Johns 2004)

Reflective cue	Way of knowing
• Bring the mind home	
• Focus on a description of an experience that seems significant in some way	Aesthetics
• What particular issues seem significant to pay attention to?	Aesthetics
• How were others feeling and what made them feel that way?	Aesthetics
• How was I feeling and what made me feel that way?	Personal
• What was I trying to achieve and did I respond effectively?	Aesthetics
• What were the consequences of my actions on the patient, others and myself?	Aesthetics
• What factors influenced the way I was feeling, thinking or responding?	Personal
• What knowledge did or might have informed me?	Empirics
• To what extent did I act for the best and in tune with my values?	Ethics
• How does this situation connect with previous experiences?	Reflexivity
• How might I respond more effectively given this situation again?	Reflexivity
• What would be the consequences of alternative action for the patient, others and myself?	Reflexivity
• How do I NOW feel about this experience?	Reflexivity
• Am I more able to support myself and others better as a consequence?	Reflexivity
• Am I more able to realise desirable practice monitored using appropriate frameworks such as framing perspectives, Carper's fundamental ways of knowing, other maps?	

Thinking within such a frame demands a very broad perspective. Johns (2004: 238) presents an account by Sally, a deputy ward manager, of issues of conflict that have arisen in her role. She explains how nurses in the pressurised National Health Service are constantly being exhorted to maintain high productivity without sacrificing quality. The reduction in bed capacity in the interests of increased occupancy has led to the appointment of staff called 'bed managers', who are responsible for accommodating, for example, those patients who need to be admitted from accident and emergency departments. In the scenario reported by Sally, she turns down a request to place a patient who had been brutally assaulted with resultant serious head injuries on her ward as she regarded this as compromising the safety of other patients. She was already short staffed and there was no capacity to identify a special nurse for this one patient, who would also be accompanied by a police guard as he was considered to be in continued danger from his assailant.

Initially her argument was accepted by the bed manager, but later she was again contacted and instructed to take the patient. She was overawed by the appearance on the ward of 'an assembly of senior management'. Sally was left feeling angry and frustrated, caught in an organisational web in which she perceived her values and the ethics of the profession to be compromised by the authoritarian style of senior management. She experienced a sense of having let down her staff. Later, the chief executive appeared on the ward, out of hours, to thank Sally for her cooperation and this she experienced as something of a 'band aid' applied to her wounds.

A broad perspective on this issue would take into its scope the economics of a society in which health care is free 'at the point of delivery'. The level of spending on such a service is a political matter, subject to the prevailing political ideology, and to economic drivers such as the profit motive of drug companies and limits on public spending. Successive governments have introduced targets as a means of convincing the electorate that the health service is improving. Developments in medical science mean that more and more costly interventions are possible. There is a parallel with the world of information technology where continuous development ratchets demand and maintains a perhaps inevitable sense that current resources are inadequate. And perhaps crucially, we live in a society in which doctors are perceived to have the answers to our every malaise. No wonder the health service is described from time to time as creaking at the seams.

The structured model offered by Smyth (1991) is characterised by 'a number of moments that can be linked to a series of questions'. In this structure, the process of reflection is carried out in response to the four stages 'describe', 'inform', 'confront' and 'reconstruct'. This involves four associated questions:

- 'What do I do?'
- 'What does this description mean?'
- 'How did I come to be like this?'
- 'How might I do things differently?'

Smyth (1991) offers a series of guiding questions which focus on an interrogation of the prevailing social and political values that underpin practice: the interests served by habitual practices and the value-laden context in which professionals operate:

- 'What do my practices say about my assumptions, values and beliefs?'
- 'Where did these ideas come from?'

- 'What social practices are expressed in these ideas?'
- 'What is it which causes me to maintain my theories?'
- 'What views of power do they embody?'
- 'Whose interests seem to be served by my practices?'
- 'What is it that acts to constrain my views of what is possible?'

Reflective practitioners who examine their place in the health care system within its political and cultural context will question the very foundations on which the service is based. In a more caring and less materialistic society, would we have less need of doctors? One of the difficulties with extending the beam of reflection into such wide and dark corners is the potential difficulty of translating the results of reflection into practice. Structures that invite us to ask questions like 'whose interests seem to be served by my practices?' encourage us to deepen our understanding of the impact of implicit cultural imperatives, and to gain a perspective on the forces that may be constraining and sometimes prescribing the scope of our actions at work.

The starting point in Smyth's series of questions may be too far away from the immediate experiences of practitioners unused to taking a broad critically reflective perspective on their work. In my experience, these sorts of questions are rarely asked by busy practitioners and they are not always welcome. They relate to the ideas of Habermas, who saw critical reflection as a means of emancipation (Habermas 1984: 310). He was interested in the way that prevailing social discourses shape and constrain the expectations that people have about their lives. While prevailing ideologies may appear to be benign, they may serve as powerful agents of social control, limiting the roles to which large sections of the population might aspire, and their capacity to realise their potential.

Johns' structure seems to me to be in tune with the idea of the practitioner's experience being at the heart of reflective practice. There is less of a central focus on a critical examination of cultural context than is suggested by Smyth's structure. Johns' framework has been criticised for conveying an overly tidy linear view of learning and for providing set questions rather than prompting health care professionals to create their own (Ghaye and Lillyman 1997). It is also too long to be drawn on 'in practice', though not too long to be used in reflecting 'on practice'.

Hierarchical structures of reflective practice

Hierarchical frameworks describe levels of reflection that imply greater or lesser depth and complexity. The number of levels differs between models. Jesse Goodman (1984) described three levels: reflection focused on practices in order to reach given objectives, reflection on the links between principles and practices, and reflection that also incorporates ethical and political concerns.

Mezirow (1981) proposed a structure with seven levels of reflection, the 'lower' levels involving the way that learners think about things (consciousness), and the 'higher' levels (critical consciousness) where learners pay attention to and scrutinise their thinking processes. These two categories might be described as 'thinking' and 'thinking about thinking', sometimes known as meta-cognition. Mezirow argued that cultural ideologies that we have assimilated become manifest in a set of rules, roles and social expectations which govern the way we see, feel and act. These have become habits. Perspective transformation involves becoming aware of these culturally based assumptions at a 'meta'-level, i.e. becoming aware of our awareness and critiquing it.

Mezirow provides an example of reflection at a level of critical consciousness upon the assertion, 'John is bad.' Questioning whether 'good' and 'bad' are adequate concepts for understanding or judging John would constitute *conceptual reflectivity*. *Psychic reflectivity* would entail recognising the habit of making precipitate judgements about people on the basis of limited information about them. Deciding that this judgemental habit derived from a set of taken-for-granted cultural or psychological assumptions and experimenting with alternative ways of seeing would constitute *theoretical reflectivity*, a process which Mezirow regards as central to perspective transformation.

Mezirow's seven levels of reflection

Consciousness level

REFLECTIVITY

Reflectivity is the act of becoming aware of a specific perception, meaning or behaviour of our own or the habits we have of seeing, thinking and acting.

AFFECTIVE REFLECTIVITY

Affective reflectivity involves becoming aware of how we feel about the way we are perceiving, thinking or acting or about our habits of doing so.

DISCRIMINANT REFLECTIVITY

Discriminant reflectivity is the process of assessing the efficacy of our perceptions, thoughts, actions and habits; identifying immediate causes; identifying the contexts in which we are functioning (such as a play, dream or musical experience) and identifying our relationships in the situation.

JUDGEMENTAL REFLECTIVITY

Judgemental reflectivity involves becoming aware of how we make value judgements about our perceptions, thoughts and actions and what we make of them in terms of them being liked or disliked, beautiful or ugly, positive or negative.

Critical consciousness level

CONCEPTUAL REFLECTIVITY

Conceptual reflectivity involves questioning the adequacy and morality of the concepts that we use to evaluate our experiences.

PSYCHIC REFLECTIVITY

Psychic reflectivity concerns recognising our own prejudices, tendency to make judgements based on limited information, and the impact of these prejudices on actions taken.

THEORETICAL REFLECTIVITY

Theoretical reflectivity means becoming aware of the influence of underlying taken-for-granted cultural or psychological assumptions on our judgements and developing ourselves by experimenting with other ways of seeing which might lead to more desirable courses of action.

Mezirow (1981) argues that reflection at the levels of critical consciousness and theoretical reflectivity is a uniquely adult capacity related to perspective transformation which becomes a major learning domain in adult education.

Holistic models

Ghaye and Lillyman (1997: 33) argue that holistic models 'have yet to become established in the reflective development of health care professionals'. From the context of nursing they present a structure of interrelated reflective cycles underpinned by eight learning principles. The first principle is that the model 'is enabling rather than prescriptive' and this led me to muse on their use of imperatives such as 'should', 'requires', and 'must' in their subsequent principles. What might be the influence on their vocabulary of an ethos of imperatives from the authors' working context?

Ghaye and Lillyman's learning principles

- The model is enabling rather than prescriptive.
- Reflection should begin with a consideration of individual and collective professional values and what it means to be a professional and that after

this the learner is free to engage in any other reflective cycle as long as the choice is a conscious and justifiable one.

- Improving practice requires the health care professional to see holistically and think in a multidisciplinary way.
- Improving practice requires a high level of skill in being able to transfer, apply and customise knowledge from other fields.
- Just as work conditions change so do the concepts and categories that we use to make sense of our professional practice. This requires nurses to interrogate the ways in which they habitually make sense of their practice.
- Reflective and reflexive practice must interact if meaningful, relevant and sustainable improvement is to take place.
- Improving practice requires us to reflect upon the very nature or essence of our professionalism.
- Practice can be improved and learning facilitated through the establishment and nourishment of a community of reflective health care professionals engaging in peer group dialogue.

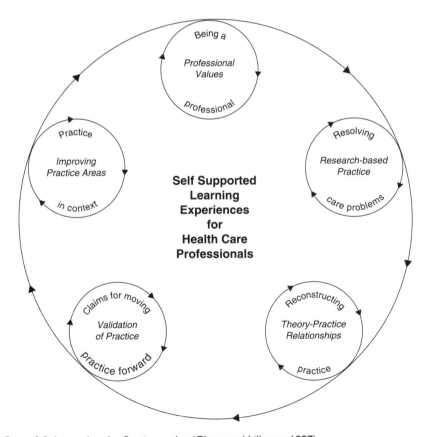

Figure 2.3 Interrelated reflective cycles (Ghaye and Lillyman 1997).

Ghaye and Lillyman (1997: 34) offer a matrix of five areas of reflective focus shown in Figure 2.3. These can be addressed by five different types of reflection: critical, interactive, receptive, perceptive and descriptive. Margaret Farren (2005) in her PhD thesis gives a clear account of how the work of a master's degree student in developing problem-based learning could be understood within this framework. Ghaye and Lillyman (1997) argue that holistic models capture the complexity of reflective practice and its relationship to ethical imperatives. I would find this framework difficult to keep in mind as I work but I can see its value given sufficient time in which to engage deeply with my experiences at work.

Critical incident analysis

Critical incident analysis is often presented as a method rather than a model or framework for facilitating reflective practice. It seems to have been much adapted in various forms from its origins as a qualitative research method. Now it has the characteristics of a framework within which a variety of methods for the encouragement of reflective practice might be employed.

John Flanagan (1954) originally described what he called the 'critical incident technique' as:

> a set of procedures for collecting direct observations of human behavior in such a way as to facilitate their potential usefulness in solving practical problems and developing broad psychological principles. The critical incident technique outlines procedures for collecting observed incidents that have special significance and meet systematically defined criteria. By an incident is meant any observable human activity that is sufficiently complete in itself to permit inferences and predictions to be made about the person performing the act. To be critical, an incident must occur in a situation where the purpose or intent of the act seems fairly clear to the observer and where its consequences leave little doubt concerning its effects.
>
> (J. Flanagan 1954: 327)

He did not regard the technique as new but set out to describe the development of the method, its fundamental principles and its present status. The main purpose of the approach was to gather specific incidents of effective or ineffective behaviour with respect to a designated activity in order to try and determine the critical requirements for successful job performance. The motivation for these studies in relation to Flanagan's work was to try to reduce the high failure level of trainee pilots in the United States Army Air Forces in 1941. The technique was defined by a series of stages:

- *Stage 1: Identify and make a statement of the general aims of the activity.*
  'It is clearly impossible to report that a person has been either effective or ineffective in a particular activity by performing a specific act unless we know what he is expected to accomplish' (J. Flanagan 1954: 336).
- *Stage 2: Create plans and specifications for the observers.*
  Flanagan argued that it was important to ensure 'objectivity' which meant that independent observers needed to be following clear and specific rules for data collection. This stage involved delimitation of the situation to be observed, a decision regarding the relevance of the activity to the general aim, a decision concerning the importance of the effect of the observed incident on the general aim of the activity, and the selection and training of observers who were to make the judgements.
- *Stage 3: Collect the data.*
  Flanagan devised forms detailing specifications for the observations to be made and argued that the behaviours or results observed should be evaluated, classified and recorded while the facts were still fresh in the mind of the observer. He argued also that it was helpful if the observers were motivated to make detailed contemporaneous observations and evaluations.
- *Stage 4: Analyse the data.*
  In this stage, the aim was to increase the usefulness of the data while sacrificing as little as possible of their comprehensiveness, specificity and validity. Data analysis was an inductive process in which frames of reference were sought and categories created, at first tentatively in a process of repeated modification until all of the collected incidents had been categorised.
- *Stage 5: Interpret and report the data.*
  Flanagan emphasised that the original researchers were in the best position to interpret the data but encouraged them to consider the limitations of the study and to provide information that allowed the credibility of the interpretation to be questioned.

While this original exposition involved independently trained observers and a clear specification of the aims of the work being evaluated, Flanagan also reported uses of the technique that deviated from these requirements. For example, Nicholas Hobbs (1948) reported the collection of over a thousand critical incidents involving ethical problems of psychologists who belonged to the American Psychological Association (collected first-hand rather than by observers). This was regarded as the first attempt to use empirical methods to establish ethical standards. The findings of the study were that psychologists believed that ethics of professional practice were important, that the ethics of the profession cannot be prescribed by committee but must emerge from the day-to-day value commitments made by psychologists in the practice of their profession, that a good code of ethics cannot be a description of current practice but needs to embody the ethical aspirations to bring performance ever closer to aspiration, and that the process is often more important than the product in influencing human behaviour. The four years of consultation with the psychologists were regarded as having been more effective in changing behaviour than the publication of the final report.

Flanagan regarded the technique as a 'flexible set of principles that must be modified and adapted to meet the specific situation at hand' (J. Flanagan 1954: 335). Butterfield et al. (2005) argued that this statement has encouraged the proliferation of approaches and terminology while allowing for innovative studies in many fields. The adaptations and departures from the original are described by Butterfield et al. (2005) as follows:

- Initially the technique was focused specifically on observations of behaviour. It has subsequently been adapted to the study of psychological states and experiences.
- There was an initial emphasis on direct observation rather than self-report.
- There has been deviation from or non-reporting of the data analysis process of establishing tentative categories which are subsequently modified.
- Processes for establishment of credibility of the data deviate from the original.

Where the technique has been adapted in order to foster reflective practice, it has generally become a process of self-study rather than other-study. The determination of what constitutes a critical incident no longer necessarily relates back to a clear statement of the general aims of the work, the data that are examined are not usually collected to a clear plan and specification, analysis is conducted in a variety of different ways, and the establishment of credibility, if carried out at all, is by feeding back the results of the analysis into future practice and seeing what happens.

Within the reflective practice literature, critical incidents have been defined in a number of ways:

A positive or negative experience recognized by the counseling student as significant.

(Furr and Carroll 2003: 485)

'snapshots', 'vignettes', brief episodes which epitomise a situation or an encounter which is of interest (for whatever reason).

(Beattie 1987: 23)

they are mostly straightforward accounts of very commonplace events that occur in routine professional practice which are critical in the rather different sense that they are indicative of underlying trends, motives and structures. The incidents appear to be 'typical' rather than 'critical' at first sight, but are rendered critical through analysis.

(Tripp 1993: 24)

incidents considered by the respondent to be positive or negative with respect to the quality of nursing.

(I. Norman et al. 1992: 596)

Ian Norman et al. (1992) argue for the use of the term 'revelatory' instead of 'critical' since this suggests that the experience in question is significant or meaningful to the person describing the incident, rather than indicative of a dangerous situation.

From my reading of the literature I have concluded that what are variously described under the headings critical incident technique (Butterfield et al. 2005), critical incident analysis (Collins and Pieterse 2007), critical event technique (Kunak 1989) and critical incident reflection (Francis 1995) involve a generic process. Within that process a variety of methods have been used for the collection and analysis of data within a reflective practice paradigm. I describe some of these methods in later chapters. The process typically involves the following stages:

- *Identification and detailed description of an aspect of practice which is of interest to the worker.* This can be an incident described in relative isolation but equally could be an account of an episode in context. Schluter et al. (2008) argue that the most meaningful data emerge when people recount their 'story' without clear demarcation of a beginning and end. Workers tend to describe situations as a whole and often find difficulty in identifying something called a 'critical incident' with its connotations of something going wrong.
- *Analysis and exploration of the practice.* This can be carried out in many different ways. The methods used by Edana Minghella and Ann Benson (1995) included brainstorming, role play and other experiential techniques, work in pairs and group role taking. Other reported methods include personal theory analysis and ideology critique (Tripp 1993), 'platform identification' (Osterman and Kottkamp 1993) which involves making a statement of espoused beliefs, repeated asking of a 'why' question (Tripp 1993), classification of dilemmas (Tripp 1993), role play, games and group exercises (A. Smith and Russell 1991, 1993) and seeking for counter-instances of typical events (Gray 2007).
- *Reaching conclusions.* These conclusions may be in the form of tentative hypotheses and have greater or lesser implications for practice.
- *Feeding the conclusions back into practice.* Implications for practice can range from a decision to keep things as they are, to make small changes

to an existing practice, or to go for a complete overhaul or change of direction.

This process looks very similar to Kolb's learning cycle with a particular emphasis on the identification of critical or potentially revelatory episodes or incidents of practice.

David Gray (2007) describes a method for identifying critical incidents by looking out for two contrasting types of event: typical and atypical. The latter includes events that are counter-instances or 'exceptions to the rule' which might be highly personal in nature. He argues that analysis of such incidents has the potential to trigger deep, and sometimes discomforting, introspection, even becoming 'developmental turning points' (Skovholt and McCarthy 1988: 69). Some critical incidents can be perceived as 'mistakes' (Cormier 1988). If practitioners are to share such material with tutors and/or colleagues, the context needs to provide the conditions that would allow such potentially shameful disclosures.

In a study of critical incidents brought to their course tutors by mental health nurses, Minghella and Benson (1995) found that there was a change in the type of incident presented that related to stage of training.

> Incidents brought by students at the beginning of the course were frequently about feeling tested, learning a new role, feelings of inadequacy, and generally focused on the self. Situations were presented as one-dimensional and specific. Students considered that they had a problem and sought answers from the facilitator.
>
> (Minghella and Benson 1995: 208)

Minghella and Benson gave an example of a student who struggled to keep a session going beyond ten minutes with a client who was described as having difficulties with social interaction. The student was disappointed in herself and wanted her tutors to provide a solution to this specific difficulty. She did not question the purpose of the interaction with the client or the validity of the task that she had been asked to undertake.

In the middle part of their training course Minghella and Benson (1995) reported:

> The presentation of incidents during this time became more complex. Frequently more people were involved. Situations were seen as multifaceted and problems sometimes presented as so complicated that there could be no solution. One recurrent theme was the impact of the work on the students' own emotions, e.g. when working with clients of a similar age or with similar experiences to their own, or who were suicidal. Issues around mental health care and ethical concerns were also frequently expressed.
>
> (Minghella and Benson 1995: 208)

An example from this stage was that of a patient being prescribed electro-convulsive therapy (ECT) by a consultant. The patient was in physical ill health and the anaesthetist refused to administer the ECT. The student nurse was distressed by her perception that among the multidisciplinary team, only one member of staff was advocating for the patient. The student was struggling with feelings of distress, powerlessness and anger.

By the end of the course the students had learned to process the critical incidents themselves and their primary interest lay in telling the complete story of the event, including their own analysis, to course staff and peers. Student anxieties at this stage tended to be about endings and leaving the course. In one example a student working on a children's unit had been involved in implementing a care plan that included 'time out' for a child. The incident had lasted for the best part of an hour and had involved restraint. The student had been very upset by the episode which had prevented her from ending the practice placement in a way that she would have found satisfactory.

This section has explored the origins of the critical incident technique, current definitions and processes, and the way in which fears of personal exposure and stage of training can influence the material offered for analysis. Methods for the exploration of such incidents in supervision are described in the chapters that follow.

Despite the value of the many structures that can support reflective practice, sometimes I find it helpful just to work out what is bothering me, what is important to me and how I am feeling in an unstructured 'splurge' of ideas which I might later subject to more formal analysis and consideration within one of the frameworks described above. Gillie Bolton (2005) advocates the use of free word association as a process for accessing these experiences. Once I am clearer about what is bothering me, I have a useful starting point.

Bolton (2005) gives an example from the work of Angela Mohtashemi, a management consultancy coach who had been working with a new consultant who was struggling with the challenges of a complicated business change project and his new role as consultant. He was encouraged to write in a free word association exercise. Mohtashemi inferred that his perception of the culture of the company merged with his own state of mind:

> NewCo pointless old tired stale dark cold unfriendly confusion anxious bleak stagnant slow protracted conflict going round in circles repeat same old parochial trivial dread going through the motions denial escape flight withdraw individual shell distance myself scared bitten stress pedantic macho picking holes unhelpful barrier don't care apathy ridiculous small-minded prejudiced siloed blinkered unappreciative arrogant waste of space obstruction denial deaf clueless machine hierarchical fragment disintegrate plural infighting political playing games Machiavellian agenda effort failure antagonism conflict embarrassment hide away secretive

behind closed doors inefficient paper-pushing overly complex dispersed resentful bitter stuck repeat

(Bolton 2005: 175)

Part of the process of reflective practice is the selection of the means by which to support reflection, and this is likely to vary according to the amount of experience that I have had as a reflective practitioner, my current state of mind, the purposes for which I am engaging in reflection on this occasion, and the means available to me in my work world.

Implications of the frameworks

Learning the practical skills of being a professional helper or educator is embedded in experience, and we learn through applying a body of theory and our own theories-in-use to practice with a greater or lesser degree of thoughtfulness. I find that engaging in 'learning by doing' is motivating and can make my learning relevant through real life problem solving. Through adopting a systematic approach to reflecting on learning experiences, we can assimilate experience with existing knowledge and skills for a process of lifelong learning and professional development.

While I believe that there are many advantages to the adoption of these descriptive frameworks or structures, so are there challenges to acknowledge. Deborah Gordon (2001: 228) says, 'the formal model is a substitute for practical mastery, much as a map serves the outsider who lacks the first-hand knowledge of a native'. She cautions that the formal model can become an end in itself. It can be reified and there is a danger that the model replaces the ongoing judgement of experienced practitioners.

> Particularly in sensitive situations like caring for dying patients, formal models can close off deep understanding rather than open it, thus providing a false sense of certainty and control rather than ambiguity and vulnerable involvement. When helping patients, involvement and openness to complexity are sometimes critical. The reductionism of formal models can then go both ways: it simplifies and orders, but when taken too far or used in the wrong situations, it can obscure and exclude important dimensions of the situation.
>
> (Gordon 2001: 234)

As Kolb (1984) outlines, learning does not occur simply through having experiences, and *description* is not enough for developing understanding. Many disciplines have encouraged or required a formal writing style which discourages the use of the first person 'I'. Impressions, feelings and personal reactions have rarely been encouraged in these formal submissions either in coursework assignments at undergraduate level or in reports and statements post-qualification. Staff may find it difficult to adapt to the differing require-ments of reflective practice. There are potential issues of self-disclosure, a fear of negative evaluation, and the influence of a power inequality resul-ting from supervisor's roles as both facilitator and evaluator (Scaife 2001). Nevertheless, helping adult learners to develop their reflective capabilities can be motivating and empowering for all concerned. And some structures, though not strictly necessary for reflective practice, may be very helpful and supportive to the process.

Conclusion

To conclude this chapter, here is a piece of reflective writing that was pro-duced without the aid of a structure, but within the context of a conversation between myself and a student who was struggling to put pen to paper in completing a coursework assignment. The piece suggested to me that she had been reflecting on this work over a quite substantial period of time and in great depth. The difficulty lay in organising her thoughts into something coherent on the page. The conversation acted as a stimulus to the organising process which was accomplished without recourse to a structure.

> When I first met this client, she seemed like a comedy character – 'Yes but, no but' . . . At first I did have a bit of a feeling of being all over the place. But I had had a client with similar touches of this in my first year and I drew on the skills I had learned to bring into a new case.
>
> A really big thing was that early on, because it was a learning disability placement, I was thinking about issues of choice and respect at the front of my mind. I said, 'Where would you,' (I had been seeing other clients at home) I said, 'Where would you like to be seen?' And she said, 'At home.' It made me realise I was offering her a choice; it made me see what I had in my head – it was not really a choice. If I had seen her in adult mental health I wouldn't have asked this question so it made me think, 'Why am I asking this client where she wants to be seen?' Left with a dilemma of having offered her a choice, she'd made it and then I was uncomfort-able. I explained my reasons to her '– I've said choose but these are the reasons I think it would be better if I saw you at College Street,' and we agreed to try that. We did try that and then she said she wanted to be seen at home which I went with.
>
> I learned to really think about whether something is really a choice or have I decided what I want to happen and I'm offering the client a false choice. There is something about it being a learning disability placement and because I saw this young woman in this context it influenced me. What assumptions am I making? Why am I making special consider-ations for this woman? It was almost as if I wasn't respecting her by offering the choice – condescending – or was I making adjustments for

her disability? I wanted to make sure I wasn't railroading her but maybe went too much to the other extreme.

Part way through the work the client told me that she had written a poem. In the first year it would have been, 'What model are we using and stick to it more rigidly. We need to do this, this, and this according to the text book.' Whereas when she mentioned this poem and she would talk at length I went a bit with my gut to look at the poem. I was lucky as well and it turned out to be a really good move because it made the client feel empowered and it made me feel a bit more – whatever we're doing here it seems to be moving in a more positive direction – feedback for me. Around this time there was a shift in her mind set. She had written a poem called 'Take Me As I Am'. I viewed this poem as a reflection of a growing self-confidence. It seemed to be a more self confident thing to be saying and at the same time the client reported to me that she felt that she had really tried all she could to save the relationship with someone she had classed as a friend, but now she stepped back from the situation and said, 'I'm not going to run after her. She knows where I live. I will continue to be present but I'm not running around after her.'

I've learned there's still room for me to fine tune. It encouraged me to just go with what's in front of me and it was my decision to look at the poem – it's not got a model around it as such – but it was more spon-taneous and I think that I could use this again in the future. It might not work as well with another client but I think my spontaneity helped the client to be herself. It was also more collaborative rather than enforcing ... when you're new to something, and this is nothing like I was expecting. I was aware of this but not overly concerned by it. You can deviate from the plan – it might have been a dead end but it was worth going down to see.

Also there's not necessarily danger in making spontaneous decisions in the session. Before I would have been more hesitant about whether it would be the right decision but chose to be more confident – no we're going to do this and see where it takes us.

When I saw this client something I thought about quite a lot and changed my mind about was whether to take notes in the session or not. Especially when I first saw the client and she was all over the place I decided to take notes and quite near the beginning we'd established a bit of a relationship and the client said, 'You're writing down a lot, you will run out of paper.' I said, 'No, it's fine, I've got plenty of paper.' It felt like the client was saying, 'My problem's too big for you to sort out with ten sheets of paper.' She seemed concerned that I was not bringing enough with me to sort this. What I did – she knew I would only be there till Christmas so we wrote in the diary all the sessions we were having – the comment seemed to suggest that she felt uncontained. This was to try and provide some containment. I haven't really had a moment like that before – I had a strong feeling that she wasn't just talking about a paper situation. Maybe that suggested more of an ability that I might slightly stand back in a session. When you're just starting all your attention is taken up by the basics of it. I learned more about being able to make use of information given to me there and then. I was making an interpretation, but not voiced to the client. I've never used a psychodynamic model and I kept it to myself. Further down the line I might. I didn't feel it was quite appropriate because of my lack of experience and not having worked in this model. I took it back to my supervisor to test it with him first. I learned something about the practical meaning of transference having previously encountered the theory.

Chapter 3

Reflective practice and personal and professional development

'It doesn't happen all at once,' said the Skin Horse. 'You become. It takes a long time. That's why it doesn't happen often to people who break easily, or have sharp edges, or who have to be carefully kept. Generally, by the time you are Real, most of your hair has been loved off, and your eyes drop out and you get loose in the joints and very shabby. But these things don't matter at all, because once you are Real you can't be ugly, except to people who don't understand.'

The rabbit sighed. He thought it would be a long time before this magic called Real happened to him. He longed to become real, to know what it felt like; and yet the idea of growing shabby and losing his eyes and whiskers was rather sad. He wished that he could become it without these uncomfortable things happening to him.

(from *The Velveteen Rabbit* by Margery Williams 1996: 6)

What is personal and professional development?

When humans work with other humans, practitioners themselves may be regarded as the 'key instrument' impacting upon the patient, client or student. I think that this behoves them to consider the personal qualities that they bring to the endeavour. To me the term 'personal and professional development' (PPD) indicates a process in which my personal qualities (sense of humour, capability to be assertive, warmth), my values and beliefs, my feelings, my habitual ways of being and relating are critically examined with a view to achieving personal growth in the service of becoming a 'better' professional. I may develop personally outside work – I hope that I continue to do so – and this may serendipitously benefit my work, but when I make a purposeful effort towards personal growth specifically in relation to my work I regard this as personal and professional development. It has been argued that a keen sense of self-awareness, insight, and control of feelings and behaviour are necessary if practitioners are to be empathic and understanding with clients (Middleman and Rhodes 1985). Falender and Shafranske (2004: 92) argued that personal influences accompany every technical intervention, and that interventions 'are guided by science and yet are influenced by our humanity'. While personal growth is not necessarily a primary goal of *supervision*, it is an instrumental goal that works in the service of making the supervisee a better practitioner (Bernard and Goodyear 1992). In this chapter I will try to illustrate aspects of PPD using accounts from practitioners' experiences, some published and some that I have compiled on the basis of observed and first-hand experience.

The term PPD acknowledges that I am not engaged in a solely technical task, but that how I carry out my work is an expression of who I am. Who I am is not static, and if I bring myself into focus I can work out what strengths I can usefully develop and what blind spots might be hindering me in my practice. This can present a challenge. 'Only when you've struggled with yourself are you free to bring your person, not just your therapist's uniform, into the room' (Whitaker and Bumberry 1988). Sometimes I recognise a reluctance to subject my experiences even to my own critical examination, particularly when I am feeling ashamed, uncertain, angry or vulnerable. I can feel particularly exposed if I show to colleagues, like supervisors, what may be some of my most intimate thoughts and feelings.

Much of the work of practitioners in the caring and helping professions involves dealing with other people's distress and the effects of this can be accumulative. The dynamics of employing organisations and relationships with other staff may be a perceived source of stress. It is not always easy to recognise or acknowledge the impact of these factors, perhaps until we find ourselves unable effectively to function in our jobs. In the following passage Sheila Youngson (2009) describes how she was eventually forced to recognise the need to take better care of herself and to look more closely at her personal landscape.

> However, even with this support and supervision, I did not take enough care of myself. In retrospect, many personal issues were being triggered, and many patterns and coping strategies, once adaptive but now not so, were being brought into play.
>
> My world view narrowed, and I found myself in dark places, an obvious (now) parallel to the experience of my clients. My body dictated that I stop, and after some minor surgery, I simply did not recover, and was away from work for 9 months.
>
> This was a time when reflection was thrust upon me! I realized that I had paid no attention to my own personal development. I had not looked at the road I had travelled or the person I had become; I had no sense of my personal landscape . . . I had not listened to any clues or nudges from inside me or from friends and family and colleagues; I had not acknowledged the patterns I created or in which I got stuck.
>
> I chose to enter personal therapy, which proved enormously helpful. I began to see patterns of being and relating that had been established

years ago, that did not need to remain set in stone. I began to discover my personal landscape and see that it could and would be fluid and flexible in response to life's experiences. I began to recognize patterns in my work-life, some of which were useful, some not so. And I saw and felt, clearly at last, the privilege and the cost of being a therapist; of spending much of my days in deep communication with people experiencing considerable psychological and emotional distress.

(Youngson 2009: 18)

Many authors have attempted to define the elusive concept of personal development and to develop profession-specific models (Sheikh et al. 2007). Definitions of PPD are reviewed in Hughes and Youngson (2009). I find it helpful (following Donati and Watts 2005) to make a distinction between personal development and personal growth, the former being a process that results in the latter. David Mearns argues that in order to work with clients in a relationship with depth, the counsellor will need to forgo the security of 'portrayal' and learn to relate more fearlessly. Three key features of the personal development process are identified by Mearns (1997: 94):

- A preparedness and willingness to become more and more aware of oneself and one's fears.
- A preparedness and willingness to try to understand one's self, often by examining 'ghosts' from the past.
- A preparedness and willingness to explore and experiment with one's self, i.e. to risk doing things differently, face fears, invite challenge, examine one's character and personality, learn to confront, etc.

Mearns (1997) argues that engagement in a process of personal development has the aims of increasing self-awareness and self knowledge within one or more of four basic domains: self-structure, self in relation, self as counsellor and self as learner.

- *Self-structure:* This domain is essentially about who we are, how we got that way and who we might become. It includes our beliefs, personal constructs, self-concept, personal identity, degree of self-acceptance, level of maturity and personal responsibility.
- *Self in relation:* Mearns states that we need to understand how and why we behave towards others as we do. Important here are our beliefs about others, our past patterns of interpersonal relating, assumptions and prejudices, understanding of roles, and how we appear or want to appear to others.
- *Self as counsellor:* Mearns' model was developed in the context of person-centred therapy. I think that his domains have relevance across a wide range of professions and this domain might be renamed 'self as

practitioner' in the context of health and social care. In this domain the self as practitioner monitors and evaluates the personal impact of work, the impact of personal life on work, perspectival blocks, barriers and prejudices that affect our work, and the overall influence of personal life history, values, beliefs and personal characteristics on how we do our jobs.

- *Self as learner:* The self as learner not only is emphasised in formal training but also is viewed as important as a lifelong state of mind. Mearns draws attention to the desirability of developing personal learning goals, adopting an attitude of willingness critically to appraise our learning, having the confidence to tolerate uncertainty that may follow from this appraisal, and taking responsibility for our own learning and behaviour.

It may be helpful to illustrate the idea of personal and professional development with an example. In order to have become skilful, teachers will have studied their subject/s, theories about teaching (pedagogy), have learned appropriate techniques and practised in the classroom with the support of colleagues and supervisors. It may be possible to know everything that there is to know about pedagogy, have flawless technique, and yet fail to teach with sensitivity to the learners in the class. There is something more to being a teacher that derives from the teacher's personal qualities and sensitivities. This kind of knowledge was categorised in Shulman's (1986) 'knowledge base for teaching' as 'knowledge of learners and learning'. The following example is an explanation given by a class teacher of her decision to prioritise focusing on a child's distress rather than 'getting through the curriculum'. One of the children had arrived at school that day upset because her pet had been found dead on the lawn that morning. The teacher decided to give priority to helping her and the other children to cope with grief and dying rather than teaching to her prepared plan. She kept in mind not only the needs of the individual child but also how this might benefit the rest of the class.

> Well, I could see she was upset straight away – she didn't have to say anything, it was just obvious wasn't it? She's always such a chirpy, sweet little thing. I knew it had to be something really significant.
> Why did I act that way? Well . . . I know that we're supposed to get through the curriculum (and there's precious little time to manage these days!), but, apart from being concerned about her (she's such a poppet) and just wanting to help her, there's absolutely no point trying to teach someone who's feeling like that, is there? They just won't take it in. No, I knew that I needed to sort it out straight away, she was obviously so upset. When you're a teacher you have to be concerned for the whole child, not just focus on the teaching aspect.

And as for the lads in the class, well, I have to keep a firm hand with them 'cause they're so easily distracted. I always have to make sure they are completely occupied with activities that they're challenged by and interested in otherwise their behaviour can be quite difficult. So I suppose all those things went through my mind really . . . the girls being upset, the boys' behaviour, the day's tasks . . .

. . . Yes, I suppose all of that flew though my mind and I chose what I saw as the best course of action for all of them – all of us, I mean. It worked out OK, I felt that we all learned something from the experience and I think it was really important to talk about their grief and dying. It can be so scary for children when they are confronted with death like that, don't you think? Everyone was fine after play and we got a lot done later that morning.

(Chapman 2000: 34)

When I use a service I prefer to be dealt with by someone, like this teacher, who keeps me in mind. I am frustrated when a bank clerk, garage mechanic or government official fails to recognise my need for an individualised response, sending me a recorded message, losing my documentation or passing me from one member of staff to another. How much more distressing if the person from whom I am seeking help cannot discern or remember what is important to me, turns up late for our meeting, loses my notes, does not take action promised, looks bored or discourages me from talking about what I need to discuss. The professions we practise require that we fully engage with our clients as people, from a position of developing self-knowledge that involves ongoing scrutiny of what is happening to us.

To summarise, the essence of my personal and professional development is an ongoing learning process about me in my work. My aim is to develop the capacity simultaneously to be affected by a client's communications, while reflecting on what the communication might mean and choosing how to respond to the benefit of the client. Without a good understanding of myself, I am likely to participate in habitual patterns of responding that close down rather than open up possibilities for how our relationship might develop, for making use of all of my experiences including my internal ones, and for optimising the possibility of useful change. This is the case not only in my relationships with clients but also in understanding what is happening between me and my colleagues, and in relation to the organisational imperatives which I experience.

The relationship between reflective practice and personal and professional development

Because reflective practice includes the practitioner in the frame, I think that it is a process well suited to achieving personal growth and facilitating personal and professional development. The following two vignettes both illustrate that critical reflection may lead to developments in workers' practice but they differ in the extent to which the focus is on personal development.

Vignette 1

I have been a member of the selection panel for a clinical psychology training course over the past several years. This year I am the coordinator for the committee. I thought that this was a straightforward task; arranging meeting dates, finding people to take part in selection, designing suitable questions to ask the interviewees and reviewing the process at the end. My first problem was the lack of volunteers. I had not realised that people would need so much advance notice in order to set aside their usual work and devote a full week to the process. Then they needed permission from their heads of department. I have learned that I need to start looking for people much further in advance than I had thought. I have also learned that I had not thought enough about the interview timetable. In order to see enough candidates and give adequate time for discussion, people on the panels had to stay beyond their usual work hours. Not having a family myself, I had not taken sufficient account of staff's after-work commitments. Next year I will discuss this fully with each panel member well before the interview week. I have learned to be more respectful of their time.

Finally, I was pleased to have allowed plenty of time to discuss and decide on the questions that we wanted to ask the candidates who tend to be very well prepared for the interviews. They often have rehearsed answers that make it difficult to see the personal qualities that they might bring to the job. Because the questions were thoughtful and non-standard I think that they allowed us to discriminate successfully between candidates. People on the committee had queried the length of time that I had scheduled but I have learned that this process cannot be rushed. Next year I will try to give a better explanation in advance as to the reason for the scheduling.

Vignette 2

This year I participated as usual in the selection of clinical psychology trainees. Usually I am involved in assessing the candidates' capability to show their academic and research knowledge and skills but this year I was on the 'personal' panel, evaluating the personal qualities that they might bring to the job. After the first day of interviews I could sense that the other panel members were becoming irritated with me and by the end of the week one of them seemed totally exasperated. My first inclination was to think that they must bear a grudge against me for some reason but I couldn't think of any explanation for why they might. I did wonder whether to ask them if I was doing something that was causing the irritation but I struggled to think of a form of words.

I found that the other panel members were much more critical of the candidates than I was myself. I felt that any of the interviewees could have been appointed and there was really little to choose on the basis of their personal qualities. As time has gone on though, I have thought more about what happened and I am beginning to realise that I might have a long-standing need to be seen as a 'nice' person. Why couldn't I ask my colleagues about their reaction to me? I guess that this might have meant that I would have needed to revise my opinion of me and try and see me from their perspective. As a clinician I take a non-judgemental stance and I think that I carried this over into the interviewing process, thinking of the candidates as I might think of a client, rather than taking an evaluative position. This has made me wonder whether my need to be seen as 'nice' is sometimes a handicap in my work as a clinical psychologist because I have noticed that I rarely challenge clients although I'm sure that they value the support that I give them. This is really a new departure for me. I don't know how to challenge people openly and it makes me cringe to think about doing it. I have decided to go and talk to one of my colleagues who was on the interview panel with me to try to get a better understanding of what was going on and I have decided to talk to my supervisor about learning how to be more challenging. I want to think some more about why I am reluctant to make judgements of people and where the roots of this might lie. I think I need to work out when it is helpful and when it is unhelpful to be judgemental and non-judgemental, and how to challenge constructively rather than avoid opportunities where I might be more useful to clients.

To my mind, while both of these vignettes involve reflective practice, only the second involves development of the person and while the development, if it results in personal growth, may have been prompted by experiences at work, the outcomes may reverberate throughout the person's life.

Below are some illustrations of the kinds of personal development that might take place through reflective practice with the aid of supervision. These are catalogued under the headings of 'Cultural and professional context, life history, values, beliefs, self-concept and personal characteristics', 'The personal impact of working with other people', 'The impact of events outside work' and 'The impact of being a learner'.

Personal development through reflective practice

Cultural and professional context, life history, values, beliefs, self-concept and personal characteristics

When I joined the profession of clinical psychology, there tended to be an assumption that the activities in which we were engaged were of universal applicability. As an example, there was no talk of 'culture fair' IQ tests – this only came later. Later still, the whole concept of IQ came under greater scrutiny along with many other assumptions that could be regarded as 'ethnocentric'. In my view we cannot help but be influenced and constrained by our culture-bound experiences, culture referring to our family culture, social culture and professional culture.

In my childhood, households were typically characterised by a division of labour in which men were the breadwinners and women the homemakers. My mother never wore slacks or trousers throughout her entire life. Divorce was rare and unmarried mothers castigated. One black girl lived in the neighbourhood. She was subject to what would now be regarded as intolerable racist abuse. I had a 'golliwog' money box. You put a coin on the black man's hand, pressed a lever at the back and he swallowed your money.

The General Mills advertisement was not atypical of the 1950s: see Figure 3.1 overleaf.

This all took place not that many years ago. These cultural imperatives are insidious and influence how we construct our ways of being, including how we carry out our jobs. They are at work constantly through the media and reinforced in our daily interactions. They are consolidated in our use of language and we may thoughtlessly reinforce stereotypes on a daily basis. Recently I listened to an item on the radio discussing the decision to terminate pregnancy when the unborn child had been diagnosed with Down's syndrome. In my neighbourhood lives a young man with Down's syndrome and I idly wondered how it would feel to hear this report if I were him. Unless we set out deliberately to scrutinise them, these often implicit cultural values constrain our creativity and may sustain us in working practices that are discriminatory and potentially destructive. What is your first reaction to the cartoon in Figure 3.2 on page 57?

What assumptions, if any, did it reveal at first glance? We like to think of ourselves as enlightened compared with our fellow humans who lived in past eras, but I think that history will show that we are just as bound in our thinking by culture as were the people who have lived in any other time and place.

Social or cultural values can sometimes be revealed by phrases in popular usage. I ask myself whether it would be necessary to discuss 'quality time with the family' and 'work–life balance' if I lived in a society where my job allowed me sufficient leisure time. In my view, these phrases have emerged out of a professional culture in which my work and home lives no longer have a sharp

Figure 3.1 General Mills advert.

division. Until the late 1980s, with the arrival of a personal computer on my desk at home, there was a clear boundary between my work and home lives. By 2005 I was regularly emailing back and forth to colleagues even on Sundays. It became much easier and more tempting to bring my work home and mingle the two kinds of activity with a computer on my desk and the opportunity for instant communication and information retrieval, particularly at times when my workload threatened to be overwhelming.

Figure 3.2 Tell me doctor.

Reflective practice encourages the identification and questioning of values and beliefs whether these are of social and/or familial origin. It could therefore be regarded as a subversive activity, undermining the tenets on which professions and organisations are predicated. Thomas Kuhn (1962) identified the tendency for researchers to act congruently with the 'school' in which their training had taken place, arguing that 'scientific revolutions' were typically brought about by forces from outside the discipline. Without such challenges to orthodoxy, there is a risk of stasis and the persistence of outmoded ways of working. Reflective practitioners include within their scope the full range of their experiences, examined from a position of curiosity encompassing themselves, their social, cultural and work environments. Here are some vignettes that attempt to illustrate learning about values, beliefs and approaches to work through critical reflection resulting in changes to practice:

Vignette 3

I was brought up in the north of Ireland in a Catholic family. As a child I lived through 'the Troubles' and was taught that as a group 'the Prods' were an oppressive and dominant minority. At their hands we suffered discrimination that prevented us from obtaining good jobs and decent homes. My family were great supporters of the Irish Republican Army (IRA), even though the campaign resorted to violence.

After I moved to England I developed a successful career as a speech and language therapist and I was happy in my job. Then I was offered the opportunity of promotion. My colleagues assured me that I was worthy of the post and that they would look forward to being members of my team. But over and over again I kept worrying that I wasn't up to the job and I was overwhelmed with feelings of discomfort, even reconsidering if the profession of speech and language therapy was for me. I couldn't even decide what to wear to work and although I wasn't aware of making a conscious decision I started to 'dress down' almost as if challenging the smart informal code.

Eventually, my partner was sick of listening to my ruminations and I took the issue to supervision. My supervisor suggested that I might try drawing a genogram (a map of my family), including not only their names, ages and occupations, but also any repeated sayings or beliefs of which I was aware. She suggested that I bring the results of my reflections to the next supervision session. We began to discuss the strength of feeling in my family about the issue of oppression and gradually I began to realise that if I were to be promoted this would put me in a position of power relative to my fellow workers. In my family, positions of power were automatically assumed to be occupied by oppressors. Perhaps if I were to accept the promotion I would be identifying with the oppressor. Could this account for my discomfort with the whole idea? This led me to read about and discuss with colleagues a style of leadership that emphasised collegiality and offered support. I have continued to keep in mind the possibility of abusing positions of responsibility but I have grown into my promoted post and have learned to be comfortable with the exercise of authority in ways that I think are helpful to my team.

Vignette 4

I joined a Child and Adolescent Mental Health Service (CAMHS) multidisciplinary team as a clinical psychologist at about the same time as a new consultant
psychiatrist was appointed. We were both keen on family therapy approaches
and she favoured a collegial style of management. Some of the team members
were quite young and newly trained, others had been in the team for many
years. One of the older community nurses told me that her expectation was for
the consultant psychiatrist to take responsibility for all decisions. A senior nurse
shared this view, as did the senior administrator.

The psychiatrist, for whom this was her first consultant post, tried hard to
lead the team democratically. Tensions escalated as the traditionalists resisted.
The administrator could not grasp the new style of management. Eventually, so
frustrated by what she saw as a failure of the consultant to lead, she began
to invite families experiencing any kind of frustration with the service to make a
complaint.

The conflict between the progressives and traditionalists escalated, making
the team a very unhappy place to work until the psychiatrist had to put an end
to the misery and resigned. The team was without a consultant for a period of
about two years during which there was an atmosphere of relative peace and
harmony.

Had I been asked at the time what was happening I would not have given this
account, but I lived through another cycle involving the same process with
different personnel. On this occasion both 'leaders' left their posts. Kurt
Lewin's change theory (Schein 1996) helped me to understand the process and
I learned that in a conflict of ideology, it is generally unhelpful for me to follow
my inclination to become 'glued' to one side of the argument – the one that is
congruent with my personal views. Rather, it is wise to try to undermine the
forces that maintain each or either position. By adding force to an argument I
merely reinforce the strength of the opposition.

Vignette 5

I was once asked to say what kind of client I found difficult to work with and the
first thing that came to mind was those clients who are quiet and say very little.
It makes me feel like I'm doing all the work. Unlike some of my colleagues,
I never minded those who seemed aggressive or forceful because I always
felt that there was material to work with. When I was completing a post-
qualification course I had to submit some work as case studies and I realised
that I would have to write during sessions in order to be able to illustrate
my assignments effectively. I was also trying to carry many new ideas in

my head and I started to find it helpful to jot things down as I went along so that I could come back to them if it seemed pertinent at a later point in the session.

Sometimes I found myself still writing a little time after the client had stopped talking. If I waited I found that often clients would say something further that helped me to understand better what they were experiencing. The mechanism of writing has helped me to learn the skill of leaving silences in a way that no longer feels awkward for me and that seem helpful in the work. It's not exactly a personal quality but there is something different about the way I am in the sessions. I don't seem to have the same imperative to feel that someone must always be talking.

The personal impact of working with other people

When we work with other people we are inevitably faced with the subjective worlds that they inhabit. Even though we may have a variety of 'objective' measuring instruments at our disposal, they are not invariably useful in taking the work forward:

> Supposing you're the therapist and I'm the client and I say that I want some therapy because I'm grossly obese. You're looking at someone who clearly isn't grossly obese and yet is reporting this as a perception. It is the client's reality but not that of the therapist. You would have to have measurements and a set of norms in order to define whether the client is obese or not. That could be done. But in a way it doesn't matter what the facts are, it only matters whether I *think* I'm obese. The interesting thing is that the therapist's instruments don't see the pink elephants that are flying all around the room. I can see the pink elephants.
>
> (J.M. Scaife 1995: 69)

As a practitioner who works with other people, I have been on the receiving end of a wide range of human emotional expression. I find some of these more difficult to manage than others. It can be very unpleasant to be the recipient of a client's anger, whether this is expressed overtly or more subtly when a client gives the message that the way in which the worker is attempting to help is ineffectual. The latter is sometimes expressed by way of questions such as, 'Do you really think that this is going to help?'

In the example of internal and external dialogue from Redmond (2006: 112) in Table 3.1, Carmel, a nurse, has been working with a child whom she suspects warrants a diagnosis of autism. She has not shared this with the parents as she does not regard it as her brief. When a diagnosis is made, the child's parents express anger that Carmel has withheld vital information from them. She has been encouraged to write about this experience under the

Table 3.1 Internal and external dialogue

Internal dialogue	External dialogue
	Mother: 'I'm really annoyed with you, you should have told us that she had autism, why didn't you tell us?'
What should I say now?	*Carmel:* 'I'm very sorry if I've upset you. Yes, I did suspect that Susan had autistic tendencies. But I do not make or give diagnoses.'
	Mother: 'But you should have informed us and told us what you thought.'
She didn't realise that Susan had a serious problem.	*Carmel:* 'In my profession, I do not make or give diagnoses. The diagnosis is not given without much consideration and is generally made by a psychologist or psychiatrist. You know that what I've been doing with you is talking about Susan's behaviour and management.'
	Mother: 'Oh yes, but when I told you about Susan's behaviour and what she was doing now you said, "*Good, great*". You didn't tell us the truth and I expected you to be honest with us.'
This woman is really angry. I wish she would only listen.	*Carmel:* 'It is true that Susan has made some progress. She will now use eye contact, concentrate for short periods and is using much better self-help skills. This has to be acknowledged.'
	Father: 'You should have told us what you thought about Susan. You've been coming here for the past three months and you're the one that knows Susan best.'

headings of 'internal dialogue' and 'external dialogue' as part of a method for encouraging reflective practice.

In this example, the parents expressed their anger directly and Carmel apologised, explained (although she did not feel heard) and subsequently was able to continue her work with Susan. Through discussion with her peers she was able to gain a perspective on the interchange from the angle of the parents. From their standpoint, Carmel had failed to share important information with them and this conflicted with the kind of relationship they thought that they had with her; one of partnership.

Struggling with feelings aroused by the work that I do is one thing; deciding to take them to supervision is another, particularly given the supervisor's mandate to ensure that I comply with the norms and standards of the profession and do not pose a risk of harm to the people with whom I am working. What might my supervisor make of my own confessed anger or distress?

Many other students are really afraid to tell their supervisors if they're really upset about something, for fear it'll be held against them somehow ... you know ... being seen as weak or not capable. Grades are important, and often there's a fear that the supervisor'll mark them down if they're seen as not coping.

(Kavanagh 2000: 66)

Phil Mollon (1989) gives examples of how clients' behaviour towards novice therapists in particular can generate feelings of inadequacy that interact with the more general feelings of incompetence associated with early stages of professional development. He described the case of a client who complained that her novice psychologist was cold and distant. She wanted him to be warmer and friendlier. He attempted to be what she claimed to want and began to act inauthentically. Despite his efforts, the patient complained of feeling worse and worse. In a further effort to allay his guilt and to demonstrate that he really did want to help her, the psychologist began to visit her at home. The relationship continued in a painful way, eventually being terminated by the patient writing a letter to the psychologist's secretary, denouncing him as a destructive man who was doing her harm. Mollon (1989) argued that one of the tasks of supervision is to bring the supervisee's anxiety and mental pain into the conversation so that feelings of incompetence and disillusionment become just like any other material that can inform the work. I think that the capacity to recognise and provisionally label feelings and then use them to take the work forward is central to the art of being a reflective practitioner. Sometimes the feelings can be really horrible when I am angry, upset or ashamed. It has been argued that such feelings can lead to 'withdrawal', 'avoidance', 'attack on self', and 'attack on others' (Hahn 2001). Resultant ambivalence towards clients can result in them being passed up the team hierarchy to those regarded as senior practitioners (Gill Wallis, personal communication 2009). Reflective practitioners ask themselves, 'What's going on?' and if they are unable to answer in a manner that leads to constructive paths forward, will invite colleagues to ask them pertinent questions until the matter has been explored from a range of perspectives.

It is not only novices who experience the emotional impact of working with other humans who are in poor health, who are suffering and in distress. There is a whole research literature addressed to staff burnout, vicarious traumatisation and compassion fatigue (Bennett, et al. 2005; Figley 1995, 2002; Myers and Wee 2005; Rothschild and Rand 2006). Figley (1995) argued that professionals who listen to clients' stories of suffering may feel similar fear, pain and suffering because they care, and that those who have the greatest capacity for feeling and expressing empathy tend to be more at risk of compassion stress. In my view, the process of critical reflection can help to inoculate practitioners against these negative by-products of the work through normalisation (they are a natural and inevitable consequence of the work that we do) and by putting them out into the public domain so that they do not eat away at us in isolation. Being 'out there' allows them to be examined as material from which useful intervention strategies can be devised.

It is not just that working with clients can generate *negative* feelings that can be problematic for someone trying to occupy a professional role. Goffman (1968) asserted:

A . . . general way in which human materials differ from other kinds, and hence present unique problems, is that however distant the staff tries to stay from these materials, such materials can become objects of fellow feeling and even affection.

(Goffman 1968: 79)

It is this kind of feeling, kept secret, that can lead even highly experienced and caring practitioners to transgress professional and ethical boundaries.

The impact of events outside work

As I reflect on my career I am aware that a number of personal events have changed the way that I practise in quite profound ways. One of the most significant, given that my clinical work has been with children and families, has been the experience of being a parent myself. This is not to say that I was incapable of doing good work before I had this experience, but rather that it has changed my perspective now that I know first-hand the anxieties, emotional highs and lows, and the intensity with which I feel towards and about my children. I need to guard against the danger of thinking that my clients have had an identical experience to myself while keeping in mind what it might feel like to be the parent of a child presenting to health or social services.

Many years ago, unable to find a child of a suitable age for the trainee on placement with me to practise cognitive assessment, I suggested that she give a test to my son. This we videotaped in order to be able to review the process. In retrospect, this whole thing was not a good idea and I have learned through it and other experiences that occupying a dual role (in this case parent and professional) makes life very complicated and is best avoided. I have learned to maintain much stricter boundaries between my personal and professional life than many of my friends and colleagues.

My son chose to respond in a fairly unconventional (it seemed to me) way for a five-year-old. Even by this age, influenced by the culture of right-answerism in schools, he showed reluctance to engage with activities in which he perceived himself to be failing and responded by turning the tests into games of his own devising that ultimately involved hiding behind the curtains and disappearing!

I was mortified. I was willing him to give an outstanding or at least adequate conventional performance although until the testing commenced I had no idea that this was how I would feel. I later learned that the trainee was also mortified. What was she doing wrong that led this child to disobey the implicit rules of testing, namely that the tester asks questions or poses problems and the testee gives predetermined 'correct' answers and actions? I was more recently reminded of this episode when a colleague who had suffered a stroke was the subject of a psychological assessment. As he said, 'I could never do that test before I had my stroke but now it's evidence that my brain is scrambled.'

These kinds of experiences – becoming a parent, losing a person to whom we feel close, experiencing a relationship breakdown, suffering ill health, or falling in love – have massive potential to influence the ways in which we work. We are provided with new perspectives that can lead to transformational learning. It is not only such major life experiences that provide material from which we can learn through critical reflection, but also more minor transitions such as moving house, or taking a holiday in a different culture. Reading novels, poetry, watching and discussing films can help us to develop empathic awareness of similarities and differences between ourselves and others. A selection of films that might prompt other-awareness has been suggested by Bhugra and De Silva (2007). They include *The Shining* (1980), *The Madness of King George* (1994), *King of Comedy* (1982), *Taxi Driver* (1976), *Shine* (1996) and *Twelve Monkeys* (1995) as aids to developing understanding of the experience of people with mental health difficulties, *The Naked Lunch* (1991) and *Trainspotting* (1996) on the experience of drug dependence. Rohinton Mistry's novel, *Family Matters* (2002), illustrates complex kinship situations. For the reflective practitioner, all of life's experiences offer learning opportunities that may lead to developments in practice.

The impact of being a learner

I spent much of my secondary education in trying to protect myself from appearing to be stupid by sitting at the back of the class and trying to make myself invisible with the hope that the teacher would address questions to others and not to me. This ethos, in which schooling is about getting the right answer rather than developing understanding, seems to have maintained its grip. When I lead workshops, it is almost inevitable that the front row is the last to be filled. When I ask for volunteers to help in a demonstration, I cannot ever remember being swamped with offers, even if the role involves silently sitting in a chair facing the 'audience'. This could be down to my lack of skill, and sometimes I conclude that it is, although I have observed the same behaviours when I have been a participant myself and someone else has been the leader.

Here is an example of the kind of experience to which people may have been exposed in the history of their education:

> Take Mrs Howard for instance, the German teacher. She practises teaching German in her own individual way every year. When the term starts,

she gives the pupils their daily homework of German grammar, then checks carefully every day to see whether they have really learnt what they were assigned. Those who have not done the work properly (and there are always some, as you know, who for different reasons have not) she makes a fool of them publicly in front of the class, in an ironic way, trying to make them feel embarrassed. In other words, she 'puts them down' before the very eyes of their class-mates. And this is repeated until nobody will risk coming to her classes unprepared in German grammar.

(Handal and Lauvås 1987: 26)

Mrs Howard justifies this approach by saying that her students obtain very good examination results, having been responsive to the social motive of peer-approval. Salzberger-Wittenberg (1983) and Lee and Littlejohns (2007) argue that an adult entering a new relationship with a teacher is inevitably anxious and that feelings associated with earlier relationships with authority figures are likely to be evoked. Salzberger-Wittenberg (1983: 12) stated: 'Any new relationship tends to arouse hope and dread, and these exist side by side in our minds. The less we know about the new person the freer we are to invest him with extremes of good and bad qualities.' She argued that helpers such as teachers, counsellors and doctors are often imbued with immense power for good and evil.

Feeling vulnerable might prevent me from making the most of the learning opportunities with which I am presented. My defences might be solidly present. If I can be aware of feeling vulnerable, understand it as a normal reaction to my situation as a learner, I may be able to take responsibility for managing my defensiveness and not allow it to rob me of the opportunities open to me. As an aspiring reflective practitioner I aim to take responsibility for identifying my learning needs, adopt a position of openness to learning, try to recognise my defensive manoeuvres, show willingness to share my known strengths and weaknesses with colleagues and work out how to show my fears and anxieties without undue apprehension.

In this chapter I have attempted to illustrate the concept of personal and professional development and show how the outcome of personal growth can be accomplished through reflective practice. Personal growth may result from an examination of cultural and professional contexts, life histories, values, beliefs, the worker's self-concept and personal characteristics, the personal impact of working with other humans, the impact of events outside work and the impact of being a learner. Work offers a rich tapestry of experiences from which such growth may result, the outcome of which may be improved practice but also important personal developments that transcend contexts.

Chapter 4

Supervision conditions that support reflective practice

Figure 4.1 Dragon cartoon.

The cartoon (Figure 4.1) illustrates to me the central issue in supervision – the nature of the relationship between supervisor and supervisee. How did our relationship come into being? What are our responsibilities for the task? What are the constraints? What are my fantasies about my supervisor or supervisee? How scary is it going to be? In this chapter I aim to explore some of these questions and raise matters for consideration both that have been of importance to me and that are highlighted in the supervision literature.

I often find that by observing the work of others I learn more about what is important to me and so I begin with some short transcripts against which you might like to explore your reactions. I offer a few prompts in the form of questions but you might prefer to create your own.

What do you like and dislike about each extract? What is the supervisor doing in each case? What can you infer about how the participants view the supervision task? What do your reactions tell you about your preferences in supervision both as a supervisor and supervisee?

Supervisee: She was saying she is useless, incapable and can't do anything. She looked disheartened, avoiding eye contact, speaking quietly. I knew this was just her biased thinking so reminded her of the stuff she had achieved recently. While I was giving her these positives she seemed to sink further . . . And I got a bit lost.

Supervisor: Tell me a bit more about that?

Supervisee: She was down already, being hard on herself. I intervened by reminding her of this stuff she had been doing and her mood went down further. And that's what I was trying to avoid, making her more distressed . . . I think at that point I felt quite panicky, lost . . .

Supervisor: So noticing her low mood, avoiding eye contact with you, speaking quietly, and her stating these negative comments, you thought?

Supervisee: I need to make her feel better, improve her mood, get her out of that dark hole.

Supervisor: And failing to do that would mean?

Supervisee: I wasn't doing my job properly . . . I should be able to make her feel better.

Supervisor: What does that sound like?

Supervisee: (Giggling) Yes, I know, it's one of my own beliefs. 'I should be able to make her feel better,' yes that's a particularly strong belief I have.

Supervisor: So part of you was thinking, 'I need to make her feel better.' And in that situation, it sounds like that belief contributed towards you feeling panicky, and lost?

Supervisee: Ah huh, that's right. I was trying to make her feel less distressed, but the opposite was happening. I wasn't doing my job.

Supervisor: I'm wondering if that had been around when you'd been met with her thinking she was incapable, useless?

Supervisee: Absolutely, those words felt quite powerful, and I wanted to steer away from them.

Supervisor: So staying with her sense of being incapable, useless would mean?

Supervisee: She'd end up feeling worse, more distressed ... And I was unsure about that.

Supervisor: If you'd stayed with her sense of being incapable, your concern was about making her worse, does that sound right?

Supervisee: Yes that's right.

(Sloan 2007: 103)

The following example is from my own experience:

Supervisee: I've been working with staff in a residential setting and the director keeps contacting me. I have an email from him every morning about one of the clients he's keen to discharge. This resident has been described as disruptive and unsuited to the milieu. At the same time I keep getting daily telephone calls from the resident's mother. She thinks that he should stay in his placement and that everything would be OK if only the staff would understand his needs better.

Supervisor: And how is this making you feel?

Supervisee: Well, there is an issue of risk. Some of the staff are very angry with the client and I think there's a risk of mistreatment. There has been a complaint made to me by the mother which should have gone through the regular complaints procedure.

Supervisor: Have you dealt with the issue of risk or is that something it would be helpful to discuss?

Supervisee: No, I've redirected the letter through the correct channel and explained it to the mother. And I've already arranged a meeting between the director, myself and the mother. I know the staff well because I've been involved for a number of years. We can handle it like we have on previous occasions and I have that in hand.

Supervisor: Where would you like to get to in relation to this situation by the end of our session today?

Supervisee: I don't think the demands that are being placed on me by the director and the mother are reasonable. I don't want to have to talk to each of them several times a day. I'm frustrated and it bugs me outside work.

Supervisor: How do you think you got into that situation?

Supervisee: I know the director very well; I sometimes meet with him socially, so I feel obligated to help if I can. I tend to agree with the mother about the lack of understanding that the staff have about her son and as she's relatively unsupported I feel that I can't leave her to fight on her own. So I guess I end up feeling I have to respond to them both every day.

Supervisor: I'm thinking that there are a number of possible focuses for this supervision. We don't need to think about how to handle issues of risk and the complaint because you've told me that you have that in hand. Would it be more useful to address your frustrations and how to manage those, how you've come to be in a position where both the director and the mother are contacting you every day and whether this is unique or a position you've experienced before, or should we look at your formulation in this case and your coming meeting with the director and the mother or something else?

Supervisee: I think I'd like to review how I get into these situations; it's not the first time.

This example is from Elizabeth Holloway (1995):

Supervisor: I think you might be on to something. Let me tell you what I understand from your experience with the client. You felt that as we talked about the client's dependency needs that maybe what you hadn't discovered was the fact that you can give to someone and it won't take away her self-sufficiency. It won't mean that you're taking away your respect of her as a person who can take care of herself.

Trainee: Yeah, my hunch is that my experience of what that should have been was something that penalized me at times and therefore that's the way I sort of think about it.

Supervisor: And it sounded like it had some of those strings attached just, someone overprotecting you, someone taking away from you something, is that right?

Trainee: Yeah.

Supervisor: Taking away those things from you by saying, 'I'll take care of you because you can't take care of yourself, nor will you be able to.'

Trainee: Yeah, yeah. It was really dumb. It was a really contradictory message. It was on one hand you're not handicapped, you're going to live like a nonhandicapped person; you have all those expectations. Plus you're the first child and you're not the boy you were supposed to be. But on the other hand, you really can't go outside and walk around on your own.

Supervisor: So you were both things.

Trainee: There's a real lack of trust.

Supervisor: How were you ever going to be independent within that frame and yet to be loved you had to be. So you were stuck.

Trainee: Well, I got a different person.

Supervisor: Well, in that moment, it was a way of not being stuck. And with this client, then she's asking, she's touching upon something that is not clear within you. We can't articulate exactly what she is asking, but it is something to do with 'taking care of me.' Something to do with dependency. Maybe why you're saying 'I don't want to give her that' is perhaps because you're afraid it will put her in a bind, she won't be able to grow and develop and be that independent, self-sufficient person.

Trainee: Let me tell you a keyword that my mother uses – 'duty.' This is what you do because you have to do it. I don't want that type of relationship either. I don't want to do certain things because I have to.

Supervisor: Uh, but translate that to the client now. What do you not want to do for her because you think you might be obligated out of duty as the counselor?

(Holloway 1995: 109)

The final example is from Val Wosket (1999), who is supervising Shaun:

Shaun: You're smiling at me. Why?

Val: Because I want to say: 'I wish you'd shut up. I need some space to think about what you said at the start.' [We both laugh.]

Shaun: And I'm not letting you by giving you all this stuff that you don't want.

Val: I'm just getting confused. I can't make sense of it all – but I *am* wondering if this is what your client does – gives you lots of stuff to keep you from thinking about what you need to think about when you are with him.

Shaun: He does it all the time! Every week he brings something different and I don't know what it will be. He just pours it out, like a confessional.

Val: And what do you do with it?

Shaun: I guess I just receive it. It's quite flattering to feel that I am the only person he tells any of this to.

(Wosket 1999: 226)

Maybe you asked yourself some questions about what you would want from the supervision if you were the supervisee, and what direction you might pursue as the supervisor. What could you tell about the supervisory relationship from the extracts? My experience of supervision has led me to view the following things as crucial in trying to make my supervisory relationships work.

Factors related in my experience to effective supervision

Creating a climate of trust and safety

The very process of showing my work to someone else, particularly when it is personal, can feel like a very dangerous act. I have to know what the other person is going to do with my work and my vulnerabilities about my work. This usually means clearly delineating the role of the supervisor as assessor and conveying an attitude of open mindedness, curiosity and acceptance both of supervisees as people and of their thoughts, feelings, actions, attitudes and beliefs, however different these might be from my own. I am not alone in having experienced workplace interactions as unsafe. 'I tended to dread supervision. I did not want to reflect on my actions and feelings for fear that my supervisor (and I) would discover what a terrible job I was doing' (Benrud-Larson 2000: 103). 'Nervously insecure in those days, I took many suggestions as muted or all too explicit judgements on what I was doing wrong' (Coles 1989: 8). George Prince (1975) found that people frequently responded defensively to close questioning about their ideas, or even to a non-response or well-intended joking. He concluded that adults at work are much more susceptible to hurt feelings than is commonly acknowledged, and that in all vocations there is a tendency for staff to see themselves as engaged in a competitive struggle to preserve and enhance a fragile sense of self-esteem. Sebastian Barry (2008) described with an evocative metaphor the response of a staff group which felt threatened, rolling itself into a ball, needles outward. I readily identify with a workplace populated by metaphorical hedgehogs. No wonder it is necessary to take great care.

Melanie Jasper (2003) reminded me how frightening it can be for students entering the workplace on day one when almost every task is a first. It put me in mind of my first day in a new job based in a Victorian mental hospital. The corridors were long and forbidding; it was difficult to know when and whether to make eye contact and which side to pass others who were approaching. I could see from a distance a large stooped figure loping towards me and as he drew closer I could hear him muttering repeatedly under his breath, 'Fucking cunt, fucking bastard.' I assured myself that if there had been danger he would not have been walking down the corridor unaccompanied, but it was an unnerving beginning. The newness of the practical environment can be daunting, encouraging the donning of emotional 'armour'. The supervisor may be perceived as yet another intimidating figure and it is as well to bear this in mind when trying to establish an atmosphere of safety and trust in the supervisory relationship.

The development of trust is aided by holding and conveying a positive attitude to colleagues in general. If I 'bad mouth' a colleague to supervisees, how do they know that I will not do the same to them? It is all too easy to join in with others' complaints about colleagues, but outlining their strengths and/or positive motivations for what are perceived as negative actions can redefine colleagues or reframe their behaviour in a positive light that encourages a more constructive ethos in general.

Trustworthiness requires me, in the absence of dangerous situations, to keep confidences, and to show congruence, to the best of my ability, between what I say about what I do and what I actually do in practice.

Delineating the formal assessment role is likely to be particularly relevant in pre-registration supervision. I find that supervisees value being provided with information about what is important to me, the supervisor. What will the supervisee be assessed for, and against what standards or criteria? These may be specified by a training institution in the form of intended learning outcomes. Even so, I am sceptical about there being consistent agreement about the qualities that make someone fit to be a professional helper. There are difficulties resulting from poor inter-rater reliability (Shaw and Dobson 1989), poor association between measures of competence and client outcome (Svartberg and Stiles 1992) and difficulties in reaching agreement about what features are central to the task (Fordham et al. 1990). At what level need a skill be demonstrated? Should a predetermined criterion be reached or is the judgement norm-referenced? Is the supervisor assessing an average or best performance? What if the skill is demonstrable within one context but not in another; on one occasion but not on another? These difficulties show no significant signs of resolution (Falender and Shafranske 2007; Rubin et al. 2007) so to reduce anxiety and make supervision a safe space, an open discussion of my approach to assessment can assist. And assessment is not only one-way. I also appreciate reassurance that the supervisee's assessment of my supervision will be managed with sensitivity.

Giving my full attention

Giving full or undivided attention to someone else has been described with the word 'presence'. Presence has been defined as 'a gift of both time and space . . . a way of being rather than a technique that can be applied' (Freshwater 2007: 272).

For the time that I am in supervision, I have found that I need to clear my mind of all other matters. There are contexts in which I have only half a mind on what someone is saying to me and I notice that I am simultaneously carrying on a conversation with myself that seems to be of greater moment. I have learned usually to give my full attention as a therapist and supervisor but still struggle from time to time if something is really bothering me. I find it essential to banish such other subject matter from my mind, sometimes by making a note to assure myself that this important issue will be given attention at a later time and that I need have no fear that it will go away. For the duration of the supervision session it is the material brought to supervision that will have prime place.

Providing containment

One of the features of working with or 'on' people as materials is that the work generates feelings – of love and affection, anger and frustration, fear and anxiety, amusement, happiness and sadness. These feelings are information about what is happening in the work although it is not always easy to think of them in this way. One of the tasks of supervision is to contain the feelings of workers so that they do not overwhelm, and so that they can be used constructively in the service of the work. It makes sense for the supervisor to assist in containing such feelings, bearing listening to and experiencing them, and responding in ways that acknowledge, normalise and legitimise them. Peter Hawkins and Robin Shohet (2006) drew my attention to the work of Jampolsky (2004) and how his acknowledgement of his own fears made for a common bond with a patient on a locked psychiatric ward to whom he had been called out at 2 a.m. one Sunday morning. He says:

> I looked through the small window in the door, and saw a man six feet four inches tall weighing 280 pounds. He was running around the room nude, carrying this large piece of wood with nails sticking out, and talking gibberish. I really didn't know what to do. There were two male nurses, both of whom seemed scarcely five feet tall, who said, 'We will be right behind you, Doc.' I didn't find that reassuring.
>
> As I continued to look through the window, I began to recognize how scared the patient was, and then it began to trickle into my consciousness how scared I was. All of a sudden it occurred to me that he and I had a common bond that might allow for unity – namely, that we were both scared.
>
> Not knowing what else to do, I yelled through the thick door, 'My name is Dr Jampolsky and I want to come in and help you, but I'm scared. I'm scared that I might get hurt, and I'm scared you might get hurt, and I can't help wondering if you aren't scared too.' With this, he stopped his gibberish, turned around and said, 'You're goddam right I'm scared.'
>
> I continued yelling to him, telling him how scared I was, and he was yelling back how scared he was. In a sense we became therapists to each other. As we talked our fear disappeared and our voices calmed down.
>
> (Jampolsky 2004: 125)

Practitioners work on a daily basis in contexts of risk. Supervision can work to keep everyone engaged in the endeavour safe, not by avoiding risks but by encouraging supervisees to face up to them and make both intuitive and reasoned responses to individual clients that may take workers away from the confines of their original training. Supervision can help to distinguish between actions that have been categorised as 'boundary crossing' and 'boundary violation' (Gutheil and Gabbard 1993; D. Smith and Fitzpatrick 1995). Boundary crossings are regarded as relatively frequent occurrences that involve a professional in departing from what might be regarded as common practice. In my view, supervisees considering professional boundary crossing are well advised to share this and their reasoning about it with their supervisor. Like Val Wosket (1999: 133), I believe that, 'rules can limit therapeutic effectiveness even as they also importantly define the boundaries of safe practice'.

There are many actions that can be taken by supervisors with a view to providing containment, which can range from ensuring a regular protected space without interruptions to providing clarity about the purpose and tasks of supervision. Imagine finding yourself in a room with another person. Neither of you know quite why you are there or what you are supposed to be doing. How would that feel? It could be quite exciting but on the other hand pretty anxiety-provoking. Sharing my understandings of and structures within which supervision might take place can reduce the experience of anxiety in supervisees.

Being prepared

Being prepared pertains when I am supervisor or supervisee. It involves taking the supervision seriously, taking responsibility for getting my needs met and using the time set aside to good effect. I will have engaged in self-supervision between formal sessions and may have noted some issues that I wish to review with my colleague/s the next time we meet. I will not be happy only to 'get what I'm given' but rather take an active part, whatever my relative status, in making sure that the supervision 'works'.

Bearing in mind that the people I am working with are trying to do their best

Why would someone not wish to do their best at work, particularly when they have chosen a job that involves minding about people? If they are not being successful, this is probably because they can't rather than won't. In terms of supervision this orientation makes it the supervisor's task to encourage and support, to point out strengths and to encourage development. One of the difficulties with criticism in the health, social care and educational professions is that it can have the effect of deflating the person as a being, not taken only as a critique of work carried out. It is all too easy for supervisees to take umbrage when they perceive supervisory interventions as a comment on their personhood. I have inadvertently and unhelpfully hurt supervisees with statements that begin with the word, 'You'. Maybe you are still smarting from a supervisory intervention made months or years ago which continues to strike you as unfair. If workers feel accepted for themselves they are likely to be open to the challenges posed directly by the work itself, and to identifying their own points for development.

I like people to notice my strengths, even if I often experience what I think of as a very English embarrassment if they are pointed out. I find it helpful to assume that supervisees also like to have their strengths noticed and to feel that I, as their supervisor, am interested in them as people. Helping supervisees to recognise and own their strengths can be a very rewarding task for a supervisor.

Being prepared to exercise the authority vested in the role of supervisor

This may seem to contrast with the previous point. I accept that there are times that my role will involve barring a student or trainee from joining my profession. This will be because they have behaved in ways that are unsuited to the job and have been unable to make the changes at this time that would befit them for the profession. Sometimes I will need to impress upon qualified workers my opinion about what they are doing if I consider it harmful to themselves or their clients. I can do this in a way that still acknowledges their intention to do their best. Particularly in the case of pre-registration training the responsibility for client welfare remains with the supervisor and this may require me to give instructions and ensure that they are followed. In some cases, such as situations involving child protection or public safety, it may be necessary to act in haste. Usually a longer discussion and explanation is merited when time allows. If it is possible to anticipate such situations, suitable responses can be discussed during the initial contracting process with information provided about whom to contact and how in an emergency.

Recognising that the only concerns that can successfully be addressed in supervision are those owned or accepted by the supervisee

Supervisors can encourage, support and model through their own reflective practice, but it is the supervisee who determines how and whether to use the opportunities provided. I may have many ideas as a supervisor about the learning needs of supervisees but unless I am able effectively to draw their attention to these, my interventions are likely to lack effectiveness. If supervisees bring a dominant belief that they are responsible for making clients change I have to start with this rather than try to impose my view that clients are the people responsible for deciding about and making changes to their lives. If supervisees don't see a role for themselves in helping an isolated depressed client with the paperwork involved in a benefit claim, telling them to do so will most likely generate resentment. I need to be more creative in exploring the issue with them.

Thoughtfully managing feedback

Supervisees often express the wish to have feedback about their performance and in my experience this can be a dangerous thing, since they risk exposing themselves to evaluation of any aspect of their work or person, and this can be shocking. The same goes for supervisors who offer an open-ended invitation to supervisees to give them feedback. I have often found unsolicited feedback to be unwelcome, both to myself and to the people I supervise. This is the case even when I have been asked to give feedback. Feedback may be at its most effective when it relates to the concerns and issues of the supervisee who makes a specific request.

- 'How clearly do you think I explained the procedure to the patient?'
- 'Was it wise for me to hand the client a tissue when he began to sob?'
- 'Do you think that Ben felt put down when I made a joke about him swearing at me?'

The impact of specificity is that of containment. More general requests, such as a supervisee asking, 'How do you think it went today?', open up broad swathes of possible and unpredictable response.

If I have a concern as a supervisor that I feel obliged to raise, I find it works best for me to challenge strengths and to link my concern to something about which I can be complimentary.

- 'I thought that you did very well to stay with the issue despite the student's reluctance to hear what you had to say.'
- 'Would it be helpful to think more about planning exactly what to say when you intend to raise difficult issues?'
- 'When Kelly disclosed that her mother had slapped her face and asked you to promise not to tell, I think it showed how effectively you have built up a trusting relationship. Then you had the dilemma of not being able to make the promise. Let's think again about how to introduce the limits of confidentiality to children so that they understand that you are always going to act to keep them safe.'

While the supervisor holds an assessment role, particularly in relation to pre-registration supervisees, the skills of self-assessment are a useful habit to acquire that will serve students well in their future careers. I explore this more fully in Chapter 10.

*Being prepared to show my own practice and acknowledge
my imperfect performance*

I have found watching other people work to be one of the most effective methods by which I learn. When people watch me work I prefer them to have an active role to play, and to adopt an orientation of doing their best to help me do good work. It can be unnerving to imagine that an observer is bent on critique, particularly when I am trying out something new.

Being open about my errors or lacklustre work is important whether I am the supervisor or supervisee. Sometimes I find that supervisors feel an urge to present an 'expert' persona – I used to myself. My position now is that I have to believe that I know *something* but that it would be unreasonable to expect me to know everything, or even if I did, to be able to share it in a way that was useful to the supervisee. I try to comment on areas both where I have a certain view and where I am unsure, modelling that the uncertainty of not knowing is a professional inevitability with which supervision can assist. Apologising for mistakes and being willing to bear uncertainty some of the time model this position and make it more possible for others to do the same. I agree with David Tripp when he says:

> A profession is not much valued for helping others or for the sheer amount of essential expert knowledge that its members have to acquire. Rather, members of a profession are valued for their ability to act in situations where a lack of knowledge (there not being the 'right' answer) demands sound judgement (Schön 1983). Professional judgement is thus a matter of 'expert guesses' and has more to do with reflection, interpretation, opinion and wisdom, than with the mere acquisition of facts and prescribed 'right answers'.
>
> (Tripp 1993: 124)

Sometimes it can be helpful also to be open about past practice so that the supervisee is aware that you too were once a novice; also to show yourself as a human being beneath your professional bearing.

Creating and reviewing the psychological contract

The supervisory contract addresses the expectations that people bring to the supervisory relationship. Some of these are conscious and formal such as the timing and duration of supervision sessions. Many topics need to be negotiated in agreeing a formal contract for supervision, which, in the case of pre-registration supervisees, will include the requirements of their training course in terms of type of work, exposure to work suited to coursework requirements, costs if any, and anticipated learning outcomes. But of greater importance I think, is what the parties believe about supervision, their entitlements, and implicit expectations which may not at the outset be conscious or verbalised. These issues can contribute to discussion of what has been called a 'psychological contract' (Guest and Conway 2002) and I have found it helpful to explore these in depth early in the relationship. I like to ask questions such as the following:

- 'What have you found helpful and unhelpful in your previous experience of supervision?'
- 'What kind of balance would you expect between my asking questions, listening and telling you things?'
- 'What might I do that would offend or hurt you?'
- 'If I were to offend you how would I know?'
- 'How would you advise me to respond?'

This means that if we later run into difficulties we have discussed the fact that this might occur and have some ideas about how to move on from a rupture in the relationship. It is possible for supervisors to provide supervisees with information about how best to 'manage' them if supervisory interventions lead them to feel threatened. The process is permission-giving in terms of making the topic one that can be raised, with a commitment from the supervisor to attempt to respond non-defensively.

This kind of conversation can seem to be taking up valuable supervision time and it may be desirable to spread the initial contracting over several sessions, particularly if either party is showing signs of frustration. Most supervision relationships work to the satisfaction of the parties involved, but careful attention to the contracting process has served me well when problems have subsequently developed since it has provided a structure within which to explore the difficulties.

One of the potential difficulties with raising things that might go wrong in the relationship is the risk of unnecessarily heightening anxiety. I think that it is worth the risk, and the tone of the conversation can convey a certain lightness, especially with the judicious use of humour so that the focus is on keeping all the parties to the work safe.

Agreeing the purposes of supervision and staying on task

A highly succinct statement of the purpose, aim or goal of supervision as 'to enhance professional functioning' was offered by Bernard and Goodyear (1998: 10). This answers the 'What is it for?' question. I can think of no better overall purpose than this because if workers' professional functioning is enhanced then their clients and students are likely to benefit. When I am in supervision I value keeping in mind the three interactive functions of supervision described by Inskipp and Proctor (1993), which are educative (formative), supportive (restorative) and which deal with accountability (normative). These help me to answer the 'What am I trying to do?' question.

John Driscoll and Julia O'Sullivan (2007) gave an analysis by supervisory function of the kinds of issues that were discussed by a supervisee in clinical supervision as follows:

Formative function

- How to be a supervisee and get the most from sessions
- Articulating what clinical supervision is to others
- Writing as well as talking about practice
- Use of a structured framework to help with reflection on practice
- Being more assertive in practice
- Use of own experiential learning to develop further knowledge about being a carer within a family and increased awareness of patient/client needs
- The importance of networking in a post that is often isolated from immediate peers (i.e. other Macmillan radiographers)
- Development of a deeper insight of the impact of self on others at work.

Restorative function

- The danger of becoming too involved with caseloads to see objectively
- Personal feelings that can surface from everyday working with the patient/client
- Personal effects of trying to be all things to all people in the caring situation
- The need to recognise as well as establish a support network in the immediate work environment to survive the stresses and strains of working in oncology
- Giving oneself (and actively seeking) permission to take time out on a regular basis to reflect on practice with someone outside of practice.

Normative function

- Examining how a 'small fish' swims in a big pond
- Roles and responsibilities in practice
- Clarification of role boundaries in practice
- Establishing the legitimacy of clinical supervision by 'finding the time' in busy practice
- Less defensive and more open about strengths and limitations in own practice
- Questioning own leadership potential.

When I read these I was struck by the degree to which the articulation of the functions of supervision mapped onto potential functions of reflective practice in this instance.

The overarching aim of jobs that involve providing a service to other people is to enhance their lives, whether this be through facilitating learning, development and change; maintaining health; easing pain and suffering; or giving them a sense of being noticed and heard. Keeping this in mind and retaining it as the overarching imperative helps keep the supervision on task. There are some approaches to supervision that risk turning the supervisee into the client, an orientation against which it is important to be on guard. A style of supervision designated 'therapeutic' (Rosenblatt and Mayer 1975) led supervisees to feel problematised when their struggles in their work appeared to be attributed by their supervisor to personality deficiencies in themselves.

Agreeing on 'how to do' supervision

There are very many models and frameworks within which supervision may be conceptualised and these help me to think about the 'How am I going about it?' question. These include literature directed exclusively to supervisees' role in making supervision work (Carroll and Gilbert 2005), framework-specific texts (Falender and Shafranske 2004; Frawley O'Dea and Sarnat 2001; M. Gilbert and Evans 2007; Hawkins and Shohet 2006; Holloway 1995; Page and Wosket 2001; Stoltenberg and McNeill 2009) and works that describe a range of alternative frameworks (Bernard and Goodyear 2008; Butterworth et al. 2001; Milne 2009; J.M. Scaife 2009; Watkins 1997).

Frameworks for thinking about and planning supervision have the advantage of giving structure to supervision sessions in order to keep on track with the aims and objectives. I prefer to keep in mind something relatively simple that does not distract me from giving maximum possible attention to my own and/or my supervisee's issues. Some of the frameworks mirror approaches to the work being supervised, particularly in psychotherapy and counselling. They draw on theories of change and theories of learning. So, if the supervisor works in a cognitive behavioural model, a significant focus for learning and development is likely to be supervisee cognitions, and the supervision session will follow a similar structure to cognitive therapy sessions (Liese and Beck 1997; Rosenbaum and Ronen 1998). Person-centred models emphasise the primacy of active listening, congruence, empathic understanding and unconditional positive regard in both therapy and supervision (Tudor and Worrall 2004). Psychodynamic models stress the importance of the supervisory alliance and the impact on the participants of transference and counter-transference (the process whereby emotions and patterns of relating are transposed from one relationship to another) through a parallel process (Binder and Strupp 1997; Frawley O'Dea and Sarnat 2001).

Two generic frameworks are illustrated in Figures 4.2 and 4.3. I like them because they are relatively simple and I find them to be pretty much self-explanatory.

The General Supervision Framework (J.A. Scaife and J.M. Scaife 1996; J.M. Scaife 1993a) comprises the three dimensions of supervisor role, supervision focus and the medium that provides data for supervision (Figure 4.2). While the framework emphasises the role of the supervisor, reciprocal roles tend to be played out between supervisor and supervisee. The role relationship may be dictated by the actions of either or both parties. For example the supervisee might invite inform-assess role behaviour while the supervisor intends to adopt an enquiring stance. This dimension can help the parties to notice what is happening between them in terms of reciprocal roles, and to decide whether this interplay honours the agreed contract.

Supervisory focus comprises the material upon which the parties agree to concentrate. The discussion is likely to shift between the three dimensions in any one supervision session. The possible options for the medium

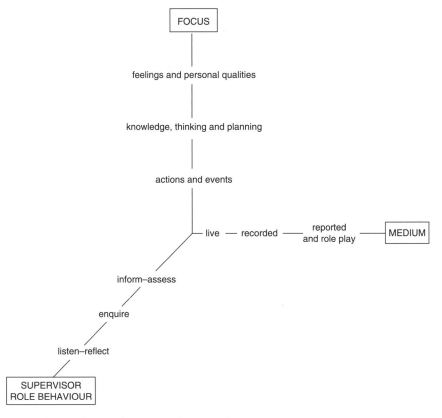

Figure 4.2 The General Supervision Framework.

of supervision include non-participatory observation, role play, simulated therapy sessions (West 1984), sitting in with the supervisor, bug-in-the-ear (earphone), bug-in-the-eye (whereby information is provided to the worker via a computer screen shielded from the client: Klitzke and Lombardo 1991), audio- and video-recordings, verbal reporting, telephone and email communications, and video-conferencing (Wood et al. 2005). This model and the one that follows are described more fully in J.M. Scaife (2009).

The cyclical model of supervision (Page and Wosket 2001) is addressed primarily to the structure of supervision sessions (Figure 4.3). The model delineates a number of stages through which each supervision session proceeds, and can be used to help the supervision stay on track, ensuring that there is movement towards the agreed goals. The supervision process is presented as a cycle of five stages proceeding from contract to focus, space, bridge and review.

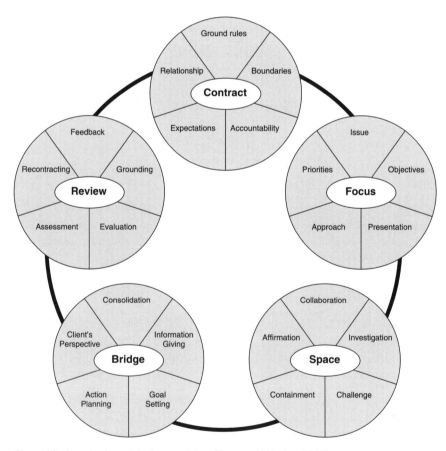

Figure 4.3 A cyclical model of supervision (Page and Wosket 2001).

In my experience issues brought to supervision are sometimes given insufficient 'air space', there being an apparent degree of urgency to reach a destination. This model emphasises the 'space' as the part of the session that is likely to take up the most time. The space is the primary stage in which reflection can take place. Keeping the framework in mind can ensure that the products of the reflection are taken forward via the bridge into action. The process of review begins another cycle. Not all supervisions will follow the process in this order; there may be recycling or stages omitted. Like each of the frameworks, it operates as a mind map through which to keep a check on the supervision journey.

Using material that enables review of performance

Some materials lend themselves particularly well to the process of review: audio- and video-recordings and 'live' supervision or observation being examples. The benefits of recorded material are that they aid the supervisor and supervisee in becoming joint observers, working together to try and understand the processes taking place. Review of recordings can also help to remove doubts about competence through endorsement of seen practice. Recordings are unique in allowing participation followed by review; a slowing down of the interpersonal processes taking place which I regard as ideally suited to reflective practice.

Live supervision can be containing for both client and clinician, if agreed in the contracting process, since changes of direction, or interruption of unhelpful interactional patterns between client and worker can be accomplished in-session rather than through post-session discussion. The client can benefit from the presence of an experienced practitioner and/or a different perspective during the session. Openness of practice is a safeguard in itself. Nevertheless, the presence of an observer can be nerve-racking and I find it useful and desirable to prepare extensively for such 'live' supervision. This is discussed more fully in Chapter 8. For a first experience it is helpful to be the worker who is taking the least active role.

Being mindful of the organisational culture

Supervision may be a voluntary or mandated activity in professional practice. When I lead supervisor training workshops I sometimes encounter participants who have attended as conscripts and they may let me know through their social behaviours that this is the last place they want to be. I am not as brave as a colleague of mine who begins such events by inviting anyone who has more important things to do to leave. And even then, who would have the nerve to go when this may be seen as breaking the rule that says you have to be present even if you are really somewhere else? As far as supervision goes, did your supervisees choose you as their supervisor? Do they want to learn to be reflective practitioners? You may need to work around a supervision contract that addresses 'how to keep the organisation off my back'.

'Watch your back' is a type of organisational culture described by Hawkins and Shohet (2006). I think it often develops out of fear of making mistakes and being the butt of public criticism. It contrasts with the learning culture that I think is necessary to support reflective practice. In my experience a 'watch your back' culture emphasises rules and procedures that encourage a shut-down of thinking and stifling of creativity. Reflective supervisors can encourage practitioners to look behind these procedures and to circumnavigate the constraints that they impose. I have experienced very productive and enlightening conversations in my supervision that have confirmed the organisation as a legitimate focus of the supervisory conversation. Knowledge of the cultural constraints under which supervisees are practising keeps the supervision focused within the bounds of what is possible.

What the literature says

For researchers, the investigation of the key factors in effective supervision has presented a significant challenge. While ultimately it might be considered desirable to demonstrate a relationship between supervision and client outcomes, the multiple links in the chain from supervisor interventions to client change, and the impact of variables unrelated to supervision make convincing evidence difficult to construct. Multi-variable systems with inherent time lags between actions and outcomes, and in which complex paths of causality may pertain, do not readily lend themselves to the types of study that seek a clear and simple causal relationship. There is a risk of trying to study a phenomenon using unsuitable methods. By trying to impose on the activity of supervision manualised interventions and the 'gold standard' randomised controlled trial, we fail to study the activity in question, but rather are in danger of changing the activity to something else in order to make it more researchable. This leaves me very sceptical about what the results of such studies might tell me.

There is a parallel in the field of education where few would argue against the idea of education often being efficacious for learning. However, there is little consensus about what factors reliably lead to intended learning outcomes (D. Hargreaves 1996; Muijs and Reynolds 2006). Class size, setting or mixing, single sex or co-educational, learner or teacher-centred methods all have their proponents. Established causal links between teacher education, including supervision of practice, and student learning are even harder to find. What has emerged from research is the crucial role that *beliefs* play in teaching in all sectors of education (Kemp 2008; Norton et al. 2005).

Given the complexities of the supervisory system, I don't find it surprising that extensive systematic reviews of the literature (descriptive and often statistical meta-analyses of a number of individual studies within a topic area such as those carried out by Bogo and McKnight 2005; Ellis and Ladany 1997; Ellis et al. 1996; Gilmore 1999; Holloway and Neufeldt 1995; Milne and James 2000; S. Wheeler and Richards 2007) have excluded many studies on the grounds of methodological imperfections and have reported some disappointing outcomes of supervision. Milne and James (2000) did conclude that there was evidence to suggest that supervision benefited clients through the 'educational pyramid' of consultant, supervisor, supervisee and client.

In order to address the balance between rigour and relevance, Milne et al. (2007) argued the case for an approach to reviewing the literature entitled Best Evidence Synthesis (Petticrew and Roberts 2006). The reviewer works with whatever evidence is available so studies are not excluded for lack of rigour, but those with findings based on sound methodology are given greater weight. The approach combines the meta-analytic approach of extracting quantitative information from a series of studies while taking into account study quality and relevance. Also promising are small-scale qualitative studies which I think are well suited to the study of supervision.

Studies of supervision within many professions (psychology, counselling and psychotherapy, nursing, psychiatry and teaching) have consistently found the relationship or supervisory alliance between the parties to be the most crucial determinant of outcomes and satisfaction (Beinart 2004; Hensley 2002, reported in Bogo and McKnight 2005; Kilminster and Jolly 2000; Ladany et al. 1999; Lizzio et al. 2005; Sweeney et al. 2001). Worthen and McNeill (2001) conducted a national survey examining the attitudes and beliefs of experts in the field of supervision concerning what constitutes effective supervision. The opinions expressed in the survey considered effective supervision to be reliant on the development of a facilitative supervisory relationship characterised by empathy, warmth, trust, mutual respect and flexibility. An effective supervisory relationship was believed to encourage thoughtful experimentation and reflection on mistakes so that they become learning opportunities (Worthen and McNeill 1996). Trustworthiness was identified as the central most important feature of the supervisory relationship when trainees described characteristics of influential supervisors (Green 1998, cited in Beinart 2004). Supervisor style – attractiveness, interpersonal sensitivity, and task orientation – were found to be related to the strength of the working alliance by Efstation et al. (1990). Modelling openness to differences of opinion and willingness to work at resolution has been found to be a characteristic of highly competent supervisors (Nelson et al. 2008).

What else does the literature have to say about what supervisors can do to accomplish the normative, formative and restorative purposes of supervision? The setting of clear boundaries at the outset was found to be facilitative of effective supervisory relationships (Beinart 2004). She found that the wisdom and experience of the supervisor seemed to be of less importance than opportunities to observe the supervisor's work and engage in stimulating conversations from a position of curiosity. Flexibility was important to supervisees who found didactic supervision or inflexible adherence to models less helpful.

The findings in the literature suggest that novices and experienced supervisees have different preferences for the supervisor's approach and the focus of supervision. Typically, beginners have been found to prefer more formal structure (Stoltenberg et al. 1994; Tracey et al. 1989) whereas more experienced supervisees prefer a focus on case conceptualisation (Heppner and Roehlke 1984) and more emphasis on personal development than technical skills (G. Allen et al. 1986; M. Winter and Holloway 1991). Beginners had a greater preference for didactic teaching than did experienced workers (Worthington and Roehlke 1979). The need for structure was found to be important for all workers if they were dealing with a clinical crisis (Tracey et al. 1989).

In a study of community mental health nurses, the perceived quality of supervision was higher for those nurses who had chosen their supervisors, and where sessions took place away from the workplace (D. Edwards et al. 2005). These nurses obtained higher scores than their peers on the sub-scales of trust/rapport and supervisor advice/support.

From a survey of clinical psychology supervisors and trainees, Delia Cushway and Jacky Knibbs (2004) found that there was a striking similarity between the top ten ranked issues identified by supervisors and by supervisees. Establishing good rapport and giving appropriate positive feedback were ranked as the top two most helpful behaviours by both groups. Supervisors rated the holding and containing aspects of supervision a little more highly than did supervisees. Trainees rated teaching, critical appraisal and direct observation of the supervisor more highly than did supervisors. Supervisees also valued being helped to develop self-confidence, being provided with relevant literature, being offered suggestions for alternative ways of working with clients and help with experimentation and discovery of their individual style. Cushway and Knibbs (2004: 177) state: 'It may be that unless a good rapport is established, little else of value can happen.'

When there are difficulties in supervision there can be a tendency to assume that these have arisen because the supervisor has been unable to create the conditions that foster the necessary rapport. Michael Carroll and Maria Gilbert (2005) helpfully remind us that the supervisee has responsibilities too. They write of the need for supervisees to take responsibility for their supervision and their learning which requires supervisors to allow them to do so. The following reflection on supervision reported by Jan Fook (1999) illustrates how taking responsibility can lead to routes forward following a rupture in a previously satisfactory supervisory relationship.

> The discussion with the supervisor of the critical incident and the ensuing handing back of the client was expected. The unexpected was the tone of the discussion. The interpretation made by the supervisor was that I had pushed the client into divulging too much, thereby allowing

the client's power to flow on to me. To have my supervisor (who is known to be one of the foremost supervisors around) say this just stopped me in my tracks. My first reaction influenced what happened next as I did not regain my equilibrium enough to question the initial analysis. This probably allowed her to think her assumption was correct. If I had interpreted the supervisor's analysis as inquisitive questioning rather than an accusation of incompetent practice, the emotional element would have been controllable on my part. I had intended to report in detail what happened and then debrief, but this never happened . . .

A main theme emerging from this session was my inability to assert myself. I allowed my inability to 'name' things to take over, and did not claim my own professional skill base . . . In my recently recognised 'victim' mode, I gave up my narrative for hers, just accepted the tabled analysis of the situation and withdrew. My withdrawal had two negative functions: first, it allowed me to indulge in a safe space of 'the victim', therefore I did not have to take a chance in debate; and second, by not extending myself, the supervisor was denied a constructive space where she could mirror her argument. Foucault (cited in Sawicki 1991: 52) claims power is 'exercised rather than possessed . . .' The power I exercised against myself would otherwise be known as sabotage. This demonstrates the fluidity of power: it has so many interpretations, allowing its influence to go unrecognised through biography, therefore hardly ever challenged.

(Fook 1999: 196)

To conclude, it seems that at the heart of the supervisory enterprise, as at the heart of the educative and helping professions is the quality of the relationship between the involved parties. When the relationship is working, deep exploration of practice can take place:

In interpersonal relationships, empathy is a tool of civility. Making an effort to get in touch with another's frame of reference sends a message of respect. Therefore, empathy plays an important part in building a working alliance . . . When clients are understood, they tend to move on – to explore substantive issues more widely and deeply.

(Egan 1994: 117)

Chapter 5

Approaches to supervision of reflective practice (I)

Enquiry

> Confidence, like art, never comes from having all the answers; it comes from being open to all the questions.
>
> (Stevens 2008)

Confidence can be reflected in the capacity of a practitioner to endure a mind state of constant questioning and uncertainty. I think that this is the state of mind of a reflective practitioner. It contrasts with an attitude of firmly cling-ing to a fixed idea or putting up a defensive wall to challenge. The reflective practitioner asks, time and again, how her or his experience might be con-ceived and understood from different viewpoints so as to create multiple options for action. Consistent with this position, Earl Gary Stevens (2007) discourages us from looking to external authority 'from above' for answers, arguing that individuals are quite capable of creating their own questions and making their own decisions. Underlying this view is the constructivist idea that no one can claim to know the single, real or correct interpretation of experiences, rather there are multiple perspectives, accounts or stories which may be more or less useful to the practitioner.

Barry Mason (1993) argues that at times we are all caught up in a desire for certainty but that it can contribute to a state of paralysis and lack of creativity. Instead he proposes we adopt a position of 'safe uncertainty' as a framework for thinking about our work so that we 'fall out of love with the idea that solutions solve things' (Mason 1993: 194). Safe uncertainty is con-sistent with practitioners viewing themselves as respectful listeners who do not understand too quickly, if ever. This position can help to counter the desire for certainty sometimes expected by employers. It is easy to get caught up in seeking the 'right' answer.

In order to foster this state of mind, supervisors may use questions as their key resource. Particularly when questions generate an element of surprise they can promote changes in understanding and new vantage points that can make a difference; the supervisee is prompted to construct new meanings. There are times when I have carried around in my head an apt and challenging question for days after it has been asked. For me, questions are at the heart of the process of reflective practice, whether these are posed by the person doing the reflecting or by a peer, supervisor or educator. What do I see as the benefits of questioning over being told? Thoughtfully posed questions encourage the making of links, challenge people's stories about themselves and their lives, encourage openness to new ideas, and can lead to deep learning about oneself and the impact of oneself on others. The respondent is invited to be an active participant in the dialogue, constructing ideas and making connections, resulting in a sense of ownership and personal agency that I think is more likely to bring about desired changes than usually results from being told. Questions can also provide support for a hitherto tentatively held view and help to consolidate learning.

Although this chapter is about questions, supervisors also have available the resources of listening and informing. I have at times been surprised by the power of someone's undivided attention as a listener to help me make sense of my experiences. Questions benefit from being asked by an attentive listener who allows the answers to guide the posing of the next question. This helps to maintain a focus on the needs and concerns of the supervisee. In supervising the reflective practitioner, the parties struggle together from a position of curiosity to make meaning of the supervisee's experiences at work. It is in the context of this mutual attempt to understand that questions derive their usefulness and power.

It is not only from words themselves that the listener derives meaning; this is also inferred from the emotional tone or posture in which they are posed, and the relationship context in which they are asked (Tomm 1988). If enquiry is to be a mainstay of the supervisor's approach, therefore, it is as well to have explored this thoroughly in the initial contracting process. I believe that effective initial contracting has much to contribute to the subsequent quality of the supervisory relationship (outlined in Chapter 4) and it is wise to address not only the task of supervision itself but also the preferred methods and approaches of the participants. Initial agreements can be reviewed and adjusted as the relationship develops.

Questions that I have found useful to the development of reflective practice are asked from a position of genuine curiosity. Even if the questions are leading, the 'correct' answer is not in the supervisor's head. The sorts of questions that can stimulate reflective practice go beyond those employed in everyday life: open questions enquiring into what, how, why, where and who. In this chapter I will describe some approaches to questioning derived from different psychotherapy traditions, all of which aim to stimulate or affirm changed perspectives either through highlighting difference or by drawing connections. I want to sound a note of caution, though, in adapting questions from the psychotherapeutic context for the purpose of encouraging critical reflection. Some of these questions are deliberately contrived: contrived with the original intention of helping clients to make significant changes in their lives. When adapting such questions in order to encourage reflective practice, keeping in mind the *purposes* of the questioning will help to ensure that supervision stays within the boundary of facilitating the development of people in their *work*. It is, in my mind, crucial that supervisees are fully aware of what they are signing up to when they agree to such questioning, and it may be helpful to forewarn by providing written materials and examples lest they begin to feel 'therapised' rather than supervised. I see this aspect of the contracting process as ensuring informed consent and permission. Supervisees need to know that they will not be assessed negatively should the questions prove too detached from current experience or too unsettling to be of value to them. As the following extract shows, some questions, particularly 'why' questions, can be experienced as inciting rather than inviting:

> He was giving me a lot of information. I don't need the reasons behind it to know what my next step is, whereas before I would look for the reasons behind things. They are not always known. That is one of the things that reflection has brought out. The reasons are not always known and when you ask him 'Why?' you put him on the defensive. So I try to avoid that question.
>
> (Osterman and Kottkamp 1993: 167)

Differences of approach to questioning within therapeutic traditions appear to lie not so much in the specific questions asked, but rather in the theoretical frameworks to which the practitioner subscribes, the precise purposes for which particular questions are asked, and the philosophical underpinnings and value bases on which the practice is based, none of which can be directly observed. I have therefore organised the questions in this chapter according to the supervisor's aims. This cuts across the traditions on which I am drawing of cognitive behaviour therapy (Socratic questions) systemic (circular and reflexive questions), narrative and solution-focused approaches.

Questions that aim to facilitate the contracting process

In the beginning stage of a cognitive behavioural approach (Padesky 1993) 'informational questions' are asked. This stage aims to make the subject under consideration concrete and understandable to both parties. A broad sweep is taken to try to identify the place of the client's issues in the wider context. The initial contracting process in supervision provides an opportunity for information exchange which can facilitate mutual understanding and sets the scene for future development of the supervisory relationship. Such a conversation usually begins with general questions that explore the supervisee's previous experiences of supervision and how these might relate to the current situation:

- 'In previous experiences of supervision, what have you found to be particularly helpful to your learning?'
- 'What might I do that you would find unhelpful?'
- 'How will you let me know about what you are finding helpful and unhelpful?'
- 'What kind of issues should I be particularly careful about?'
- 'What do you think it's important for us to discuss at this time?'

I have found questions that explore the future of the supervisory role-relationship (mutual partnership; teacher–student; consultant–client) to be of particular value in heading off potential problems. They encourage the exploration of hypothetical challenges to the relationship, giving a message that these are matters that may be discussed and resolved:

- 'How will you let me know when you want me to enquire into your ideas and when you want me to tell you what I think?'
- 'What is your feeling about me offering critical feedback?'
- 'Would you prefer to invite me to give you feedback or give me a free rein?'
- 'How will I know if I am being insensitive?'
- 'How might you react if I were to hurt your feelings?'
- 'What kind of response might I make that would repair the damage?'

Carroll and Gilbert (2005) offer very helpful ideas about being a supervisee, among which are posed a range of questions that supervisees usefully can ask themselves. The authors suggest questions to ask when interviewing a prospective supervisor, and more to think about following the interview. Further questions suited to initial contracting that explore the focus of supervision, boundaries, issues of diversity, current skills and points for development are described in Scaife (1993b).

Questions that aim to enhance supervisee confidence

Questions that use time to promote different perspectives can be encouraging to supervisees who are experiencing difficulties or a crisis of confidence. They serve as a reminder that whatever I am worrying about now is unlikely to be worrying me in five days', five months' or five years' time, and is not the same as my worries from five years ago. Questions may invite respondents to examine an experience from the perspective of any time difference, however long or short, looking either into the past or the future. When something that feels 'big' is looming on the horizon, questions oriented towards the future may put the anxiety-generating context into a frame in which it has shrunk. Looming events can be dominating and often generate anticipatory anxiety, but after they have happened they are history. Imagine that a supervisee is worrying about an impending interview or viva. Asking questions about looking back from the day after the interview reminds supervisees that much of life will be just the same; the sun will still shine, traffic lights will still turn from red to green and something else of import will be dominating their thinking. This particular focus on time is known in narrative approaches as 'historicising the near future'. Future-oriented questions can help supervisees to create a story or narrative about themselves which releases them from the constraints of the present. The future holds multiple possibilities.

Questions that compare the past with the present can serve to remind people of changes that they have made. From a cognitive behavioural perspective Christine Padesky (1993: 1) described how a list of 'good' questions included, 'Have you ever been in similar circumstances before?', 'What did you do then?', 'How did that turn out?' and 'What do you know now that you didn't know then?' She cautions that a list of 'good' questions, which have generally been found to stimulate thoughts experienced as useful by clients, is only a beginning, and that such generic questions are not enough once students have progressed beyond the basics.

From solution-focused therapy comes a specific hypothetical question known as 'the miracle question'. Solution-focused supervision is based on the assumption that if supervisees come to feel that they are basically competent, then they are more likely to be receptive to learning (O'Connell 2005). The miracle question is both hypothetical and time-related, in that it asks respondents to project themselves into the future as if a miracle has happened and their difficulties have dissipated. Here is a sequence from O'Connell (2005):

Supervisor: If you were working better with this client and your current difficulties had been overcome, what would be the first signs for you that a miracle had happened?

Supervisee: My heart wouldn't sink when I saw him in the waiting room.

Supervisor: After the miracle, how would you be feeling and what would you be thinking when you saw him there?

Supervisee: I would smile at him the way I do with most clients and sound a bit more enthusiastic in asking him to come in.

Supervisor: What else?

Supervisee: When he started talking, he would let me get a word in edgeways, rather than just launching into a verbal attack, as he usually does.

Supervisor: What difference would that make to you?

Supervisee: I'd feel that I had something to offer rather than just being a dumping ground for all his complaints, without him being willing to let me help him change.

Supervisor: What else would be happening once the miracle had happened?

Supervisee: I wouldn't be feeling so weary and hopeless after seeing him.

Supervisor: How would you be feeling at the end of a session?

Supervisee: I would feel that he had worked harder than me and that it was worthwhile trying to help him.

Supervisor: If you were to bring this client to supervision three months from now and you were telling me that things were much better, how would it have come about? What would have happened to make it happen?

Supervisee: I would have found ways of keeping him on the subject and listening to what *I* have to say for a change.

Supervisor: I wonder how you would have managed to do that?

Supervisee: I would have an agreed agenda for a session and interrupt him once he went off on a tangent. I also think that I would have given him things to do between sessions and started off a session by asking him whether he'd done them or not. I think if I could get him to keep to the point most of the time I wouldn't mind if occasionally he went off on a monologue.

Supervisor: So you would have more of a structure to the session than you have at the moment?

Supervisee: I think that I would have limited the sessions to less than an hour as well. Then I wouldn't feel so drained at the end of them. I think I could do a better job with him in half an hour than an hour.

Supervisor: That sounds as if you are thinking of ways that will help you to be more effective and look after yourself at the same time. How will you do this in a way that impacts positively on your client?

(O'Connell 2005: 93)

Solution-focused approaches to therapy specifically emphasise the use of pre-suppositional questions which are leading and express a belief or expectation. For example, a question such as, 'Can you think of a time that you were more in tune with the client?' can be turned into a pre-suppositional version: 'Tell me about a time when you were more in tune with the client.' This type of question was designed in order to enhance people's awareness of the inevitability of change and of their own personal strengths (O'Hanlon and Weiner-Davis 2003). Pre-suppositional questions asked by the supervisor such as, 'How did you know to do that at just that moment?' help to create a positive mind-set in both the supervisor and supervisee (Swann et al. 1982). Presbury et al. (1999) suggest that from day one the supervisor is best advised to phrase questions and statements to include the assumption of competence. Later questions in this chapter can often be adapted to pre-suppositional form.

While the sequence above comes from a solution-focused tradition, I think that it could also be seen to exemplify Socratic questioning. 'Through sensitive questioning, clients are encouraged to use what they know, to discover alternative views and solutions for themselves, rather than the therapist suggesting them' (Westbrook et al. 2007: 90). A supervisor working in a cognitive behavioural model, and using a congruent approach to therapy and supervision might adopt such a questioning process in order to facilitate a supervisee's learning.

Sometimes I find that supervisees bring to supervision actions that they believe were 'wrong' or feelings, such as guilt, about not being good enough. This is a time when it may be helpful to create questions that reverse the meaning of 'wrong' or 'guilty' from their implicit undesirability to a state of potential usefulness. The supervisor can take the action seen as wrong and ask what was right about it. This might have to be in the form of a hypothetical question:

- 'If there had been something right about what you did, what might it have been?'
- 'What other wrong actions might have had a worse outcome?'

Not infrequently I have assessed a session with a client as particularly 'good' only to find that at the next session nothing has changed. And after particularly difficult sessions following which I have felt down-hearted or depressed, the client has returned on the next occasion having made significant steps forward. The worker's assessment is one of many and clients use the material from sessions in unknown and sometimes unintended ways to generate their own solutions. There is a folk song expressing the difficulty of judging 'good' and 'bad' outcomes. The son of a farmer takes a horse to market to sell, and en route the horse is lost. He returns home and everyone says, 'What bad luck'. The next day the horse returns to the farm, bringing with it another horse and everyone says, 'What good luck'. The son goes riding on the horse, falls off and breaks his leg and everyone says, 'What bad luck'. This means that when he is conscripted he is unable to join the army and everyone says, 'What good luck' and so on. The refrain is, 'How do you know, how do you know?' This overarching question underlies a process of enquiry that challenges assumptions about meanings already made, particularly when these have the effect of undermining confidence. Paul Gilbert (2009: 297) encourages clients to take a compassionate perspective on themselves and suggests self-questioning which includes, 'What holds me back from really taking on board my own wisdom and understanding that things are not quite as I'm telling myself they are?'

Hypothetical questions typically begin with 'If' or 'Suppose'. 'If you did or said this, if you thought this, if you felt differently about, if that had happened instead of the other . . .' Such questions are designed to release respondents from a closed or set view in order to reveal hopes, fears and aspirations. I have taken the following example from an exposition of Socratic questioning (Padesky 1993: 3): 'What things would you do differently if you were less depressed or a better father in your eyes?' This type of question adapts well to supervision:

- 'If you were less anxious and a better therapist/teacher in your eyes, what things would you do differently with your client/students?'
- 'If you were Sigmund Freud working with your client, what ideas might you have about where to go next?'
- 'If you thought that your client was only going through the motions of wanting to change his life, what would you say to him?'
- 'If you weren't fearful of hurting your client, what risks might you take with her?'

A pre-suppositional version of the last question, made by substituting 'when' for 'if' and changing to the present tense can orient supervisees towards their strengths.

Questions with embedded suggestions can be hypothetical in the sense that the supervisor introduces her or his ideas in the form of a question. Instead of making suggestions or stating opinions such as, 'I think that you should challenge your client more,' the ideas are presented in the form of a question, 'If you were to challenge your client more, what do you think would result?' (When you challenge your client more what is the result?) 'If you thought that your client would benefit if you were to be more challenging, how would you find the voice to do this?' This form allows the supervisee to accept or reject the supervisor's ideas with less pressure to conform to the views of a person who might be regarded as an authority. It can also be difficult to have the confidence to refute the views of a supervisor who has an assessment role. One of the dangers that I have found in pressing my own opinion is that supervisees tend to think that my ideas are superior to theirs. This does not help them to gain confidence in their own thinking. Alternatively, supervisees may pay lip service to my ideas but do what they were going to do anyway.

I am not trying to make a case always to use questions rather than make statements or offer opinions, rather that it is helpful for supervisors to develop an extensive repertoire of enquiring skills in encouraging reflective practice. But an unreflective habit of invariably turning telling into asking could be very frustrating for supervisees and inauthentic on the part of the supervisor. The supervisee's current views are central to the direction of possible learning and the supervisor's questions can act as windows on a variety of paths from which the supervisee might choose. There is a genuine opportunity for the supervisor also to learn from the exchange and from what the supervisee can see through the windows. This kind of enquiry can help supervisees to become increasingly confident in their own reflective judgements.

Questions that aim to encourage the setting of realistic goals

Scaling questions derive from a solution-focused approach. 'The primary purpose of scaling questions is to help clients set small identifiable goals, measure progress (beginning, middle and end) and establish priorities for action' (O'Connell 2005: 53). They invite respondents to locate on a scale their position in relation to an issue. The end points of the scale are secured by the use of referents such as 'the worst it could be' and 'the best it could be'. David Campbell and Marianne Grøenbæk (2006) refer to these as 'semantic polarities' and explain how they can be used to aid staff in thinking about their positions in organisations. Scaling can draw the attention of clients to small differences in their experiences according to precise times and circumstances, and for this reason it is advised that questions address such specifics. By allocating a numerical value to indicate the severity of a problem in the initial session, often in conjunction with the 'miracle' question, small changes can later be highlighted. For example, if the identified issue is the intensity of pain being experienced (either physical or emotional), a small reduction indicated by a shift of rating from 9 to 8 may otherwise go unnoticed. Clients may decide that they are happy with the aim of a reduction to a rating of 3 rather than being satisfied only by a change to zero. Thus, scaling can help to avoid 'all or nothing' thinking. The questions can be used in supervision to measure confidence, motivation and progress. O'Connell (2005) suggests the following:

> On a scale of 10 to zero how confident are you that you can improve your
>   work with this client?
> Is that good enough for you to make a start?
> If not, where would you need to get to for that to happen?
>
> (O'Connell 2005: 94)

Scaling questions can help supervisees to set themselves small identifiable goals, particularly in relation to learning tasks that they are interested to pursue. These can involve skill development (e.g. the use of scaling questions in therapy), emotions (feeling more confident about managing sessions or handling a class of students), and cognitions (understanding constructivism). Self-ratings can be revisited by either party as supervision proceeds, with a view to flagging up development and change.

Questions that aim to encourage a sense of agency

Narrative therapy is based on the notion that the person is not the problem, the problem is the problem (Carey and Russell 2002). Problems are located as a product of culture and history. The problem becomes 'externalised' from the person and the therapist asks questions about the relationship between the person, the problem and the person's strengths and personal qualities. In a narrative approach, respondents are encouraged to notice actions and intentions that contradict their 'dominant story', often a story about themselves that has been retold and consolidated in the telling. Contradictions are developed through the identification of 'unique outcomes'. The questioning process encourages further development of these contradictions into new narratives which include a perspective in which respondents are encouraged to see themselves as having agency in bringing about desired changes. Here is an example from Sallyann Roth and David Epston (1995) in which the respondent is being encouraged to question her or his relationship not with another person, but with a state which he or she is experiencing now; one which could be experienced differently in the future.

- 'How does busyness feature in your work life? In your life beyond work? Your relationships?'
- 'When it is having its way with you, what happens to your dreams for the future?'
- 'Are you satisfied or dissatisfied with the way the busyness is "wrecking my relationship" and leaving you no time for friends?'
- 'Have there been times that you have thought – even for a moment – that you might step out of busyness's forced march?'
- 'Given everything that busyness has got going for it, how did you protest against its pushing you around?'
- 'Can you imagine a time in the future that you might defy busyness and give yourself a break?'

The following questions from the same article illustrate how the alternative narrative might be developed from a single exception to the dominant story into a different future narrative.

- 'Where do you think you will go next now that you have embarked upon self-delight?'
- 'Is this a direction you see yourself taking in the days/weeks/years to come?'
- 'Do you think it is likely that this might revive your flagging relationship, restore your friendships, or renew your vitality?'

I can see a place for these particular questions in supervision. I know of no one in my professional field who does not experience work overload at times, and it is easy to become down-hearted when faced with seemingly insoluble problems. This kind of question seems to me more likely to encourage self-reflection and generate different perspectives on busyness and workload pressure than would telling, mutual moaning or sympathy alone. Their aim is to encourage the construction and telling of a different story in which the teller has the wherewithal to bring about desired changes.

Questions that aim to develop enhanced empathy

Observer-perspective questions invite respondents to try to stand outside their own experiences and to hypothesise or speculate from a distance. This distance may be accomplished by attempting to enter the experience of others; their actions, thoughts, feelings and beliefs. Such questions might be described as 'mind reading'. This perspective might involve empathy: the capability to imagine the experience of another. Observer-perspective questions might achieve distance by focusing on how other people may be experiencing the supervisee, or how inanimate objects might report their observations if they had a voice. The questions might encourage supervisees to become observers of their *own* actions, thoughts, feelings or beliefs by taking a 'bird's eye' perspective. I believe that this type of question can be particularly useful in enabling respondents to include themselves in their reflections.

In the tradition of systemic therapy, mind-reading questions are designed so as to discourage a sense of one person being asked to speak for another in the context of a family interview. That could arise if the question were asked in the form, 'What does Jon think about how you handled the situation?' Questions like this asked in family interviews invite the response, 'Why don't you ask him?' The question would, however, be appropriate to an interview or supervision session with an individual. In a family interview the question would more likely be phrased in the form, 'If I were to ask Jon what he thought about how you handled the situation, what do you think he would say?' This version might work well in group supervision.

In narrative approaches, the presenting 'problem' is given an identity and can be afforded a voice with such questions. While reflecting on their practice supervisees may identify something that they define as a problem such as feeling anxious in the presence of a particular client, or having difficulty in bringing sessions to a close. A 'problem perspective' might be taken with questions such as:

- 'How would the problem (e.g. anxiety) say it affects you when you are together?'
- 'What would it notice about how you attempt to banish it from your session?'
- 'What would anxiety have to say about the times that you are vulnerable to its influence?'
- 'How would anxiety know, when it came knocking, that you are not at home?'

Such questions may be focused on the relationship between the conditions that allow the problem to have a significant influence and on those that reduce the influence.

Observer-perspective questions designed to encourage a 'hawk in the mind' perspective often enquire about what respondents have *noticed* about their actions, thoughts, feelings or beliefs.

- 'When you noticed how exhausted you were feeling, what did it make you think?'
- 'When you saw how much effort you had put into encouraging your client to make changes, what did you think about how hard you would try in the future?'
- 'When you noticed that you felt angry with Sven, how did you think that would affect your ongoing relationship with him?'
- 'Now that you have acknowledged your disappointment in yourself, how will that influence what you do the next time you're faced with this situation?'

In my experience, supervisees often enjoy engaging with observer-perspective questions that give voice to inanimate objects such as their desk, telephone or a piece of work in which they are engaged, such as a coursework assignment or dissertation. Workers often spend much time in the company of these objects which 'see' and 'hear' much of their occupant's work. Not infrequently I am confronted by supervisees who are feeling exhausted and demoralised. Questions invoking the voice of inanimate objects can lift sessions and introduce some fun into the workplace:

- 'What does "desk" notice about you at work?'
- 'What does "desk" most enjoy about seeing you coming into the office?'
- 'How much joy has "desk" seen in recent times?'
- 'What has "desk" noticed that lifts your spirits?'
- 'What would "desk" have to say about what helps you to keep your spirits up?'
- 'Who would "desk" recommend that you keep at a distance?'
- 'If your dissertation had a voice, what would it be more likely to say, "Get me perfect" or "Get me finished"?'
- 'What would your dissertation's advice to you be about what section to write next?'

Questions that aim to broaden perspectives

While at times supervisees bring puzzlement to supervision, they may also bring ready-constructed explanations for their experiences or the experiences of the people with whom they work. I find that closed explanations – she's a hopeless gambler because it runs in her family; he's depressed because he'll never get over the loss of his child – tend to shut down options for change and in such instances it can be helpful to attribute agency to the organising properties of the 'problem'. Another alternative is to reverse the meaning made of an experience with a reframe: it is because gambling runs in the family that she will be able to draw on a great deal of experience of keeping it under control; it is the experience of losing his child that provides him with so many opportunities for growth. Such reframes can then be turned into exploratory questions:

- 'What opportunities for growth is the loss of his child providing?'
- 'What has she learned from her family's experience of keeping gambling under control?'

Karl Tomm (1987), who describes various categories of 'reflexive' questions in a systemic tradition, refers to this type of question as 'unexpected context-change questions'. They may explore opposite content from that brought to the session – the therapist asks questions about happy events and celebrations when a couple brings the problem of a partner's depression. The questions may address opposite meaning. A problem of incessant arguing is explored thus:

> Who in the family enjoys the fighting most?
> Who would experience the greatest emptiness and loss if it all suddenly stopped?
> Who would be the first to recognise that father gets angry because he cares too much rather than too little?
>
> (Tomm 1987: 177)

Tomm (1987) suggests that such questions can also introduce what he calls 'paradoxical confusion' and gives the examples of: 'How good are you at stealing? How come you get caught so easily? Can you not steal any better than that?' Or in relation to someone who has been suicidal: 'Why is it that you have not killed yourself already? Which ideas and thoughts need to die?' I can imagine circumstances in which such questions might introduce much-needed humour and a possible sense of liberation into a session while, as Tomm himself proposes, it would be important to use them with caution and in the context of a trusting relationship.

Like some of the earlier questions, these challenge current perspectives on an experience with a view to opening up a range of options for understanding and action.

Questions that encourage the making of connections

It is easy to become entangled in the details of work at the expense of the bigger picture – struggling to see the wood for the trees. Questions can serve to encourage a broader view that includes and draws on the wider context.

Connecting questions encourage the experience to be seen more broadly, by encouraging a search for 'patterns that connect' (Bateson 1972).

Jac Brown (1997), from a description of circular questioning in a systemic tradition, suggests five categories of connecting questions that link behaviours, feelings, beliefs, meanings and relationships. Examples from any category can be linked with another:

- 'When your client asks how his sessions with you are going to help him, what feelings are going on for you?'
- 'How do those feelings connect with what you believe about how counselling works?'
- 'What effect does this sort of statement from your client have on your relationship with him?'
- 'What feelings or beliefs do you think your client might be trying to communicate when he asks those kind of questions?'

The first stage of a narrative approach is to map (explore the extent of) the influence of the 'problem' in the person or family's life and relationships. That is, to identify how the problem affects the person and to consider where it fits in the broader context. This is with the aim of helping the participants to develop a mutual understanding of the 'problem-saturated story'. Roth and Epston (1995) argue that it is:

> crucial to take enough time to develop this, for people to feel that their experience is 'known' and for them to 'know it' in a way that offers them a different, more detailed perspective on the problem's effects on their lives. A broad mapping at this stage opens multiple opportunities for exploring unique outcomes (times when the problem does not have these effects) later. It also gives a rich sampling of people's language habits around the problem.
>
> (Roth and Epston 1995)

Coles (1989: 105) encourages patients to make broader connections when they present to their physician with pain. He tells the patient to stop describing the pain and tell him about the onset of the pain and what they were doing at the time in order to gain greater insight into life before the pain and a broad picture of what has happened. He begins with the question, 'When the pain knocked on your door, interrupting your life, what were you doing?' It would be simple to substitute the words, 'frustration', 'animosity', 'anxiety', or 'your computer' for 'pain' in this example.

I have also found it helpful, when focusing on an account of a specific session or event, to take the session back a step and to enquire into what happened, what the supervisee was thinking and feeling before the client came into the office or as they created a teaching plan.

- 'What thoughts were going through your mind as you were planning for this session?'
- 'How enthusiastic were you to see your client/students again?'
- 'What were your feelings when you saw your client in the waiting room?'

It can also be productive to take the process of making connections forwards in time in a similar way to the time-comparison questions described earlier.

Questions that aim to discourage generalisations and challenge assumptions

Theories of personality have reflected a view that people are blessed or cursed with more or less fixed qualities; he is intelligent, she is kind, he is aggressive, she is shy, they are lazy. This kind of essentialism is also very readily observable in folk psychology – people's informal psychological explanations about why things are as they seem. Essentialism may be challenged by questions that encompass an assumption that such qualities are not fixed but, rather, are shown by people, and that what they show will differ according to circumstance and by the 'take' or interpretation of the observer. This means posing questions in terms of observed behaviours, inferred attitudes and motivations as opposed to fixed personal qualities. Such questions can also imply that the quality is in the eye of the beholder.

- 'At what times do you most notice her aggression?'
- 'What have you noticed are the limits of your kindness?'
- 'When your kindness is exhausted, what do you tend to show instead?'
- 'Is your patient's/colleague's tender side or strident side easier for you to see?'
- 'When he is showing his strident side how do you encourage his tender side to reveal itself?'

This kind of question can also be useful in challenging a position in which a supervisee is taking an 'all or nothing' view or showing prejudice.

- 'What would be your client's view of your describing her as *suffering* from her disability?'
- 'What advantages might she say derived from her experience as a wheelchair user?'
- 'When you describe this bad parent who shouts at her son, what else does she do that would lead you to call her a good parent?'
- 'What might be her motivation in shouting at him?'
- 'How do you think he experiences the shouting?'

The task of the supervisor in these examples is to notice assumptions that are being made by the supervisee (that wheelchair users must be suffering; that parental shouting at children makes them bad parents) and to challenge them with questions that encourage consideration of different perspectives while trying not to raise their defences.

In health, education and social care contexts there are many examples of labelling that suggest fixed or permanent conditions, some of which may implicitly condemn the person labelled to the fringes of society. He or she is an alcoholic, schizophrenic, special needs student, bully, control freak, or victim. I have found there to be occasions when some labels can serve a useful function but more often they serve as a full stop to further thinking. Robert Coles (1989) gives a pertinent example:

> When I put that youth's 'history' into a theoretical formulation, the familiar phrases appeared, none of them surprising, each of them applicable not only to that person but to many, many others: 'domineering mother' (and sister), 'poor masculine identification,' 'aloof father figure,' and so on. When I named his 'defences,' his 'hostility,' the kind of 'transference' (involvement with me) he'd make, I was again consigning him (and me) to territory populated by many others. No wonder so many psychiatric reports sound banal: in each one the details of an individual life are buried under the professional jargon. We residents were learning to summon up such abstractions within minutes of seeing a patient; we directed our questions so neatly that the answers triggered the confirmatory conceptualization in our heads: a phobic, a depressive, an acting-out disorder, an identity problem, a hysterical personality.
>
> (Coles 1989: 17)

Ranking, sequencing and scaling questions invite comparisons and can involve asking respondents to judge what is more or less than, to create a sequence or rank order from most to least, or ask for a location on a numerical scale, typically 0–10 or 1–100. Comparison and sequencing questions derive from a systemic tradition in which clients typically are asked to order family members in terms of a characteristic, belief, feeling etc. This can have the effect, of discouraging generalisations and either–or positions, and can highlight differences of feeling, behaviour, thinking and belief between people. Brown (1997: 112) makes the following suggestions:

- 'Who is the most argumentative in the family? Who the next?'
- 'Who, between the two of you, most thinks that women should have the major responsibility for the housework?'
- 'Who is the most committed to the relationship? How do they show it?'
- 'Who most shows their concern about the problem?'
- 'If the problem stays around for a long time, who will be most concerned about it?'

The following examples might be appropriate to supervision:

- 'Do you feel more or less optimistic about working with this client than you did last time we spoke?'
- 'Which of your students do you think is most likely to benefit from the changes you have made in the classroom? Who next after that?'
- 'Who do you think is least likely to benefit?'
- 'Who among your colleagues would be most supportive of the changes that you are making?'
- 'Who would find the changes most difficult? How do you expect them to show their difficulties?'
- 'What strategies might you adopt to prevent them from undermining the changes you have made?'

Questions that challenge behaviours

Questions that challenge behaviours are widespread in narrative approaches when the 'problem' is attributed organising properties or a grammar of agency. Imagine working with a supervisee who, despite having expressed the view that a great effort is being made to be on time, is almost invariably late for supervision. Imagine that the supervisor wishes to encourage reflective practice in relation to this issue, rather than to take an authoritative or authoritarian stance in regard to the implications of continuing lateness both for the supervisory relationship and for the supervisee's future career. The supervisee is asked to think of a time when he or she has not been late, and a series of questions is used to explore how 'being on time' could take precedence over 'lateness' in being in control of the supervisee:

- 'How did lateness take such control over your coming to supervision?'
- 'Does lateness only take control when you are coming to supervision or does it take charge at other times too?'
- 'On the last occasion when you were on time for supervision, what made it possible for you to be able to defy lateness's prescriptions?'
- 'How easy or difficult was that?'
- 'How do you plan to connect with "being on time" for our next supervision?'
- 'What does this tell you about yourself that is new?'
- 'Who else in your life would applaud your standing up to lateness and getting close with "being on time"?'

Before adopting such an approach I would counsel discussing it with the supervisee lest the questions be seen as sarcastic and inauthentic. Timekeeping is bound up in cultural imperatives. Supervisees might experience such questioning as a game being played by the supervisor to avoid telling them to be on time. Authenticity derives from the supervisor's belief that telling often has limited impact, whereas enquiry may be more effective. It would be respectful to share this conviction, explain where such questions come from and to illustrate their use, drawing parallels with how the supervisee might adapt them to her or his practice. It is important to check that the supervisee does not experience such questioning as putting them in the role of client. Supervisees could be provided with some theoretical background reading and asked to construct their own questions and answers around the issue of lateness and being on time.

Questions that aim to amplify new ideas and consolidate change

As supervision proceeds and new ideas emerge, sometimes fleetingly, it can be helpful to ask questions that aim to amplify a new account. This type of question derives in particular from a narrative tradition in the form of 'unique circulation' questions which include other people in the newly developing story, 'experience of experience' questions which invite people to be an audience to their own stories by seeing themselves through the eyes of others, those that 'historicise unique outcomes' by establishing a history of the nascent alternative account and 'consulting your consultant questions' which are designed to shift the status of a person from 'client' to 'consultant'. The following sequence is from Roth and Epston (1995):

> Is there anyone you would like to tell about this new direction you are taking?
> Who would you guess would be pleased to learn about this?
> Would you be willing to put them in the picture?
> What do you think I am appreciating about you as I hear how you have been leaving busyness behind and taken up with self-delight?
> What do you think this indicates to Judy (best woman friend) about the significance of the steps you have taken in your new direction?
> Of all the people who have known you over the years, who would have been most likely to predict that . . .?
> What would Judy have seen you doing that would have encouraged her to predict that you would be able to take this step?
> Given your expertise in the life-devouring ways of busyness what have you learned about its practices that you might want to warn others about?
> As a veteran of busyness and all that that has meant to you, what counter-practices of self-delight would you recommend to those in the service of the busyness?
>
> (Roth and Epston 1995)

The idea behind such questions is that of enhancing the likelihood that the new story will be carried forward by establishing a 'history of the alternative present' (White 1993). To my mind these questions are relatively highly inter- ventive; they are designed to lead the respondent in constructing a changed life story. In supervision this would translate to leading a supervisee towards a changed work story, for which their consent would be needed. Roth and Epston (1995) propose that this be accomplished by interjecting 'preference' questions throughout sessions. These encourage respondents to evaluate their responses and make their own decisions about the directions in which they wish to proceed.

- 'Would you consider this to be an advantage or disadvantage to you?'
- 'How good or bad would this idea be for you?'
- 'How are you finding the direction that this supervision is taking?'

Karl Tomm (1987) proposes a number of sub-types of specifically future- oriented questions. These seem to have much in common with some of the questions deriving from a narrative approach which are designed to explore and amplify 'unique possibilities'. He describes a process of questioning which he terms 'reflexive', in which questions are designed to open up new possi- bilities for self-healing. The simplest of these are straightforward and enquire into future goals:

- 'What plans to do you have for your future career?'
- 'How will you know when the goal has been achieved?'

Further questions are designed to explore anticipated outcomes and the rela- tionship of these to the views of other people in the respondent's system. For example, 'When this goal has been accomplished how will it change the rela- tionship between yourself and your daughter in five years' time?' Tomm (1987) argues that future-oriented questions can be used to introduce hypo- thetical possibilities that can help to determine what happens in the future.

Conclusion

I find that well-posed questions asked by my colleagues can kick start a reflective process that leads to or supports changes in my practice. This is particularly so when the questions seem prompted by curiosity. When I ask such questions of my colleagues these can also develop my own thinking. I like the following paragraph from Osterman and Kottkamp (1993) that summarises how they regard questions as one of the tools that facilitators can use to shift perspectives:

> In the organizational setting, the facilitator is the technical assistant, the person who tilts the mirror so that it reflects from a different angle, the

person who focuses the microscope so that an undistinguishable entity comes into view, the person who turns the prism or kaleidoscope or changes the lens from telescopic to wide angle so that the observer sees the same phenomenon from many different perspectives.

(Osterman and Kottkamp 1993: 62)

This capability, to encourage a shift in perspective, gives questions the central role that I see for them in encouraging the development of skills in reflective practice through supervision. There is a balance to be struck between enquiry, listening and telling. Relentless questioning can be experienced as oppressive. In a sound supervisory relationship, either party might highlight an imbalance. There is also a danger that questions may be prone to supporting a process of intellectualisation, of remaining in one's 'head', thereby avoiding the experience of a full emotional perspective. Where this is at issue, further methods such as those involving immersion in a role may be of particular benefit. The next three chapters are addressed to a spectrum of further approaches using a range of media that are intended to support and encourage reflective practice.

Chapter 6

Approaches to supervision of reflective practice (II)

Methods that encourage self-awareness

In Anthony Trollope's *Barchester Towers*, Mr Arabin is described as a person who, in things affecting the inner man, aims at humility of spirit. He habitually questions himself as to his actions and intentions:

> Mr Arabin, as we have said, had but a sad walk of it under the trees of Plumstead churchyard. He did not appear to any of the family till dinnertime, and then he seemed, as far as their judgement went, to be quite himself. He had, as was his wont, asked himself a great many questions, and given himself a great many answers: and the upshot of this was that he had set himself down for an ass.
>
> (Trollope 1953: 73)

Who has not, once in a while, been in Mr Arabin's position in concluding themselves 'an ass'? And how often does further reflection not fail to open up additional perspectives that shed a different light on us? Mr Arabin is described as failing on occasion to answer his own questions honestly because, 'it was and ever had been his weakness to look for impure motives for his own conduct'. One aim of reflective practice is to explore these habitual tendencies towards viewing our own practice and to challenge them by trying for fit alternative ideas, beliefs, attitudes and values.

In social sciences research a brief statement of the researcher's position is often called 'positionality' (Wellington and Szczerbinski 2007). It involves declaring the answers to questions like:

- 'What biases, assumptions and prejudices have affected how I conducted myself in this role?'
- 'What assumptions are being taken for granted by the institutions in which I am working?'
- 'What written and spoken language is being used to describe and discuss the topic?'

Jerry Wellington and Marcin Szczerbinski (2007: 54) suggest that 'both the style or tone and the actual words need to be questioned'. What might Figure 6.1 tell us about our view of the people with whom we work and the changing professional 'fashions' in labels?

In this chapter I am describing methods that aim specifically to generate alternative perspectives on our selves. These methods acknowledge the 'I' at the centre of reflective practice. Such perspectives may be particular to a unique piece of work, may relate to learning and development in professional role including perspectives on the relationship between supervisor and supervisee, or may encourage expanded understanding of our underlying ideas, beliefs and values. They have in common the aims of strengthening

Figure 6.1 Service user cartoon.

Reproduced with permission – www.CartoonStock.com.

introspection and providing new information with which to view ourselves. There are other ways in which this may be accomplished, for example through personal therapy. I have selected the following methods as suited to supervision. Some are reported in Scaife (2009) as creative methods for undertaking the supervisory task.

Inskipp and Proctor (1995) suggest that creative methods have the capacity to cut through surface presentation to something 'raw'. They therefore caution against pressing supervisees to take part against their better judgement, and charge the supervisor with careful and respectful management of the process. They also propose that debriefing, a method for disengaging from the material explored, be undertaken as a way of closing down the exercise. This may be as simple as moving position or reconnecting with the next tasks of the day.

Methods that seek to expand understanding of practitioners' underlying assumptions, ideas, beliefs and values

In the 1970s a series of studies aimed to explore the impact of context on memory. In one such study by Bransford and Johnson (1973) all participants read the same description of a man getting ready in the morning to leave his house. He had breakfast, read the newspaper, and so on. Some participants were subsequently told that he was a stockbroker, others that he was unemployed. Those told that he was a stockbroker were more likely to 'remember' that he was reading the financial pages; those told he was unemployed remembered the 'want ads', although the story did not specify either.

Both context-specific and culture-specific information have been found to influence comprehension and memory. Harley (2008) reports a study by Steffensen et al. (1979) in which groups of participants from two different cultural backgrounds read two passages describing typical weddings in each culture. Participants read more rapidly and with less distortion the information describing their own culture. This finding was replicated in a study (Lipson 1983) that compared children from Catholic and Jewish backgrounds.

These studies serve as a reminder that sometimes prior knowledge can lead us astray. In my clinical practice I have found that once a label has been applied to a person – 'bipolar', 'attachment disordered', 'personality disordered' – professional thinking sometimes seems to stop. The label becomes a shorthand way of describing someone and is passed on between practitioners, becoming an unquestioned 'truth'. This kind of assumption can be unravelled with careful re-examination of the information that led to the conclusion. When attempting to reveal culturally determined beliefs, values and ideologies constructed over the course of a lifetime, I think that the process is even more challenging.

If you were to ask me out of the blue about the ideologies that contextualise my behaviour I would have (at least) three problems. First, my cultural context and personal learning history frame the way that I think about my world and as I am unable to step outside these I would have to rely on my prior experiences of encountering alternative ideologies and of challenges to my own in answering your question. Second, even if I could tell you about some of my espoused beliefs, I am aware that these are not always reflected in my behaviour. Third, if I do not know you well, I may be unwilling to share what I do know in case this appears to show me in a bad light.

Brookfield (2001) states:

> Critical theory views ideologies as broadly accepted sets of values, beliefs, myths, explanations, and justifications that appear self-evidently true, empirically accurate, personally relevant, and morally desirable to a majority of the populace, but that actually work to maintain an unjust social and political order.
>
> Ideologies are hard to detect being embedded in language, social habits, and cultural forms that combine to shape the way we think about the world. They appear as commonsense, as givens, rather than as beliefs that are deliberately skewed to support the interests of a powerful minority.
>
> Althusser (1971) believed that people lived naturally and spontaneously in ideology without realizing that fact . . . In Althusser's view, we can claim in all sincerity to be neutral, objective, and free of ideological distortion when this is really an impossibility.
>
> (Brookfield 2001: 14)

Ideology critique

Authors such as Stephen Brookfield (2001) and David Tripp (1993) argue that ideologies are embedded in our day-to-day practices and that we unthinkingly participate in routines, 'social games', rituals and practices determined by them. Brookfield (2001) suggests:

> these practices (such as chopping up the curriculum into discrete chunks to be absorbed, measuring learning and the quality of teaching by percentage improvement scores on standardized tests, and moving people in streams and age-based grades through a system at a pace and in a manner over which they have no control) are perceived as rational and obvious but actually support certain ways of understanding and ordering the world.
>
> (Brookfield 2001: 15)

Tripp (1993) cites the examples of the organisation of land ownership and belief in an afterlife (or not) as ideologies that organise societies. He states:

> Although a number of land-occupying people may realise that freehold land ownership is but one way of enabling people to occupy it, few will question whether it is a good idea, fewer still will formulate alternatives, and almost no one will operate according to an alternative.
>
> (Tripp 1993: 55)

Ideology critique is a process addressed to the recognition of how dominant ideologies, frequently uncritically accepted, are embedded in everyday situations and practices. It is a method compatible with 'double loop learning' (Argyris 1976).

The language that we use to describe our experiences can give us clues as to the underlying ideologies within our culture. Language 'bedevils his sense of reality, so that he is all too apt to take his concepts for data, his words for actual things' (Huxley 1952: 6). During my professional lifetime I have noticed changes to the vocabulary used to describe my life and my work that seem to reflect changes in underlying ideologies. The primary responsibility of health workers now has been described as 'the business of delivering health care' (Jasper 2003: 108) whereas previously such professions were known as vocations, meaning devotion to a particular job, especially one giving service to other people. One of the current mantras of my profession of clinical psychology is that interventions must be 'evidence-based'. What constitutes evidence sometimes seems to be only what the National Institute for Health and Clinical Excellence (NICE) says whereas evidence-based medicine has been defined as 'the integration of best research evidence *with clinical expertise and patient values*' (my emphasis) (University of Toronto Libraries 2000). Clinical expertise and patient values seem to have got lost somewhere along the way. I sometimes find myself questioning the suitability and being disappointed by the dominance that some of these words have achieved as they have colonised my workplace.

I take the view that it is useful to try and identify my embedded ideologies in order to question and subject them to critical reflective practice. Such a process helps me to understand how the cultural shifts in my lifetime could have taken place and to make conscious decisions about where I sit in relation to them. Joyce Stalker (1996) has devised a method for encouraging students to understand what has shaped their perspectives on life and education. She uses this in her classes in a group context but I can also see its value adapted to individual supervision.

Stalker's framework for understanding and analysing experiences

Stalker's (1996) framework comprises four categories: consensus perspective, conflict perspective, interpretive perspective and new right perspective.

Consensus perspective

Consensus perspective evolved during the 1950s and 1960s and dovetailed with the optimism and social stability of the years following the Second World War. Money was allocated generously for the purpose of schooling and widening participation was encouraged by free education in the UK and access to grammar schools through the selective Eleven Plus examination.

> The consensus view of society is of a harmonious stable balanced and static form which functions successfully. These represent the situation in which some individuals have more power, authority and control than others. Regardless of their dominant perspective, most people acknowledge these differences. It is, after all, impossible to ignore the contrast between those who live in mansions and those who live beneath the bridges. For those who hold a consensus perspective this hierarchical relationship is viewed as completely normal.
>
> (Stalker 1996: 63)

In the consensus view, equality of opportunity is espoused and people are seen as starting from a level playing field. If they do not make use of the opportunities it is their own 'fault' and individual effort reaps its own reward.

Conflict perspective

By the late 1960s there was a sharpening of tensions in Western societies reflected in the growth of feminism, the civil rights movement, opposition to the nuclear arms race and antithesis to conflicts such as the war in Vietnam. Despite promises based on equality of opportunity, an 'underclass' still flourished, and the issue of inequality began to be traced to socio-economic variables. The conflict perspective represents a view of society as unstable, volatile and ever-changing within which different groups exist in a state of tension and confrontation. From this perspective minority groups strive to change society to a more just version in which resources, influence and authority are wrested from those in power through harsh confrontation. The vocabulary used to describe people belonging to minority groups shifts from words such as 'disadvantaged' to 'oppressed'. The issue of equality shifts from opportunity to outcomes through the notion of equity: in order to achieve equity people cannot be seen as starting from a level playing field. Analysis of experience is framed within this view at the level of society rather than at the level of the individual.

Interpretive perspective

In the interpretive perspective, the consensus and conflict perspectives are viewed as too clear cut and society is seen as a complex of negotiated under-standings within which subgroups create and maintain shared rules and understandings. From an interpretive perspective society comprises con-stantly shifting perspectives and complex structures which are interrelated. The nature of a society can be described only at a moment in time. The interpretive view is about examining society and valuing the differences uncovered. There is an emphasis on shared meanings and people's subjective experiences which are unique rather than universal.

New right perspective

The new right perspective rose to prominence in the 1980s and is based on the premise that the state has no role in intervening in the life of society but rather that market forces are best allowed to govern systems, processes and relationships. The quality and nature of services are left to regulation by the market and the privatisation of services is promoted. The opportunities afforded by the marketplace are lauded and there is corporate freedom to compete. Poverty and unemployment are viewed as resulting from individ-uals misjudging the needs of the marketplace and failing to participate accordingly.

Developing perspectives

As I write, in the midst of a 'credit crunch' and what is being referred to as a global financial crisis, it seems that another perspective may be in the process of formation. World leaders are discussing the need to regulate the excesses of the banks and to work together in managing a global eco-nomy addressed to both rich and poor nations. I await the outcomes with interest.

Joyce Stalker (1996) presents these perspectives to her students with the caveat that they are culturally bound, falsely tidy categories. She encourages students to apply the perspectives to their everyday experiences. They are divided into groups which are invited to argue from one of the four perspec-tives in relation to a series of scenarios. She suggests that they imagine a role for themselves, for example as a mother, social worker, or friend and from the role describe the problem and the advice that they might give to the central character. Here is an example of a scenario:

> Powhiri is a 35-year-old mother of two children: Rangi who is ten and Janet who is three. Powhiri separated from her partner five months ago. When she was first married, she worked as a clerical assistant for several

years, and when she had her first baby she and her partner agreed that she should work at home.

(Stalker 1996: 73)

The groups report back and then she asks them to stay in role and react to other groups' responses. She argues that these exchanges highlight the tensions and miscommunications that can arise from the different perspectives. To build on this she encourages students to examine from the four perspectives relevant television shows, films, newspaper articles and academic articles with the intention that participants explore alternative perspectives. In so doing this may shed light on aspects of their own ideology. I can see enormous potential for this in the context of supervision, whether the perspectives are those described by Stalker (1996), or derive from other lineages. Pitting an 'objectivist' against a 'constructivist' account might be similarly fruitful when responding to an academic paper.

Uncovering assumptions

Stephen Brookfield (1992) argues that reflective practice is characterised by efforts to identify underlying assumptions that are influencing people's work, and by engagement in a process of constant checking for validity. He describes five approaches to 'assumption hunting' which he recommends be undertaken in small groups since it is difficult to analyse assumptions using the same frames of interpretation and understanding within which they are embedded. He presents a series of activities that moves from the safety of discussing events that are similar to but removed from practitioners' own lives to more direct first-hand experiences. This avoids the possibility of pitching people into the potentially alarming experience of questioning long-held assumptions.

Scenario analysis

Scenario analysis is the first in Brookfield's series of activities. Hypothetical scenarios involving fictional characters at a choice point in their lives are presented. This might involve changing jobs, deciding whether to follow a course of study, or moving house. Individually all group members list the assumptions that they think underlie the character's choices and decisions. These are presented in small groups followed by a discussion about how the characters could check out the validity of such assumptions. Group members then generate an alternative interpretation of the scenario that could explain the character's behaviours but would probably come as a surprise to the characters. I have found that potentially fruitful scenarios, although possibly further removed from first-hand experience, may be based on topical subjects relevant to professional domains: deciding whether to turn off a life support machine, where to direct limited funds in a financial crisis, or the implications of the development of stem cell research. Newspapers are a good source of different opinion when readers send in requests for advice to which other readers are invited to respond. Ninetta Santoro and Andrea Allard (2008) devised scenarios based on a research project that involved collecting the stories of pre-service teachers' classroom experience. These proved to be a source of material rich with underlying assumptions and prejudices:

> Kylie is teaching Year 10 English to a culturally diverse group of students, a proportion of whom are Turkish-Australian Muslim boys. Kylie finds herself struggling to maintain a degree of classroom control as a group of boys dispute everything she says, argue among themselves and refuse to cooperate with her. She emerges from the class feeling distressed and anxious and seeks the advice of her supervising teacher. The teacher tells her that the boys in the class are 'arrogant arseholes' and that under no circumstances should she 'let them get away with anything just because you're female'. The teacher also explains that some of the Muslim boys believe that women who do not wear the hijab [head scarf] are easy and that they're 'sluts' . . . Kylie decides that in her next class with these students she will assert her authority and insist that the school rules are followed, that is: 'students must respect the teacher', 'everyone has a right to learn', 'the teacher has the right to teach'.
>
> (Santoro and Allard 2008: 170)

Viewing practice through critical debate

Critical debate is a form of modified role reversal in which participants are asked to work in teams to develop the best arguments they can from a position that they personally disavow. A debate is held, followed by a rebuttal. Finally participants de-role and discuss the experience of arguing from an unfamiliar perspective, reviewing the extent to which their original views may have changed. The exercise invites participants to step out of their familiar interpretive frames to experience a different perspective.

Simulation for making a decision in a crisis

Participants are deliberately placed in a crisis situation in which an immediate decision needs to be made. Brookfield (1992) gives an example called 'The Firing' in which the participants must decide to save one salary in order to preserve an entire educational programme. The three candidates are an exceptional teacher, an outstanding researcher and a political 'wheeler-dealer' who is highly successful at obtaining funding for the department. The team is given a few minutes to choose by majority vote which one to 'fire' and then asked to make explicit the reasoning.

Heroes and villains

Participants identify and write descriptions of the practice and behaviour of 'heroes' and 'villains' known to them. In groups of three they take turns to be the storyteller and the 'detectives' whose role is to provide the best insights that they can about the assumptions underlying the stories. The trio lists the most common assumptions unearthed and these are then challenged in a process called 'assumption checking' by participants creating as many events, factors and circumstances as possible that would invalidate the assumptions. The point is to make participants more aware of the potential fragility of some of their own deeply held assumptions.

Critical incidents

Finally Brookfield invites participants to analyse incidents from their own practice. The format and roles follow the heroes and villains exercise except that participants choose events involving emotional highs and lows from their own experiences. Gray (2007) describes a similar exercise in which three people write about a critical incident or scenario based upon their recollection of a news or political broadcast that made them feel angry. In turn, each member of the triad relates her or his incident, while the other two participants try to identify the narrator's underlying assumptions embedded in the description.

Platform statement and development (Osterman and Kottkamp 1993)

> A platform is a written statement that expresses one's stated beliefs, values, orientations, goals, and, occasionally, the assumptions that guide professional practice. More colloquially, it is one's philosophy of education or administration, a concise statement of what one intends to do, to accomplish, and how.
>
> (Osterman and Kottkamp 1993: 67)

Robert Kottkamp, in his chapter on preparing reflective school administrators, describes this method for enabling professionals to identify their espoused theory and compare it with their theory-in-use as shown in their writing about and actions at work. He invites course participants to write a statement about their beliefs regarding education, and this is done in a group context. In the second stage, specific feedback is provided by course participants to each other, with the directive that this be purely descriptive rather than evaluative. The rationale is to provide the writer with opportunities to develop a deeper understanding of what has been espoused in the written platform. In responding to each other the participants are given instructions to examine the platforms for internal consistency and to comment on this. If there are internal inconsistencies then these are to be described and if the reader has any queries they are to be raised in question form. The other task is for readers to identify any assumptions that they see lying behind the various statements that have not explicitly been identified by the writer.

Kottkamp proposes that while examining the platforms, readers will be responding to the value orientation of the writer in terms of agreement and disagreement with what has been stated. Readers are prohibited from responding to the writer with prescriptive responses, but rather are exhorted to use these to examine their own platforms in order to develop a fuller understanding of their own underlying beliefs and values concerning education. He uses his personal written platform to demonstrate the process in the first instance.

The third and final but potentially ongoing stage of the process is that of testing the platform against behaviours in practice. Kottkamp tends to generate such behaviours through the use of role plays in which pairs may work together before participating in a large group comprising teachers and administrators who are completing higher degrees. He has used supervisory scenarios, such as the following example, devised for the purpose.

> A teacher has been late to school and to homeroom. The situation first came to your attention when you observed students standing by the classroom doorway after the last bell had rung. You questioned the students and discovered that there was a pattern to the teacher's late arrival. You have left a note in the teacher's mailbox requesting that he or she sees you after school. In the current situation, that teacher has just arrived.
>
> (Osterman and Kottkamp 1993: 96)

When the role play is complete, the group members debrief, providing *descriptive* and not evaluative feedback. Kottkamp has experimented with recording the role plays for private personal analysis outside the group. In a revised version of Osterman and Kottkamp's book, it is suggested that while contrived role plays are valuable, the re-enactment of an actual situation is more powerful since in contrived versions the actor may dismiss the experience as an aberration (Osterman and Kottkamp 2004). Kottkamp believes that keeping the talk descriptive protects the players and prevents group members from giving advice which is liable to engender defensiveness.

Other ways of testing the platform include examining written case records; writing autobiographical accounts of experiences as a student, teacher or administrator which can generate insights into issues of power, authority and control; journal writing; completion of self-assessment instruments such as the Myers-Briggs Type Indicator; and the creation of metaphors.

A process described as 'personal theory analysis' by David Tripp (1993: 51) has much in common with the platform analysis of Osterman and Kottkamp.

He explores examples of behaviours in practice described by teachers insofar as they reveal underlying personal values. He cites an example in which a teacher describes a child who is regularly disposing of her lunch in a waste bin as 'sneaky':

> What did concern me was that I felt the idea that children are simply 'sneaky' misinformed her professional judgement about what action was best for the child's long-term well-being. Sneakiness is a 'black box' term (like 'the weather' or 'dyslexia') which labels, but does not explain. I do not believe that children do 'sneaky' (meaning 'sly, deceitful, underhand') things just because they are inherently 'sneaky'; my experience is the opposite: children are naturally honest and open about what they do till they discover things they have to hide from adults. Children generally have good reasons for breaking such procedural rules, but because they cannot change the rules and are punished if they are caught breaking them, they are forced to hide their rule-breaking, as this child did. The child's behaviour was not autonomous, but a direct response to what was being done to her. Children have all sorts of reasons for not eating the lunch they are given: they do not like it but are not able to say so or are ignored when they do; it does not match up to their friends' lunches; they really are not hungry at that time; they are given too much, and so on. But because the idea that children are intrinsically sneaky explained her behaviour, it obviated finding out why the child actually behaved as she did.
>
> (Tripp 1993: 52)

I too have found that the process of labelling is liable to shut down further thought. Personal theory or platform analysis could lend itself well to supervision, participants being on the lookout for statements that reveal underlying values, beliefs and assumptions. I have used a variant of the process of platform testing (J.M. Scaife 2009: 60) to examine a recording of a supervision session in which many of my implicit beliefs and values and those of my supervisor were revealed. I like Kottkamp's modelling as an introduction to the method; showing his own platform to the students on the course, thereby allowing them the opportunity to test it against his actions in practice. Here are two examples from platforms written by school administrators attending his courses:

> Every child is curious about the world outside and inside. As educational theorists from Rousseau to Dewey have affirmed, that curiosity is the best motivation for and source of learning there is. And it must be honoured by the teacher. Motivation is a very personal and ephemeral thing. No one can motivate anyone else. A teacher can create an environment, can stimulate, provoke, even inspire – but only you can motivate yourself. In fact, just as freedom that is given is not a true freedom, because it can be taken

away, so an education cannot be given; it must be taken for oneself. Giving without asking in return creates either passivity or indifference, attitudes destructive to both the learning process and the human personality.

(Osterman and Kottkamp 1993: 90)

The Old Testament states that those who educate others unto justice shall shine as stars for all eternity. Education unto justice for all: the rich, the poor, the sound and the disabled, the young and the old, regardless of race, creed, or dominant language. Equal education is not necessarily just or fair education. Justice requires education according to need. As a physician treats each patient according to need, the true teacher educates each student according to needs defined by aptitude, achievement levels, family support, motivation and individual interests.

(Osterman and Kottkamp 1993: 89)

This method involves a greater degree of exposure and therefore danger than that proposed by Brookfield (1992), since it requires revelation of espoused beliefs, and 'live' performance. As in most approaches to the facilitation of reflective practice, the quality of the supervisory relationship is paramount if supervisees are to put their trust in their supervisors and experience reasonable freedom to show themselves and their practice.

Text analysis

I have found it useful to examine some of my own writing in order to try to learn more about the assumptions that I am making and the messages that I may be conveying. This is a version of 'platform testing' as advocated by Kottkamp. When I read other people's writing, I am faced with making judgements about the meaning of the text. I have found in the everyday context of sending and receiving emails that I am capable of creating different interpretations of what lies behind the communication if I return to the text at a later time. I have learned to send my own emails to an outbox as an intermediate stage prior to selecting 'send', as this gives me an opportunity to reread and attempt to discern how my message may be received before it goes. Examining a piece of your own professional writing for evidence of your beliefs and assumptions after some time has elapsed since its creation can encourage identification of your theories-in-use. I have used the following text to give people practice in this process prior to subjecting their own writing to such critical examination:

Summary of concerns

I feel that Claire Brown is a loving mother who is unable to recognise or take on board any of the concerns of the local authority. She does not work honestly with professionals and as soon as concerns are raised she becomes hostile with the person concerned and I think she is suffering from a personality disorder as this is a repeating pattern. Apart from this she drinks excessively – I can often smell alcohol on her breath and she often slurs her speech and staggers. Claire has suggested that this is due to a medical condition but the same things have been noticed by Sarah's head teacher. I have told Mrs Brown that she needs to refer herself to the drug and alcohol service but there is no evidence that she has taken this forward.

Claire is often seen with bruises and cuts to her face. She denies that this has been caused by Mr Brown and says that she falls down often because of her medical condition. The neighbours say that they hear heated arguments from next door on a regular basis. One neighbour has repeatedly telephoned the local authority with concerns about what she can hear from next door. Claire says that this is her neighbour being vindictive as they have fallen out over some money that was borrowed and not repaid.

Sarah often arrives at school late, without school uniform and looking unkempt. She is always hungry at school and waits for seconds. She has chronic head lice and I feel very distressed by her vulnerability and the lack of even basic care that is being provided. I have demonstrated to Mrs Brown on many occasions how to go through Sarah's hair with the nit comb and offered advice. When I last saw her on 5th June Sarah had large live head lice in her hair and a number of eggs. Her head teacher says that Sarah used to have a best friend at school called Kirsty but Kirsty's mother got sick of the persistent head lice and so told Kirsty not to be friends with Sarah any more.

Sarah always says that she wants to stay at home and live with her mother but Sarah is a child and is not able to judge what is acceptable and unacceptable parenting so her view cannot be allowed to take precedence. Mr and Mrs Brown are unbelievably negative about Sarah's father, referring to him as 'DH' or 'the Dickhead'. Sarah has joined in with this negativity and it interferes with any possibility of reinstating contact with him. What she says to me often sounds rehearsed and I feel that her mother and Mr Brown coach her in what to say. This puts her under a great deal of pressure, entirely unacceptable for an 8-year-old child.

These concerns have been ongoing for over 12 months and I regard it as unacceptable for this child to continue living in her current circumstances. The local authority needs to seek a care order at the earliest opportunity.

In the way that I have composed this particular text I have tried to make some of the beliefs and values of the author relatively explicit while being mindful that the meanings that I make come from my own theories-in-use. More subtle expression makes the task more challenging.

Repertory grids

Repertory grids are grounded in the theory of personal constructs proposed by George Kelly and originally published in 1955. Kelly (1955) took the view that people develop individual structures for making meaning which comprise an elaborate system of interlinked dichotomous pathways or constructs that derive from their past experience. These constructs allow us to anticipate and construe new experiences in predictable or habitual ways so that we can navigate through our lives. We effectively operate on the basis of a value system or personal theory that is constantly tested by our new experiences.

The repertory grid is a technique designed to elicit or make more explicit these implicit personal theories without prejudging the terms of reference. The aim is to enhance self-understanding. The process involves a conversation that seeks to externalise or objectify in language the respondent's personal construct system or meaning-making processes.

It is the supervisee who provides the elements of the grid, the criteria for making distinctions, and who makes attributions of characteristics to the people with whom they have relationships.

Philip Candy (1990) offers a worked example concerning a person who wants to learn more about relationships with colleagues. The process for eliciting constructs involves the supervisee writing on individual cards the names or initials of the colleagues in question. One card represents the supervisee and there may also be a card for the supervisee's 'ideal' self; 'myself as I would like to be'. There are further cards for the 'best' and 'worst' person with whom the supervisee has worked. The cards are shuffled and the supervisor places three cards on the table. The supervisee is asked to say in what way two of the colleagues are similar and different from the third. For example, two of the colleagues may be regarded as helpful and the third unhelpful. This has identified the dichotomous construct 'helpful . . . unhelpful'. The supervisee then arranges all of the cards on an imaginary continuum of helpfulness and allocates each colleague a score from one to seven. The supervisor records this information on a grid.

The process is repeated with further sets of three cards and scores are allocated for each colleague on all of the identified constructs. The outcome of this first phase is a summary sheet or grid with each colleague, self and ideal self (if included), scored for each construct. An example is shown in Figure 6.2. Phase two involves analysis and interpretation of the grid. This provides information about self in relation to others. It is possible to examine relationships between constructs, and whether any co-vary. In the example above the constructs 'relaxed' and 'trustworthy' seem to be quite strongly related to each other. The grid can highlight inconsistencies and reveal habitual patterns of meaning-making. Candy (1990) argues that the process can be a learning experience in its own right since the supervisor can enquire and prompt, asking supervisees to try and be more specific, to describe how they

Work relationships

1	Colleague name							7
	Jane	Mohammed	Peter	Molly	Myself	Bobby	Ali	
Helpful	6	2	2	7	3	7	2	Unhelpful
Knowledgeable	1	6	4	4	2	4	4	Lacks knowledge
Friendly	2	1	5	2	1	5	4	Unfriendly
Authoritarian	3	2	1	6	2	1	7	Democratic
Modern	6	2	2	7	3	2	7	Old-fashioned
Uptight	2	5	3	1	5	3	7	Relaxed
Untrustworthy	2	5	4	1	5	3	6	Trustworthy

Figure 6.2 Example of a completed repertory grid.

came to develop these particular ways of interpreting their experiences, or to imagine different ways of viewing their colleagues.

Grids can be used to explore individual value systems concerning relationships with friends, colleagues, books, holiday destinations and the like. The process does not have to result in a formal record. The method can be adapted and used with groups which might involve constructive and critical debate concerning the differences in constructs between individuals.

Metaphors, symbolic expression, visualisation and pictorial representation

'My husband barges into the house like a locomotive.' So said a client to her therapist Richard Kopp (1995). This occurred in session thirteen of work carried out with a woman recently separated from her husband. She said that he would walk into the former family home unannounced. The client had expressed a wish to prevent this, and had identified the means of so doing by changing the locks on the doors, but had not taken her ideas forward into practice.

When she said to her therapist, 'He barges into the house like a locomotive,' the therapist said, 'If he's a locomotive, what are you?' The client responded, 'I guess I'm a tunnel.' When asked, 'What if you could change the image so it would be better for you?', the client, after some thought, responded, 'I'd be the derailer.' By the following session, she had changed the locks and taken other action to improve the situation from her point of view. Kopp (1995) argued for the potential transformative properties of metaphor which can allow an idea to be explored creatively and with some sense of distance, in this case when more direct exploration had been unproductive. Both metaphors and similes such as this one have been used to expand self-understanding, often by the judicious use of questions that develop the original representation.

Metaphors involve the use of a word or expression in a different sense from the literal meaning in order to give life or emphasis to an idea. They have been used in therapeutic contexts in order to help clients move on by making new or different connections without recourse to logic. Battino (2005) argued that metaphors are characterised by non-linear causal chains and the indirect nature of the relationship between people's experience and the metaphorical representation allows them to try out a new perceptual frame without having consciously to decide on its acceptance or rejection (Combs and Freedman 1990).

'Metaphors assist in simplifying and clarifying ideas and help to summar-ise thoughts, enable and limit meaning, help develop alternative ways of looking at a topic, gain insights into what is not yet understood' (Taggart and Wilson 2005: 169).

In a study of metaphor involving hospice staff, Spall et al. (2001) identified five main functions or uses of metaphor: avoidance and distancing, getting to the heart of the matter, aiding understanding, aiding communication and connection, and facilitating grief work. I was struck by the potential impact of the examples provided by the hospice staff:

> You get hit with a wave.
> Losing your parents is like losing the tent poles out of your tent.
> When you are grieving it feels like a herd of elephants rushing towards you – but when you face the fear they turn into mice with megaphones.
> Being at a crossroads and being surrounded by fog.
>
> (Spall et al. 2001: 348)

Metaphors can be created by supervisors, supervisees, workers in health, edu-cational and social care settings, or developed from the stories told by clients and students. They can be taken from literature and myth or arise serendipitously in the course of work.

> The artfully constructed metaphor permits the listener to develop her own unique interpretation. This then provides an alternative way of per-ceiving her own reality. Rather than being stuck on one response, the metaphor opens up the possibility of alternate responses, many of which may be more appropriate and healthful.
>
> (Battino 2005: 5)

This aim has much in common with that of critical reflection: to expand practitioners' ways of seeing themselves in relation to their work. I am not surprised that their use has been adapted to the context of supervision with the aims of aiding case conceptualisation, of helping supervisees to understand the developmental process of becoming a professional, and of furthering understanding of the process of supervision itself. Methods have involved not only verbal representations but also visualisation and pictures. Antony Williams (1995: 161) noted: 'The tale trainees tell about therapy is the tale they spin; when they access the world of visual images, however, the tale spins them.'

David Deshler (1990) described a method for the analysis of metaphors which were to be supplied by learners rather than facilitators. These were in one of three domains: personal (family lifestyles, parents and parenting, careers, gender and human sexuality, financial resources, sports and leisure activities, and friends or reference groups); popular culture (products, vehicles, art and architecture, popular music and literature); and the organisational domain (places of employment, educational establishments, government, social movements, religious institutions and public policy issues). These subjects are proposed since they can be pointers for identifying how the meanings in our lives have been shaped by our experiences.

He describes eight steps for the analysis:

- Select a primary subject from the three domains.
- Scan memories associated with the primary subject and try to recognise several metaphors that have been in use with the subject. Examples may be provided (such as a family being like a cafeteria, narrow boat, beach, nest, circus, or prison: a workplace being like a machine, Monopoly game, rat race, disaster area, or computer).
- Select one metaphor and write down its meaning in reference to the primary subject. If this is in the context of a group the process can be carried out interactively.
- Reflect on the values, beliefs and assumptions that are embedded in the meanings of the metaphor.
- Question the validity of each metaphor's meanings by comparing these with personal life experiences, knowledge, information, and values and beliefs that support or run counter to the meanings.
- Create new metaphors that express meanings that participants now want to emphasise regarding the primary subject under discussion. Share these with other group members.
- Consider implications for action that derive from the newly created metaphor.
- Repeat the process with further metaphors concerning the primary subject or select new primary subjects.

Deshler (1990) argues that metaphors encourage the mind to be daring, to think freely and with novelty. It is possible to use metaphors to conduct mind experiments while retaining control of the subject matter. Metaphor creation and analysis can help to challenge the impact of social forces on the process of individual meaning making. Deshler cites the story of John Newton, captain of a slaving ship who, as a result of his reflections on the voyage, turned his ship around and returned the slaves to their home. Pete Seeger, singer of a song that encapsulates this story, said that he likes to sing it because it gives him hope that other metaphorical 'ships' can be turned around.

On a cautionary note, Amundson (1988) advised the careful use of metaphors since some supervisees are inclined to respond negatively by reason of not being 'visualisers', by lack of drawing ability, or by other feelings of insecurity. Voluntary participation and informed consent in the context of a sound supervisory alliance are advisable.

Knowledge mapping

Knowledge mapping is regarded by Osmond and Darlington (2005: 11) as 'a window into the dynamic process of what another is thinking in relation to a specific subject'. In their example, it is a way for the supervisor to aid the supervisee in recognising the forms of knowledge on which they are drawing in order to understand clients' issues. The supervisee is asked to think of a recent interview with a client and to describe the client's problem or issue in focus. In the next phase supervisees detail their thoughts, ideas, feelings, reactions and considerations that had occurred during the session. The supervisor records this on a whiteboard or a large piece of paper so that the supervisee can see how the information is being organised and interpreted. Both then seek clarification, make amendments or add additional information. The diagram is used as an 'external memory' in order to stimulate reflection on the forms of knowledge that have been used to understand the client's issues. Categories of knowledge might include theory, research findings/evidence, knowledge of procedures (e.g. risk assessment, child protection), personal/tacit knowledge including intuition and feelings, practice wisdom/experience, ethics, diversity, values, beliefs and assumptions, and knowledge influenced by work context – that's the way we do it round here! The supervisor draws this from the supervisee by means of questions and may also make suggestions in a collaborative process. Osmond and Darlington (2005) argue that the method, apart from helping supervisees to clarify and develop their understanding, also allows for the identification of imbalance in the types of knowledge being used.

In a study of experienced and inexperienced practitioners working in the domain of child protection where public action is legislated, Drury-Hudson (1999) found that the students involved in her research had developed only a superficial understanding of the legislative and organisational context of child protection work. For example, when asked about the impact the legislation had exerted on a decision (to remove a child from the birth family), one participant stated, 'I don't know of any legislation. I don't know if the "Keeping Families Together" thing is just Departmental policy or is actually legislation. I'm not sure' (Drury-Hudson 1999: 165).

I can see the value of this approach particularly in circumstances where people's human rights are at issue – child protection, clients detained under the Mental Health Act, where anti-discrimination laws come into effect. In these domains policies, procedures, legislation and theoretical and empirical data dictate and constrain legitimate and safe courses of action. While some of this information quickly can be electronically researched, knowledge mapping would serve a useful function in identifying gaps in such knowledge.

Furthering understanding of self in relation to others

> I am in a dry and arid landscape with the client with no way out. We plod for hours on end. The hard work seems futile.
>
> (adapted from Adamson 2008)

I feel as if I have been in such a desert with clients at times, and how easy it is to become disheartened and give up when the situation seems so hopeless. But people do find ways both to survive and live in or find their way out of the desert. Many options present themselves: will we find an indigenous people who will show us their sources of sustenance, take us in and teach us? Do we have ways of drawing attention to ourselves? Will we decide to amuse each other in what remains of our short lives? Will we rack our brains for ideas about desert life – how other life forms survive in such conditions? Maybe we have with us but have forgotten about the means of survival or communication with others. How did we get into this place – we can't have come far from civilisation. How do I keep up my spirits when my companion despairs? Adamson (2008) argues that this metaphor offers a new perspective providing insight into the dynamics of the relationship in which the supervisee is caught up so that the stuck-ness becomes a place of possibility.

I am not particularly skilful at creating metaphors but there are plenty of ready-made ones in the literature and plenty more created by my colleagues and clients in the general course of events that provide rich resources for encouraging a wider perspective on how I experience my work with clients.

Saiz and Guiffrida (2001), reported in Guiffrida et al. (2007), described a metaphoric drawing technique designed to aid supervisees in understanding the relationship between themselves and their clients. The supervisor draws a stick figure to represent the supervisee's client and asks the supervisee to place an X on the paper to indicate her or his relationship to the client. This can appear above, below, or on either side of the client, or at any other place that the supervisee feels would accurately describe the context of her or his relationship with the client.

The supervisor then asks the supervisee to create a metaphor to describe what it is like to be in the place indicated on the drawing. Examples of responses to this question include, 'It is like carrying a heavy load on my shoulders' and 'I feel like the client is weighing me down.' If the supervisee experiences difficulty in formulating a response, the supervisor can assist by asking a series of follow-up questions. For example, if supervisees have drawn themselves above the client, the supervisor could ask if they felt that they were teaching or directing the client or if they felt superior, in some way, to the client. Supervisees who placed themselves below the client could be questioned regarding whether they felt that they were carrying or supporting the client or whether they somehow felt inferior to or unworthy of the client. Supervisees who placed themselves behind the client could be asked if they felt that they were pushing the client or if they were having a hard time keeping up with the client.

After the supervisee has suggested a metaphor to describe her or his relationship with the client, the supervisor encourages its expansion by asking questions. These might explore visual sensations (e.g. 'What do you see when you think about yourself being below this client?') or auditory sensations (e.g. 'What sounds are you making as you carry the load?'). Questions regarding affective and cognitive reactions (e.g. 'What feelings or thoughts are you experiencing as you push?') can also be asked. To help the supervisee understand how systemic and contextual factors affect the client's situation, the supervisor can ask questions such as, 'Who else is involved in the metaphor?' and 'Where might you place these other people in relation to you and the client?' The supervisee's perceptions of the client's experience can be explored: 'How do you think your client might feel about where you are positioned?' The supervisor invites the supervisee to change the metaphor with a view to progressing the work: 'If you could make some change to the metaphor, what might it be?' 'What changed positional relationships might enhance the work that you are doing with the client?' Finally, the metaphor is used to develop the formulation of the client's issues, to further the understanding of the relationship between the supervisee and the client, and to inform future directions with the client.

Although this activity can be useful with supervisees at any stage in their development, Saiz and Guiffrida (2001) believed that the activity was particularly beneficial in facilitating the development of supervisee conceptualisation skills early in training. They also suggested that this activity may encourage supervisees to find their own solutions to their difficulties rather than to rely on their supervisor for answers. They argued that the activity may allow the supervisor to gain access to supervisees' beliefs about their work in a way that is nonthreatening and respectful (Saiz and Guiffrida 2001).

Murray Cox (1992) also explored the use of metaphor in supervision with the aim of furthering understanding of work with clients. His employment at the time of writing was in the secure forensic setting of Broadmoor hospital in the UK. He recounts a vignette in which the therapy has been moved from the regular venue to an unfamiliar room. The therapist's customary 'hovering attentiveness' to the client is diverted to identifying the location of the alarm bell. The therapist tries to give the impression that he is merely glancing around the room. The patient points to the alarm, calmly stating, 'It's over there.' Cox (1992) suggests that the metaphor of the alarm bell provides a rich opportunity for exploration in supervision. It may remind the therapist of the importance of boundaries relevant to the inner and outer worlds of client and therapist. He says:

> it allows the supervision process to explore the therapists' response to their inner alarm bells. Counter-transference issues may set them too finely, so that an inner alarm rings when a fly enters the room. Alternatively, psychological defences may be so powerful and protective, that the alarm fails to ring when a bomb goes off. How is the inner alarm of the therapist 'set' in relationship to the outer alarm on the wall? And what of the patient's inner alarm system? And what of the supervisor's? He too will need to have his own early warning system monitored and adjusted from time to time.
>
> (Cox 1992: 31)

Cox (1992) describes a pictorial architectural metaphor depicting the therapist's and supervisor's hovering attentiveness (Figure 6.3).

The wall represents the secure setting in which the work is being conducted, although it may stand symbolically for the general idea of containment. The high security perimeter wall is also represented in the figure, acting as a fulcrum on which the therapist–patient and therapist–supervisor relationships are balanced. Cox (1992) uses the metaphor to explore the issue of life–work balance. I found it stimulated me to think about where the point of balance might move relative to the weights of the suspended individuals, and how the security fence might appropriately or inappropriately be breached. How would the patient and/or therapist 'escape'?

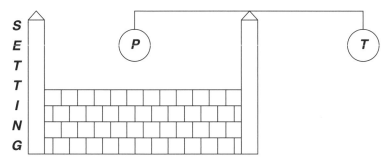

Figure 6.3 An architectural metaphor and hovering attentiveness.

Amundson (1988) described a procedure in which the supervisee's work with a client is summarised with the aid of a drawing made by the supervisee in advance, illustrating how the client and her or his problems are conceptualised. Discussion focuses on the conceptualisation and then shifts to the relationship between client and practitioner. Finally there is consideration of how the drawing might be altered to reflect a different therapeutic orientation or approach. Apart from its use in supervision, Amundson argues that the drawing and its interpretations can usefully be discussed with the client.

Ishiyama (1988) argued that Amundson's instructions for case drawing would benefit from being more specific. The supervisee is asked to respond to a range of sentence stems: 'What I see as the client's main concern is . . .', 'The way the client interacted with me is . . .', 'What I was trying to do in the session is . . .', 'What I felt or thought about myself as a counsellor during this session is . . .', 'The way this session went is . . .', 'What I think the client gained from this session is . . .'.

Metaphoric thinking is encouraged by completion of further sentence stems: 'The way I perceive the client with her or his concern may be characterised by a metaphor or image like . . .', 'The way the client responded to me or felt toward me during this session may be characterised by a metaphor or image like . . .', 'The way I conducted myself during this session may be characterised by a metaphor or image like . . .', 'The way this session went may be characterised by a metaphor or image like . . .'. Supervisees are then encouraged to draw their metaphors, to include themselves in the picture and to give consideration to present and future progress. Symbols, words and phrases can be included.

Many other authors have explored the use of metaphor, visualisation and pictorial methods to encourage reflection and expand thinking about the relationships of practitioners with their clients. These include Mooli Lahad (2000: 78), who uses therapeutic storytelling cards to depict characters and scenes. He advocates a firm structure to the process of using cards because of their capacity to introduce an unexpected surprise element. The supervisee divides the cards into five piles face down, takes five cards from any pile and places them according to a diagram:

```
      2
  4   1   5
      3
```

The cards are turned over one by one and the supervisor asks questions about the way the first card represents the client's difficulties, how the second and third cards are connected to the history of the problems, and how the fourth card represents the supervisee's fears and difficulties for the client. The fifth card deals with outstanding issues in the therapy. Later in the process, participants choose a card which most suggests, 'Stop it all, there is no hope' and a card that suggests 'Yes this is difficult but you can do it, don't despair.' The supervisee is encouraged to 'let the cards "talk" to each other' and to engage in dialogue and interview in relation to the selected characters, further exploring hope and hopelessness. The supervisor helps by holding the card facing the supervisee or by helping her or him to conduct the interview. I have enjoyed energetic and uplifting exchanges which have shed different light on and illuminated my difficulties in working with a client using this method.

Ronen and Rosenbaum (1998: 21) described a visualisation technique in which the supervisor suggests:

> Close your eyes and think of your session with that client. Try to concentrate on the room, the smell, the colors, the noises around you. Imagine you are sitting in front of a video, looking at a video cassette of your session with that client. Look at the two of you. How are you sitting? How far from each other? Pay attention to your nonverbal movements – what do you see? Listen to your voices – what do you hear? . . . Now use the remote control and lower the voices – what do you see?

and so on. The second phase of the process was used to visualise changes and the effects of these.

These methods have in common the use of visualisation and imagination, the inclusion of the practitioner in the representations, and a focus on implications for future practice. It is these features that I believe suit them to the development of reflective practice, and in particular opportunities for learning about self in relation to the client.

Robert Coles (1989: 47) reminds us that when we read or listen to the stories of others, the process tells us a great deal about ourselves. He describes an influential English professor telling his students that 'there are many interpretations to a good story, and it isn't a question of which one is right or wrong but of what you do with what you have read'. Coles (1989) argues that the discussion of stories, particularly those involving moral issues such as Lionel Trilling's *Of this time, of that place* (1979), can be a much more effective stimulus to student interest in ethical issues than a lecture format. In Trilling's story, a teacher is prompted to question himself by the contrasting behaviour of two students. Coles (1989) cites a teacher who used the story to invite self-questioning:

> to look around – and not only at the 'others', but at what they were doing with those 'others' in their minds. Oh, I wasn't giving a lecture in psychology! I noticed that when we gave those 'psychology of prejudice' lectures at the beginning of the school year [part of a social studies curriculum geared to race relations], lots of students were bored or indifferent. They fell asleep – I mean, the words fell on deaf ears, the way they

so often do during lectures. But when we got going on that Trilling story, there wasn't a heavy eyelid in the class!

(Coles 1989: 48)

Furthering understanding of self in relation to the learning and development process

Michael Barnat (1977) described his experience of 'waiting room apprehension' as a beginning student of psychotherapy. He would find himself half hoping that his client would fail to attend, being beset by great uncertainty and unreasonable expectations of himself. He said:

> Most of my sensitivity was invested internally to cope with confusion and anxiety . . . I felt quite vulnerable because of a lurking fantasy that the client might ask me to justify my presence: I have a neurosis; what brings *you* here?

(Barnat 1977: 308)

Barnat (1977) found metaphors presented by his supervisors helped to create a supportive latticework of imagery and concepts that enhanced his sense of competence. When he intellectualised too much his supervisor suggested that he was like a surfer on a board where the client was the wave. When he felt himself inauthentically to be acting a part, one of his supervisors warned, 'If you're acting, it will be dust and ashes in your mouth.' After a session with a female client in which he experienced heightened anxiety involving sexual arousal, he was asked for and gave his personal telephone number. The supervisor underscored the meaning of the moment by asking if he could get his number back. Barnat argued that metaphors carry an implicit reassurance that the rules of life have something to do with those of the consulting room. He experienced the metaphors as nurturing, supportive of action and based in humour which did not invite defensiveness in the same way that other interventions might.

In a small-scale qualitative study Marilyn Johnston (1994: 15) asked three students to describe their experiences of their two-year master's degree training programme in a metaphor with a view to trying to capture how they had changed and the differences in the way the changes had occurred. Linda used the idea of a repotted plant:

> I think of a potted plant I have sitting on my front porch. It sat in the same pot for many years neither growing nor dying, just maintaining the status quo. I decided to repot it to see if it would show some signs of new life. I removed all the old soil from the roots and discovered that it was extremely rootbound. I cut away some of the old roots and repotted it in a larger container. I trimmed away some of the older branches that were

quite bare of leaves. I put it back out on my front porch and soon it began to grow. Like my potted plant, I sat in my classroom for many years teaching my students as the teacher's manuals directed without much thought as to why I was doing what I was doing . . . In my new pot (the master's program) I started to grow in new ways and in ways that raised many fruitful questions about what I believe and how I teach.

(M. Johnston 1994: 16)

Leslie described her experience as like an artichoke. Each leaf represented an element of practice that could be understood only by peeling away and examining each layer. Some petals tasted bitter and whether edible or not they were all roadblocks in understanding practice until they were examined. At the centre of the artichoke was the heart that represented her beliefs.

Hazel saw herself as a tree that had not wished to change until there came a time of drought in which she felt alone. In order to live, her roots had to search out water until she found that with an extended root system when the rain finally came she had greater balance and security. For Hazel though, the increased complexity had also created doubts about her capability that affected her confidence and it was not until two years after the completion of the course that she became increasingly comfortable with her changed practice.

A similar process to that described by Johnston (1994) was invoked by Hagstrom et al. (2000) who invited students to respond to the sentence stem: 'Teaching is like . . .'. Responses included 'the ocean', 'making bread' and 'geology'. When I tried this out with some teachers they had no difficulty in responding, one of them offering 'advertising', explaining that both are about getting people to change their minds.

York-Barr et al. (2006: 187) reported a process of asking respondents to write down any four nouns. In their example these were cat, chocolate, bicycle and bus. Participants were then asked to complete a sentence stem: X is like Y because. Suggestions offered by participants included, 'Dialogue is like chocolate, because it is rich, you share it with people who are close to you and you want it to last a long time' and 'Co-teaching is like riding a bicycle, because it takes two strong wheels working together to get anywhere.' This activity was carried out in a group context but could be adapted to individual supervision. When I thought about this in relation to my own work as a therapist I had fun with 'treacle', 'mist', 'bubbles' and 'firework'.

A story from Greek mythology was adapted by Sommer and Cox (2003) with a view to facilitating reflection on the process of learning and development. Parallels were drawn between the challenges of training and the story of Psyche and Eros. Psyche is sent by Aphrodite to complete four seemingly hopeless tasks: sorting a large mound of jumbled seeds and legumes into separate piles, a task she completed with the aid of ants; collecting fleece from golden rams with huge and dangerous horns, accomplished by emulating the birds in the fields who collected the fleece from thorny bushes; filling a flask with water that flowed from the highest peak, in which an eagle agreed to help; and retrieving a cask of beauty ointment from the underworld. She was forewarned that on the way she would see people in terrible circumstances who would beg for help but she was to speak to no one. With assistance, Psyche ultimately completed the four tasks and was reunited with Eros.

Bolen (1984) had previously suggested some interpretations for the metaphor. Sorting a pile of seeds symbolised the conceptualisation of personal beliefs, the process of sifting through feelings, values and motives to determine what is important and what is insignificant. Bolen (1984) argued that the golden fleece represented power and that Psyche was sent to claim her power without getting trampled in the process. This symbolised fledgling counsellors who want to stand up for themselves without appearing to 'step on the toes' of individuals who are in positions of authority. Filling the flask from the highest peak was paralleled by Bolen with a struggle to maintain perspective. The broader perspective of the eagle may be provided by the supervisor. Journeying to the underworld was seen as the equivalent of supervisees learning to say no. Supervisees need to develop awareness of their limitations and to discriminate when it is appropriate to refuse unhealthy or unreasonable client requests.

Sommer and Cox (2003) argued that the supervisory relationship, especially when viewed as a collaborative process, could provide a safety net for new supervisees without tethering them too tightly. Supervisees were to be encouraged to develop their own interpretations of myths and stories. They stated (Sommer and Cox 2003: 328), 'collaborative supervision encourages supervisees to arrive at their own answers, those that uniquely enable them to be more effective counselors versus those that tempt them to become imitators of their supervisors.' The authors argued that such metaphors provide an avenue for gaining insight into supervisees' values and priorities which can be effective in enhancing the supervision process.

Sommer and Cox (2003) suggested the following questions to encourage reflection and to keep the focus on the ways in which the myth might inform the counselling and supervision tasks.

> In your development as a counselor, what names do you give to the seeds that make up your jumbled pile?
> What qualities do you bring to this task that might be helpful in sorting your seeds?
> What dangerous rams threaten to limit your power and competence as a counselor?
> What skills do you use to claim your power without being trampled?
> What would be one step you could take to further your growth as a counselor?
> What kinds of self-care tonics might your flask contain?

When you look at your work with a particular client from the perspective of the eagle, how does the counseling landscape change?

What kinds of tasks do you find overwhelming and inhibitive in terms of moving forward in your work as a counselor?

What names do you give to the voices that call out to you on your journey to become a competent counselor?

What considerations do you make in deciding how to balance your task with the needs or decisions of others?

(Sommer and Cox 2003: 330–332)

Sommer and Cox argued that sharing interpretations of the metaphor would help supervisees to conceptualise and normalise the struggles often experienced in the learning and development process.

The leaders of the Children's Learning in Science Project (CLIS) developed a set of cartoons, reproduced in Figure 6.4, that offered pictorial metaphors for the teaching and learning process (K. Johnston et al. 1990). These have been used (Jon Scaife, personal communication, 2009) to good effect in encouraging teachers to reflect on the teaching task. Jon Scaife asks workshop participants to look at the set of cartoons and invites interpretations with the question, 'Do any of the images or metaphors connect for you with any aspects of learning processes?' Next he invites a value-judgement, 'Do you like or dislike what you see, and if so, why?' In small group members discuss with each other their interpretations of and preferences for the cartoons, coming together as a large group to address further questions about what they see. These questions may address what literally can be seen: 'What do you make of the bird?' 'Who is the instructor and who is the novice?' 'Who threw the stone?' Participants make their own interpretations which may or may not be shared. Although undertaken in a group, I see this as a useful method for exploring learning expectations and preferences in individual supervision. A group may offer even richer opportunities for exploration.

Problem solving strategy appraisal

In my working life I have had the regular experience of feeling puzzled and being faced by seemingly insoluble problems. My responses to such experiences have been variously adaptive and over time I have learned more about what works for me; when to persist and when to let go. Bransford and Johnson (1972) used the following paragraph, which is often rated as incomprehensible by English-speaking listeners, to illustrate the need for a context from which to generate the meaning of linguistic input:

If the balloons popped, the sound wouldn't be able to carry since everything would be too far away from the correct floor. A closed window would also prevent the sound from carrying since most buildings tend to

A piece of clay is moulded by the potter.

A guide and a traveller are moving through hilly terrain. There are a lot of hills, and one or two are very tall indeed. The view of the landscape changes as they ascend the higher ground.

Figure 6.4 Cartoons from CLIS.

3

A petrol pump attendant is putting petrol into a car. The driver, who sometimes uses self-service petrol stations, will soon be able to drive away.

4

Many people work on the building site. They are involved in clearing, carrying, building, planning and supervising.

Figure 6.4—(continued)

A child is throwing stones into a pond, and watching the ripples spread outwards.

A gardener, surrounded by a range of garden equipment, is tending some of the different types of plant in the garden. He prefers the garden as it is, but realises that there are many types of garden.

Figure 6.4—(continued)

be well insulated. Since the whole operation depends on a steady flow of electricity, a break in the middle of the wire would also cause problems. Of course, the fellow could shout, but the human voice is not loud enough to carry that far. An additional problem is that a string could break on the instrument. Then there could be no accompaniment to the message. It is clear that the best situation would involve less distance. Then there would be fewer potential problems. With face-to-face contact, the least number of things could go wrong.

(Bransford and Johnson 1972)

This is much like the party game 'Situations' in which questions are invited in order to derive an explanation of how the situation described by one player arose. I have used this passage, and other material (J.M. Scaife 1995) as a stimulus to encourage developing awareness of strategies for responding to confusing input, puzzling experiences at work, and the associated feelings. I guess that you will already have responded in some way to Bransford and Johnson's (1972) passage, possibly by skipping it altogether, or by engaging in a variety of mental efforts to derive the context. Here's a selection of possible responses:

- 'It's a bit of a puzzle. I'll just pass it over and get on with the rest of the book.'
- 'That's a poorly constructed passage. What's the author on about?'
- 'I've spent a bit of time thinking about it. That'll do. I'll look at the answer. Of course I could have come up with it if I'd spent longer.'
- 'Let's think: there are balloons, an instrument with strings, electricity and a message. Distance is involved and something about a "correct floor". What's the significance of that?'
- 'I think in images. What mental picture am I getting?'
- 'It's Friday afternoon and I've got to pack ready to go away for the weekend. I'll just run through this quickly before I go.'
- 'I don't think I'll be able to solve that so I'll wait until the author tells me what it is.'
- 'I really think it's impossible without a lot more data.'

Being faced with a puzzle or problem can be confusing and disheartening or present a challenge, picked up and pursued earnestly with a range of different strategies. Individuals may respond with impatience, logical analysis, curiosity; a range of emotions and approaches are possible. I find that my own strategies depend on my mental state at the time, the extent to which my working context provides support in approaching problem situations, and decisions that I make about my persistence and the extent of the effort that I am prepared to make in relation to this challenge at this particular time. I have found that understanding my approaches and deciding when to give up or let go of an issue are important matters for me to know about myself.

The context for Bransford and Johnson's passage can be found in Appendix 2.

Furthering understanding of the self in relation to the process of supervision

Metaphor has been used to represent the process of supervision. Barbara Grant (1999) argues that supervision, in the context of working with academic master's degree students, is simultaneously predictable and unpredictable in its course. She states:

> It is predictable in that it is an institutionalised pedagogy predicated on the structural power and difference between the positions of supervisor and student; it is unpredictable because it is also an intersubjective relation which is subject to identity and desire – both of which mobilise, and are mobilised by, power.
>
> (Grant 1999: 1)

She stresses the importance of approaching supervision prepared for the unexpected such as when the student suddenly expresses anger and hostility towards the supervisor. Her metaphor is intended to incorporate a view of the supervisory relationship as straightforwardly defined by institutional edicts that specify mutual responsibilities, while simultaneously acknowledging the influence of issues of hierarchy, identity and desire which often take place at an unconscious level.

Grant (1999) proposes that negotiating a supervision relationship is like walking on a 'rackety bridge'; the bridge being the formally defined relationship, and the racketiness being the result of the effects of the interpersonal essence of supervision. She states:

> Once an agreement for supervision is reached, and student and supervisor begin to walk on the bridge together, to act in relation to one another, many unpredictable effects occur, threatening the stability of the bridge and those walking on it . . . When walking jointly on a *rackety* bridge, both supervisor and student need to be sensitive to the effects of their actions and responses on the other, or someone (most often the student) may fall off. At times, both need to be flexible in their tactics and willing to try new ways of acting towards the other in order to maintain a balance that allows progress to be made. This is not to say, though, that both are equal. In my metaphor, the supervisor weighs more by virtue of her/his institutional position and therefore must take greater care in how s/he walks on that bridge. A small, thoughtless move can throw the

student off the bridge. No movement at all can provoke unwise movements from the student. For instance, some students end up 'jumping' up and down to ensure their supervisor notices their presence on the bridge among all the other distractions and pressures of academic life.

(Grant 1999: 9)

I find this an apt metaphor for some of my own experiences in supervision. I can see how it could be a useful adjunct to the contracting process. Mutual study and consideration of the metaphor could enable the discussion of possible actions by each party that could lead to destabilisation and danger on the rackety bridge. Further discussion could explore how this might be overcome and mutual progress resumed. Difficulties subsequently arising in the supervisory relationship could be explored through a return to the metaphor. The method also has the advantage of demonstrating a parallel between the uses of metaphor for encouraging reflection in relation to practice with clients, and reflective practice in supervision. The rackety bridge has the advantage of attributing responsibility for any difficulties to the nature of the task rather than to the parties engaged in the task.

Guiffrida et al. (2007) reported an approach using an environmental metaphor intended to facilitate reflection on the normative function of supervision in pre-registration training, when the supervisor has responsibility for judging the suitability of the student for membership of the profession. In this approach (Valadez and Garcia 1998: 94) the supervisor was conceptualised as the sun and the supervisee as a seed or sprout. A parallel was drawn between the sun's rays causing germination of the seed, and the supervisor's evaluative comments having the potential to stimulate and awaken 'innate, growth-capable elements' in the supervisee. However, because of its intensity, the rays of the sun also have the potential to destroy the seed in the absence of adequate light filtering mechanisms. By analogy, supervisor comments, especially those that are perceived as unfair or harsh by supervisees, have the capability to hinder or destroy supervisee development.

It was argued by Valadez and Garcia (1998) that when this metaphor was described to supervisees early in the supervisory relationship, their past experiences and feelings regarding assessment and feedback could be awakened and discussed before the process was underway. Supervisees could think about their own appropriately protective filtering processes (equated with the layers of the earth's atmosphere) that would enable them to make use of supervisor feedback and evaluative comments without becoming overly defensive or projecting their past experiences onto the current relationship. Valadez and Garcia (1998) proposed that a second supervisor (the moon) might take a non-evaluative role and assist supervisees in processing the first supervisor's feedback. I think that there is mileage in exploring the multiple roles of a single supervisor as sun, moon and seed. Separating the normative from the formative and restorative functions, and locating them in two individuals stands the risk of 'splitting'; one providing 'good' supervision the other 'bad' (Pedder 1986). It may be possible to extend the metaphor to represent the two-way learning that can take place in supervision; the germinated seed and growing plant enhancing the atmosphere that both supervisor and supervisee breathe.

Furthering understanding of the worker in the work context

After taking up the relatively new post of nurse consultant, Sue Duke (2004) used reflection and metaphor to explore her struggles in understanding the role which she experienced as very different from the media vision of the 'super nurse', a *Nursing Times* cartoon character based on Superman. There were difficulties in working out where the role of nurse consultant and medical consultant met and diverged, the nature of the relationship between nurse consultant and Macmillan nurse in a palliative care context, and how to avoid adopting a purely medical model. The metaphor she developed was entitled, 'Where vampires, pirates and aliens roam'. She found that she was able to maintain a delicate balance between 'finding a place' and 'being put in my place'. Vampires are said to be corpses that come alive at night, drink blood and fizzle up in sunshine. Humans turn into vampires when bitten by one. Vampires represented the tests that she experienced of whether she could 'stand the heat' through challenges to her knowledge and skills. She had the option of bringing her role to life cooperatively or being goaded to draw blood – returning insults or putting up a fight. Pirates symbolised working outside the rules, trespassing and plundering treasure. She reported that she had needed to address the perception that she was a plunderer of other people's treasure, for example carrying the status of 'consultant' without having made the required sacrifices. Aliens signified the experience of being a stranger to the service in which she was employed, the role being alien by virtue of its novelty to staff in the employing National Health Service Trust.

She argued that the metaphors provided a safe way to discuss her struggles and to express the emotion associated with her feelings of being put in her place without feeling that she was criticising the colleagues involved.

Summary

In this chapter I have explored some methods for finding out more about ourselves at work. Alex Gitterman (1988) discusses the desirability of students breaking through theoretical and personal boundaries, arguing that our favourite theories can become so overly cherished that we come habitually to fit people and their situations to them. This is the danger if we forget or fail to learn about the need to subject our own perspectives to critical reflection:

to question and to be inquiring or curious is not a simple thing to do; the habit must be acquired over a lifetime. Professional socialization formalizes our work and stiffens our approach. Ambiguity threatens us; it ought to challenge us. We become cautious, avoid risks, develop rigid and mechanical responses and seek comfort in prescriptions and symmetries. And through these processes, we and our students may distance and detach ourselves from our clients/members.

When students enter my class, I listen in dismay and incredulously to how they talk to their clients: 'I don't have enough data to prescribe treatment' or 'Before group therapy begins, let's introduce ourselves . . .' or 'I have studied your case.' Out of their uncertainties and fears of failure, they learn to hide behind professional 'masks,' obscuring their clients' humanity behind the 'case' and their own behind their 'professionalism.' As Santayana observed: 'Nothing is so poor and melancholy as an art that is interested in itself and not in its subject.' Without a keen interest in our 'subjects' we settle for safety and mediocrity. (Will Rogers stated that the good thing about being mediocre is that you are always at your best.)

(Gitterman 1988: 36)

Chapter 7

Approaches to supervision of reflective practice (III)

Methods that encourage 'decentring' and multiple perspectives

Methods that encourage 'decentring' or trying to understand from the perspective of another person

In the course of my clinical work I was greeted in school by the five-year-old child I had arranged to see with the words, said with a sense of pride, 'I'm not allowed in the playground because I just hit James.' 'Oh,' I said, 'How does that feel?' 'Sad and angry,' he replied. He had every reason to feel sad and angry; it was a shame that James was the recipient of his feelings but I was impressed by his capability to recognise and report his emotions.

On another occasion I was visiting a student on placement in a ward for long-stay patients. As I was about to depart, the student and I chatted by the exit and a patient came up and asked me, 'What's your name?' I could just have said my name but this seemed to me an unusual start to a conversation with a stranger and wouldn't have felt authentic. I paused while I thought about how to reply and he repeated the question. Still considering a response, I said, 'I don't know whether I want to tell you my name. I'm just thinking about what to say.' 'Fuck off then,' he said and wandered away down the corridor.

I cite these examples of communication because they have both lived on in my memory, probably because they took me by surprise and presented me with a challenge; how to understand the perspective of the other person and how to respond in a way that was authentic, respectful and attuned to the experience of the other.

In my clinical and supervision work I sometimes find myself particularly moved by another person's portrayal of an experience. It is not just the words that make an impact but maybe the demeanour or the emotion with which the story is told, and I have a 'feel' for them and their situation. At other times I *think* that I understand what it would be like to be in that person's shoes. Sometimes I am at a complete loss and puzzle over the perspective being taken.

In professions that involve helping, caring for or educating others, the capacity to empathise, to decentre and try to enter into the world of another is prized. This can be in the classroom where a child is struggling to understand what to the teacher seems obvious, in the hospital where the patient is resisting a procedure that is deemed life-saving, or in the community where a child has been neglected and abused. Such situations present a greater or lesser challenge to the professional and without this attempt to experience how another experiences, it would be all too easy to ignore, insist or condemn and keep a safe distance. When Ruth Allen (2009) led reflective practice groups for health workers, one of the emergent themes was the desire to 'make things better' for patients. The physiotherapists in her groups felt responsible for patient motivation. The groups helped them better to understand why some patients did not engage enthusiastically in pulmonary rehabilitation.

Empathy is an orientation that involves using imagination to understand another's experiences. This requires us to get out of what D.H. Lawrence (1994) referred to as the 'glass bottles' of our own egos, a challenging task the more different the other's experience from our own. Although we cannot know just what it is like for others we can be attentive to other people's situations and actions, reflect on our understandings and construct a rich picture of what it might be like to be in the other person's shoes. If we can empathise we don't 'tolerate' others but 'respect' them, or at the very least when we are dealing with people who have committed base acts we do our best to 'understand'. That is, to form a coherent account of how they came to be in the situation in which we find them. Otherwise we are likely to essentialise people (they are evil) or detach ourselves from them. When I am struggling to decentre I have found the methods described below to be helpful. When I am really stuck it has sometimes been because the issue is too close to – or too far from home. Taking up, as best we can, the perspective of another encourages reflective practice; the hawk in the mind perched on the shoulder of another player in the scene.

Role play, enactment, role reversal and simulation

Small children appear to have no difficulty in adopting different roles. You only have to watch them playing games of 'pretend' in which they take up the role of teacher, doctor, nurse, train driver, soldier or princess with the greatest of facility, happily taking the simultaneous role of director. Their imaginations appear limitless. I am unsure as to when this seemingly natural and spontaneous behaviour disappears, but by the time I invite students and long-qualified practitioners to participate in role plays I am almost invariably underwhelmed with volunteers. If I circulate a questionnaire to workshop participants in advance and ask delegates if there is anything they wish to avoid, I can guarantee that the most frequently cited item will be 'role play'. I surmise that this is partly to do with performance anxiety in front of a group. Embarrassment and fear were common experiences of the students in a group studied by Wannan and York (2005) and encouragement was needed to ensure that participants took the role plays seriously. I find that people are generally happier to try things out in pairs or threesomes.

If trying out a role is to be undertaken as a means of developing reflective practice in supervision, this suggests the need for a relationship characterised by trust and safety. As a supervisor, you can be the first to take on the most challenging role and not mind making a hash of it. It is a rehearsal, a play, about trying things out and trying again in the hope of developing insights and additional perspectives. It benefits from a mind-set described by Eric Weiner whereby 'if you are free to fail, you are free to try' (Weiner 2008: 162). Such a mind-set may run counter to the state of 'being supposed to know' encouraged in our education systems and present even in the thinking of primary school children (Holt 1969).

Role play has been defined as, 'a structured, goal directed learning technique that uses the acting out of a part in a specified context to give participants an immediate opportunity to apply information or practice behaviours' (El-Shamy 2005: 4). Susan El-Shamy suggests that a simulation is usually longer and more complex than a role play and has the additional aim of letting the player experience and develop understanding of what it is like to be in anther's situation such as being homeless or feeling angry. What I envisage is something between these two positions; the aim being to develop understanding through reflection but without the necessity of an elaborate and fully planned scenario. This is similar to the view of Morry van Ments (1999: 9), who states, 'Role play is the experiencing of a problem under an unfamiliar set of constraints in order that one's own ideas may emerge and one's understanding increase.' Antony Williams (1988) refers to this procedure as an 'action method'.

Role play, role reversal, simulation and enactment have been advocated as useful methods in supervision, professional training courses and in practice settings (Errek and Randolph 1982; Meredith and Bradley 1989; Riley 2008; Strosahl and Jacobson 1986; Thobaben and Cherry 2004; Wannan and York 2005) by practitioners from a range of professions and different theoretical persuasions. It has been used to build on an intellectual understanding of experiences such as poverty and discrimination through simulation of the actual experience of feeling powerless. In some cases, former clients or patients have taken part (Hillbrand et al. 2008) and the benefits have included greater connectedness among the staff and better understanding of the patients' experiences.

I have found that one relatively non-threatening introduction to the use of role play is to provide a role description of a client which can be developed by the supervisee. More confident supervisees may prefer to create their own. The supervisor can demonstrate a specific professional task: introducing one-self and the issue of confidentiality, taking a history, giving 'bad news', assessing risk of self-harm, responding to a disclosure or explaining the role of the service. The supervisee responds in role, being as 'difficult' as he or she chooses. The process can be slowed down by the supervisor pausing at intervals to think out loud, sharing thoughts about her or his ideas and intentions as the interview proceeds. The roles may then be reversed or the supervisee may choose first to practise with a peer. The simulated experience provides supervisees with material from which to reflect on the perspective of the other and ideas for the revision of their typical practice.

When supervision is taking place between experienced practitioners such a gentle introduction may be unnecessary. The supervisee may set the agenda, inviting the supervisor to take whatever role would prove helpful to the work. Roles might include that of a client, student, a person connected to the client such as a family member or a professional with whom the client or student has had a prior relationship. In some versions of role play (described later as 'internalised-other interviewing') a piece of furniture, or a factor related to the client's health and well-being such as 'feeling guilty' or 'cancer' can be given a voice.

There are approaches to role play that can be of help if someone is struggling to engage with the process, although I would counsel against pushing too hard if this method is anathema to a supervisee or if the supervisory relationship is insufficiently robust at the time. The methods of psychodrama prescribe a 'warm-up' through the use of specifically designed exercises (Karp et al. 1998). Authenticity can be encouraged and energy generated by having the supervisee move around the room, rearranging the furniture to suit the circumstance. 'Grounding' questions, of a general nature in which the supervisee is addressed in the first person in role can also help.

Minghella and Benson (1995) used a variety of methods for analysing the critical incidents brought by their students. These included brainstorming, role play and other experiential techniques, work in pairs and group role taking. Each session also had a relevant theoretical component provided by the tutors. These components emerged from the critical incidents described by the students and included general themes such as learning skills of assertiveness. The work in pairs ranged from discussion to role taking and practice. The group role taking method was devised by the authors for situations which appeared to have two opposing viewpoints, or when they discerned a viewpoint not noted by the student. The students were asked to divide into two groups, one group taking on the role of the student and the other the role of the client. The two groups were asked to discuss their feelings about an incident reported by one of the students.

The two groups then came together and speaking as the student or client told the other group how they were feeling. In one example, the similarity of feelings generated by both groups provided a completely new perspective and enabled discussion of other ways of approaching the situation. The similarity of feelings also generated discomfort for some students who had seen themselves as very different from clients.

Role plays are followed by an immediate 'de-roling' process, and a review, debrief or processing in which the ideas that have emerged are summarised or further explored through discussion. De-roling can be accomplished through a range of methods such as changing chairs, talking about plans for the remainder of the day and discussing the character played in the third person. 'De-roling is the process of shedding the role taken on for the purpose of an activity and resuming one's usual persona' (B. Flanagan 2008: 161). I once spent a few days in the role of a depressed client as I struggled to shake off the persona that I had adopted in a simulation. I learned that it is wise to give careful attention to this stage of the process and that role play can be a very powerful medium for developing empathy. The review is a period of reflection in which participants absorb and analyse the impact of new ideas on themselves, drawing out the implications of the learning and how to build on it.

Role play can offer particular insights in the realm of interpersonal and communication skills where the interplay of verbal and non-verbal behaviours are thought too complex and subtle to be fully grasped through academic study (van Ments 1999). The method gives the participants direct and immediate feedback about the effects of their actions in role. It offers a degree of safety because it focuses on behaviour-in-role. Maintenance of this focus is crucial in the debrief, questions being addressed to the role (Why did the 'manager' (not 'you') lose her temper) and not to the player. Van Ments (1999) draws attention to the importance of allowing time in the debrief to clear up any factual errors.

The more constraints on the role play, the less opportunity there is to stray from the tutor's or supervisor's intended path while the opportunities for new insights may be fewer. Van Ments (1999) cautions that structured role plays tend to convey implicit assumptions which could include stereotypes reinforced by the choice of players to fulfil the role:

> Imagine a court room. The case before the judge is that of a cook who is married to an electrical engineer. Whilst the engineer has been working overseas on an important contract, the cook (who works in a local school) has had to call a plumber because of a fault in the central heating system at home. Whilst the plumber was at work in the empty house, a friend of the cook's, an attractive 40-year-old nurse, came to call. The plumber made advances to the nurse and in the course of a slight scuffle the plumber fell on a valve which was being repaired and a valuable Chinese carpet was damaged by water ... The prosecuting counsel, a stern-looking figure in wig and gown, rises to cross examine the plumber. The court short-hand typist prepares to take notes.
>
> (Van Ments 1999: 94)

He invites the reader to picture the characters in this scene and then tells us that the cook is a thin man of Chinese ethnicity and his wife a famous electrical engineer. We are led by the language of embedded stereotypes – 'attractive nurse', stern-looking figure', 'short–hand typist'.

One of the advantages of using role play in individual supervision is that the number of players is so restricted that there are in-built opportunities to cross the divides of gender, age, social class and the like, opportunities restricted only by the imagination of the participants.

Thinking out loud and reflective analysis

Thinking out loud is a method that I have encountered and used in role plays and in training workshops; a process designed to show what is taking place in the worker's head while he or she is conducting an interview or some other suitable work-related activity. It has also been termed 'the articulated thoughts in simulated situations [ATSS] paradigm' in the context of the assessment of cognitions in the study of cognitive behavioural therapy (Davison et al. 1997). While more perspectives may be available in a subsequent group reflection, the method can also be effective in one-to-one supervision. The participants stop the action at agreed intervals, which could be as frequently as prior to every utterance, and say what they are thinking. The aim is to slow down the interview in order to open up both thinking and action to the 'audience' which may comprise only the two participants involved. The process allows for all participants to be party to the thinking that is driving the action which may include theoretical and philosophical underpinnings and/or clinical intuition.

Thinking aloud requires participants to turn what may be vague impressions into language. Their ideas may be just fleeting thoughts or intuitions for which they may be unable to give a logical account. I think it helpful if the verbalisation process is unexpurgated and later subject to reflective examination. Such a process can show how tiny cues may be interpreted in order to make meaning of an interpersonal interaction. Participants can also verbalise the ideas that crossed their minds and were rejected.

Thinking aloud has been used in research settings when a recording may be made of the verbalisations which are then subject to more formal analysis (Osmond and Darlington 2005). The method has been used to examine social workers' decision-making in child protection work (Drury-Hudson 1999) and can also be used with recordings which are paused at regular intervals during playback. Listeners speak out loud whatever is going on in their minds as they watch or listen to the recording. In educational settings John Loughran (1996: 33) used thinking aloud to show his students what was in his mind as lessons unfolded. Some students were showing frustration at being unable to get sufficient 'air time' in class discussions. Loughran verbalised why this was a problem for him, the likely outcomes if the discussion were to continue in the same way, and suggested some solutions. This resulted in the students sitting in a circle, writing down a paragraph of their views and passing the paper on to the next person who responded in writing. Each student ended up with a record of responses to her or his views. He called this 'silent discussion'. Jon Scaife (personal communication 2009) uses thinking aloud to foreground the decisions and judgements in which he is engaged when teaching graduate students in education. This can make explicit some of the tacit thinking that is guiding the design of the teaching. Students have evaluated this as a helpful 'reflexive check' on teaching principles and methods in action.

For the purposes of supervision, the unedited articulation of thoughts can reveal to learners the breadth and depth of reflection-in-action of a more experienced practitioner and can show the diversity of what goes on in the minds of different workers when responding to a common experience. Using this method Julie Drury-Hudson (1999) found that experienced practitioners generally had a much deeper grasp than novices of the relevant theory when making judgements about critical decisions in child protection work:

> Theories I would take into account are things like Maslow's hierarchy of needs, and things like that. Systems theory. I would think about theories of child development. I think very much in terms of psychodynamic processes and the interactions between parents and children, particularly in an historical context. Also theories of power and inequality. Feminist theories in terms of this being a single mum who's been left on her own with five children and no support. And perhaps theories about mental illness in particular in relation to her level of depression. And I'm also informed by the theory that it's possible to intervene to bring about change and so I have confidence in the theory of change and that things can be different. I think that this was probably a conscious influence . . . I think that it's really important to read the literature widely and to continue reading it and to have a knowledge of the theoretical frameworks that are informing your practice and to actually enjoy that. That there's actually a clear link to theory and practice. So a detailed knowledge of what abuse is, how it occurs, the patterns underlying the intrapsychic processes, the power issues for women and children, the social position of abuse in our society, an understanding that people are abused and why, the vulnerability issues, a knowledge about change and how change occurs and what needs to happen for change to happen.
>
> (Drury-Hudson 1999: 152)

Internalised-other interviewing

Internalised-other interviewing (Burnham 2000; Epston 1993; A. Williams 1995) involves creating a conversation that invites people to respond from their internalised version of someone they know in order to promote further understanding and empathy. It involves asking the interviewee to assume the role of the other person (or it can be an inanimate object or an experience such as 'having fun' or 'feeling upset') and to answer questions posed to them from that perspective. David Paré (2001: 28) argues that 'internalized other interviewing promotes a compassionate way of knowing by inviting someone into another's experience, and drawing forth knowledges that are available to them, but not previously accessed.'

The process begins with an explanation of the stages of the interview and an invitation, which can be refused, to take up the 'other' role. This is followed by a number of 'grounding' questions, which take the form of small talk, with the aim of helping the interviewee to assume the other role. Paré (2001) gives the following example:

> Hello, Linda. Thanks for agreeing to this. Mark tells me you're an accountant; I wonder if things are busy at this time of year?
>
> As you know, I've been meeting with Mark for a while. He said there's stuff going on at home that he isn't happy about, and I wanted to check with you to get your account of what's going on. What are your concerns about what's happening at home?
>
> (Paré 2001: 25)

The stages of the internalised-other interview were identified as follows by Burnham (2000):

- Choose the person, idea, ability, problem or emotion that will be the 'other'. This choice takes place through negotiation and is best when connected with the flow of the conversation or a purpose of the interview.
- Propose the way of working as a way of fulfilling a goal of the interview.
- Explain the process as much as necessary to begin, or politely accept if the person declines the offer.
- Begin by 'grounding' the person being interviewed in the identity of the 'other'. This is accomplished by talking to the person as if meeting them for the first time and asking questions about everyday aspects of the 'other's' life.
- Continue by exploring more deeply the experience of the other in relation to the goals of the interview. These questions can be related to emotions, actions and meanings. Burnham (2000) argued that the interviewer need not be discouraged by 'don't know' responses since these are potential triggers to the curiosity of the interviewee.
- Explore the relationship between the 'other' and the person being interviewed.
- Prompt the person that this stage of the interview is ending by saying 'goodbye' to the 'other' and 'hello' to the person sitting in front of you.
- Reflect on the process and its effects in relation to the purpose of the interview.

In my experience people vary in the extent to which they are able to respond in role and often slip back into commenting *on* the other rather than *as* the other. This may be down to my lack of facility with the method. Even when this happens though, new insights often arise. These can be amplified by the reflection process and the use of skilful questioning.

Empty chairs

My first encounter with the use of 'empty chairs' was when working with my long-time friend and colleague, Mike Pomerantz. Much happier and more comfortable than I was then to work with action methods, he showed me first-hand how two empty chairs, alternately occupied by me, could be used to draw forth two sides of a debate that I was having with myself. Taking one view while seated in one chair and an opposing view while seated in the other afforded so much more clarity to the two positions. I was aided by Mike's judicious use of questions and enthusiastic encouragement to accompany my arguments with full emotional expression. Leaving the 'ifs and buts' out of the argument while seated in one chair freed me up to explore the full strength of my feelings about the issue. Then came the reflective part; reviewing what I had heard myself say, exploring what it revealed about my underlying passions, and making a plan for action.

The method has its roots in Gestalt therapy (Perls 1969) and psychodrama (Bradshaw Tauvon 1998). Scott Kellogg (2004) has described application of the method across five different approaches to psychological intervention. Internal dialogues, made external by use of the two chairs, are typically seen as useful when people experience conflicts between different parts of themselves, when they are in two minds, or when they are 'at war with themselves'. The questions posed by the supervisor can take the action into the future: 'It's a month further on in time. How are things working out?' I have found the method valued by supervisees facing indecision which may reflect a conflict between two opposing sets of values (Fabry 1988), allowing them to acknowledge the validity of both sets of views and the very many other positions between.

In a relationship that feels safe, it may be possible to explore such conflicting sets of values. It is not that uncommon for supervisees to find themselves in positions where their personal values are at odds with those embraced or implied by their professional contexts. I increasingly find this myself when what I see as rigid organisational procedures (such as the requirement for mandatory counselling interviews in response to formula-generated sickness absence data) come up against my belief in a personal and individual approach to management. My example is trivial in comparison with the experiences of many practitioners. In the following extract Nimisha Patel describes the agony of training to join the profession of clinical psychology with its primarily white middle-class values:

Well, every lecture was a constant reminder that the theories espoused, the therapies taught etc. did not include me, or people like me, or my family; there was no synergy and few meeting points between what I was being taught and my own upbringing, world beliefs, religious and spiritual beliefs, nothing that accounted for, acknowledged, childhood and adult experiences of racism, witnessing gang violence (White youth against Asian youth etc.), and nothing on social injustices and effects on people and their well-being. Worse, was that I felt so desperately lonely and alone, so alienated, so confused, so utterly over-whelmed. I did what makes sense I guess – I split things off, I abandoned (though not totally) my religious practices, I became increasingly distanced from my Black school friends, my family . . . everything and everyone who made me, who reflected me and who validated my identity, my history, my heritage and me.

(Davidson and Patel 2009: 81)

I am not for a moment claiming that Nimisha's experience could have been mitigated through empty chair work but with careful handling I could envisage a group variant of a two-chair exercise in which minority and majority views were given voice, with participants attempting to speak from the perspective of others, imaginatively playing people of genders, ethnicities, ages and faiths different from their own.

Spectrograms and play genograms

Mooli Lahad (2000) offers a wealth of ideas for creative supervision using expressive arts methods. When I use methods that involve enactment and drama, I sometimes have to 'gee' myself up – they are not my 'natural' medium. I prefer talking and listening. But I have learned to feel reasonably comfortable squatting under my desk with a child 'shooting aliens' or beating hell out of bean bags with a plastic bat provided that I have a rationale and have warned the administrative staff in advance. When it comes to supervision my instinct is to be more circumspect. Lahad describes a number of approaches that bridge talking and expressive arts methods. One of these, that encourages decentring, is the use of objects in a representational sense to create a 'spectrogram'. In order to use this method you first need a collection of suitable objects. Lahad has a rich and varied collection of small toys, some of which, in Figure 7.1, have been organised into Yosuf's (a supervisee's) multidisciplinary team. While I find such objects instantly evocative, and can imagine myself organising them into wickedly playful arrangements, this kind of approach can also be effective using a simpler collection of buttons, stones of different sizes and shapes, modelling clay or whatever else you have to hand.

Figure 7.1 Spectrogram: talking with the duke and the shepherd.

When I attended one of Lahad's workshops he gave the following instructions for creating spectrograms which I have adapted:

- Pick an object to represent yourself, a client and family members.
- Use a piece of paper as a 'sacred space' on which to arrange the figures.
- Put them the way you think that your client would have arranged them.
- Rearrange them how you think your client would want the family to be now.
- Arrange them how you think the client would wish them to be arranged when the work is finished.
- Can you see with whom you might be in coalition?
- What other alliances do you notice?
- What do the features of the creatures that you have chosen to represent the characters tell you about how you see them?
- What else do you notice about the characters' positions? Is there any mirroring?

In his book, Lahad (2000) adapts the method for the purpose of exploring Yosuf's perceptions of members of the multidisciplinary team to which he belongs. Yosuf initially noticed how he had divided the group into 'old' and 'new' team members. When asked to position the team from each staff member's imagined point of view he developed some new perspectives about who may have felt left out, who might try to block the development of new relationships and the location of old alliances and hierarchies. In his evaluation of the process he said, 'How wonderful this is, it is like chess, you can move one pawn and the whole situation changes.' He decided that he would use the learning to inform individual conversations with each member of his team.

Using a similar approach, Antony Williams (1995) gathered together a set of evocative objects attached to magnets which can be moved around on a marker board. In supervision these are used to represent people, roles, 'states' or relationships in order to illustrate the therapeutic system as currently perceived. The supervisor enquires into the arrangement with a view to the supervisee creating changes that give pointers for the future direction of the work. Mullen and Luke (2007) reported the successful adaptation of a 'play genogram' (Gil 2003) in which the supervisor directs the supervisee to select objects or miniatures to represent the client and presenting issue. Next, the supervisee includes objects to represent a perspective on the therapeutic relationship. After processing the visual/tactile representations and associative thoughts and feelings, the supervisee can add additional objects to represent other significant relationships (Fall and Sutton 2004). Other writers (Robbins and Erismann 1992) have referred to these processes as 'sculpting using objects'.

For the purposes of developing an understanding of others' perspectives, the creation of arrangements of representational objects from the perspective of a client or colleague makes sense to me. The method has the advantage of 'externalising' – taking ideas from the supervisee's mind and representing them in a material form which can be examined from multiple visual perspectives.

Diagrammatic formulations

In my work I am sometimes asked to describe clients by means of a psychological profile. I collect evidence and information from multiple sources which I often find complex to hold in mind. Diagrams help me to organise my thoughts and ensure that I include as much as I am able of the evidence which I jot down as I go along so that I can see what I think. Some approaches to psychological therapy such as cognitive analytic therapy advocate diagrammatic representation of a formulation of the client's difficulties. The example in Figure 7.2 is taken from a presentation made under the auspices of the British Psychological Society Faculty of Eating Disorders (Beglin and Bassra 2007).

Such diagrams are created cooperatively together with the client and I have found them to be a useful way of reflecting together on a lifetime of the client's experiences in order to develop a coherent and empathic understanding on which the future directions of the work can be built. Inskipp and

Sîan's diagram

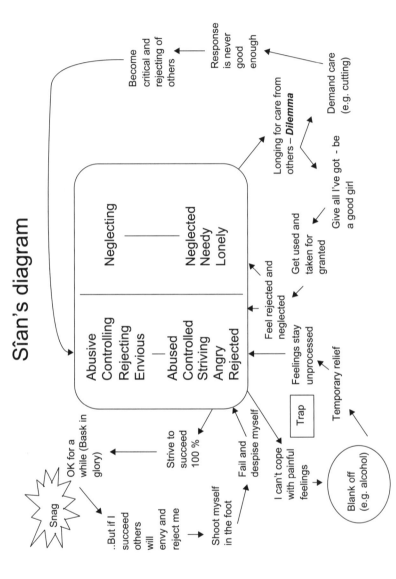

Figure 7.2 Diagrammatic formulation.

Proctor (personal communication 1997, reported in J.M. Scaife 2009) demonstrated an excellent method for getting beneath surface knowledge through drawing the client as a fish. The practitioner is also included in the drawing which I have found to be invaluable in shedding light on some of my implicit assumptions about how to conduct the work.

Methods that broaden the field to include multiple and diverse perspectives

Having explored methods that seek to explore the 'I' and 'you' in reflective practice, this section moves on to describe approaches that encourage the development of multiple perspectives so that the issues and material brought to supervision are examined not with a single lens but with the deliberate intention of looking in dark corners and from unusual and new vantage points. This involves maintaining a 'both and' position in which it is not necessary or desirable to select a single viewpoint from among different ways of seeing. The idea is to embrace difference and diversity.

One of the key imperatives for developing multiple perspectives is in order to enact the ethical principle of justice; treating our clients, students and colleagues equitably irrespective of age, gender, ethnicity, faith, sexuality, disability and culture. I have written about this more extensively in Scaife (2009). There I argued that the supervisor is in a pivotal position to facilitate the development of cultural competence, cultural sensitivity, cultural responsiveness, cultural capability, and equitable treatment. Supervision provides an opportunity to ground consideration of cultural issues in practice, not only in the direct work of supervisor and supervisee, but also as it concerns the supervisory relationship itself. Supervision that takes account of issues of diversity has been termed affirmative supervision (Halpert et al. 2007: 341–358).

Madonna Constantine (1997) describes a framework designed to aid practitioners in exploring their individual cultural identities. Some of the methods already described might help practitioners to respond to the questions that she poses:

- What are the main demographic variables (e.g. 'race', ethnicity, gender, sexual orientation, age, socio-economic status etc.) that make up my cultural identities?
- What worldviews (e.g. assumptions, biases, values etc.) do I bring to the supervision relationship based on these cultural identities?
- What value systems, based on my demographic identities, are inherent in my approach to supervision?
- What value systems, based on my demographic identities, underlie the strategies and techniques I use in supervision?

- What knowledge do I possess about the worldviews of supervisors/ supervisees who have different cultural identities from me?
- What skills do I possess for working with supervisors/supervisees who have different cultural identities from me?
- What are some of my struggles and challenges in working with supervisors/supervisees who are culturally different from me?
- How do I address or resolve these issues?
- In what ways would I like to improve my abilities in working with culturally diverse supervisors/supervisees?

(Constantine 1997: 320)

When I reflected on this framework myself it brought to mind the changes in dominant Western cultural narratives that have taken place in my lifetime. In my childhood, black people were regarded as inferior to whites. Segregation on buses in the USA was a manifestation of this belief. It was eventually outlawed in 1956, after Rosa Parks' action in refusing to give up her seat sparked a bus boycott. As I write, a black president has just been elected to the White House. Homosexuality was 'abnormal': it was removed from the *Diagnostic and Statistical Manual* of the American Psychiatric Association as recently as 1973; until 1961 'practising' homosexuality was outlawed in all 50 states in the USA (Dufour 1998). Women were housewives and mothers. Some of my former colleagues were automatically expected to give up working once they had children and had to fight to remain in their posts. My parents would never buy things on the 'never never' (credit) and the Irish were perceived as poor migrant labourers. The 'Celtic Tiger' of recent times shows just how much change can take place in a very few years. I am always trying to keep up.

The following methods are addressed generally to the development of multiple perspectives including those that might encourage enhanced cultural sensitivity.

Genograms

Conventional genograms are diagrammatic illustrations of family relationships. They may contain basic information such as gender, ages and names of family members but may be further elaborated to include beliefs and values. What also can emerge is evidence of repetitive intergenerational patterns such as number of children in a family, age of having first child, gender roles, positions of power and influence, leaving or staying at home, patterns associated with birth order, and so on. Family scripts (Byng-Hall 1995) may be revealed when repeating patterns of family interaction emerge from the representation. Such scripts are likely to influence the beliefs and values that practitioners bring both to their personal and professional lives.

Frame (2001) described approaches to the use of a spiritual genogram to raise supervisees' awareness of their own spiritual attitudes. Such a process of enquiry about the supervisor's and supervisee's beliefs with a view to understanding our faiths or life philosophies can highlight similarities and differences between us.

> By comparing and contrasting our beliefs without an attempt to determine the correctness of one's viewpoint over the other's, both the supervisor and supervisee learn about, and acknowledge, difference. The supervisee then has an internal working model of how to discuss similarities and differences in religious beliefs and is more likely to do the same with clients.
>
> (Aten and Hernandez 2004)

Questions such as whether discussion of faith beliefs is being avoided as a result of discomfort or for fear of moralising can be explored.

Brainstorming

I understand brainstorming as a technique usually adopted in groups with the aim of generating a large number of ideas for the solution of a problem. I am rather attracted to the Chambers Dictionary definition of brainstorm both as 'a sudden disturbance of mind' and 'a sudden inspiration'.

The conception of brainstorming as a process is attributed to Osborn (1963). He identified four rules designed to reduce the impact of people's unwillingness to risk appearing 'stupid' (evaluation apprehension) when expressing ideas in the presence of colleagues.

- *Focus on quantity:* Osborn (1963) wanted people to curb their tendencies to self-censor, introducing a rule that emphasised saying whatever came to mind before the censor intervened. The rule is based on the idea of 'the more the better'. Editing takes place as a later step. The aim is to produce a diversity of ideas from which creative solutions can be sculpted.
- *Rule out criticism:* This rule encourages participants to make no positive or negative comments until the group has finished generating ideas and has arrived at a later selection stage.
- *Welcome unusual ideas:* The priority is to generate a long list of original if impractical ideas. People are encouraged to look beyond or beneath their typical assumptions and to attempt to take a different stance however seemingly impossible or irrelevant this might seem.
- *Combine and improve ideas:* The three previous rules are designed to increase the diversity of ideas generated, which can then be developed through combination and improvement. Group members are encouraged to attend with an open mind to the ideas of colleagues, using them as fuel for additional ideas.

Osborn (1963) suggested that by following these rules individuals might be expected to be twice as productive as when working to generate new ideas alone. On the other hand, the research evidence suggests that groups produce only about half as many ideas as the combined total of ideas generated by the same number of individuals brainstorming alone (Paulus and Brown 2007) even allowing for the culling of duplicated ideas. By ruling out criticism and emphasising volume of ideas, a wide range of perspectives may be generated that help participants to notice their own positionality in relation to the issue under discussion.

A key finding of Paul Paulus and Vincent Brown (2007) is the importance after group brainstorming of allowing individuals time to process the shared ideas. After exposure to ideas from others, additional private time for reflection seems to be beneficial (Dugosh et al. 2000; Paulus and Yang 2000). Paulus and Brown (2007) suggest that this incubation time enables people to remember their current knowledge and integrate this with new ideas arising out of the brainstorming process.

Paulus and Brown (2007) hypothesise that when social diversity is potentially relevant to a task or problem, then the differences represented by brainstormers in a group are likely to aid the production of novel ideas. They caution that group members need to be motivated to share and elaborate task-relevant information (van Knippenberg and Schippers 2007).

A day in the life

Rhoda Olkin (1999) provides advice to supervisors concerning ways to reduce students' anxieties and increase their self-efficacy when confronted by disability. She advocates the development of a frame within which people with disabilities are seen as a minority group with civil rights. The minority model of disability places it in the social, political and economic world. There is a shift from the perception of disability as individual pathology to one of social oppression. She recommends a variety of activities that can encourage students to develop understanding of what it means to belong to a minority group. She suggests that small group activities often encourage intimate sharing of ideas, are relatively non-threatening to some students and encourage quieter students to speak more. I have found first-hand stories of minority experiences to offer significant insights into a day in the life from a minority perspective. Below are some descriptions of people's experiences that could be used as prompts by supervisors to explore the ways in which our communities and professions can function to disadvantage members of minorities. The first is from Olkin (1999):

> Nick's main problem is ABs: [able-bodied people] The counselor who told Nick's mother that she had to 'grieve the loss of the normal child' she didn't have before she could learn to love Nick. The doctor

who worked on Nick's limbs oblivious to the fact that they were attached to a whole body, much less a whole person. The mother who assured Nick that he could grow up to be anything he wanted to be, even when Nick wanted to be a football player. The colleges that refused to let him enrol and the law schools that wouldn't even send him an application. The father who didn't want him to marry his daughter. The therapist who told him he had a chip on his shoulder. People, really well meaning, perfectly nice people, use words to describe Nick such as 'resilient,' 'brave,' 'adaptable,' 'plucky,' 'courageous.' Courage requires options.

(Olkin 1999: vii)

This poem was written by Mary O'Hagan who says: I'm glad I didn't know I was going to be the chair of an international network, have a book published in Japanese, advise the United Nations or become a New Zealand mental health commissioner. If I'd told a psychiatrist I was going to do these things they would have upped my anti-psychotics on the spot.

(O'Hagan 2009)

Every morning the night nurses
pull off my blankets.
They are rough.
I can't fight back
Even their softest touches bruise me
'Face the world'
But I am facing the pain inside me.
I cannot face both ways at once.

Mary is not to hide away in her bed. She is to be encouraged to get up for breakfast and engage in ward activities (O'Hagan 1996).

(Wallcraft and Michaelson 2001: 182)

This account is from a senior hospital social worker:

if I'm in the department with two junior people talking with someone from outside, I'm talking from management, but instead of going through me the outsider talks to the two junior people until they can't cope and turn to me for answers. The outsider doesn't address me.

(Rosen 1993: 188)

Another account from the same text:

For people in my age group the whole thing was to survive in the system. This led to your being aggressive (because of kids calling you 'nigger' and so on) and then being punished for it. School was very much an escape for me, but for the major part of my primary education I was faced with a lot of hostility from classmates.

(Rosen 1993: 182)

In this article Hopfe (1999) questions whether blindness has a culture:

We use methods specific to the blind to understand and navigate the world around us, which leads many of us to develop behaviours markedly similar to one another. Why, most of us even use the same modes of transportation. Similar behaviours range from marking our oven dials to judging traffic direction by hearing. We also have mannerisms in common. This is especially evident in congenitally blind children who eye press and rock. Most people with visual impairments, young or old, seek out alternative forms of 'stimulation'.

We have internal conflict on issues unique to our group. The most notable being Print vs. Braille (sound familiar? Speech vs. Sign [sic]). Other conflicts include Cane vs. Dog. An interesting fact to note here is that while most sighted people know very little about these debates, most blind people are well aware of them and are on the front line.

(Hopfe 1999)

Mat Fraser was born with short arms after his mother was prescribed the drug thalidomide during her pregnancy. He is asked in interview if he has a mischievous streak.

Yea, because it's a much better identity than being Flid! Being one of the guys that is always there for a laugh makes you popular. When you're an isolated, disabled person in a mainstream non-disabled environment, as I was, and a hard-core one at that – you'd do anything to change your identity; anything to be not disabled; because all disabled meant was horrible . . . negative . . . other . . . different . . . pitiful! Now I can mean something else, and indeed when I . . . 'came out' . . . as disabled, it was because I managed to see the word 'disabled' as being a struggle against an oppressive society. Now I find myself being able to express disability as a political struggle of equality in a mainstream society, which I still see as that. I know that comes across fairly militant, but as you know, I'm Mr Mainstream these days; but I still think these things.

Pregnant women don't feel comfortable around me sometimes. Often they're cool, but often they think, . . . 'Oh you know, it mightn't be so bad if the baby is disabled cause look, that chap seems to be doing quite well.' . . . But a lot of the time they think, . . . 'Christ, I never thought about it, what if the baby's a mutant!' . . . – or am I being paranoid?

(Disability Rights Commission 2002)

The following extract by Catherine Butler (2004) from a text, 'Homoworld', was devised with the aim of teaching lesbian and gay awareness by reversing majority and minority group experiences:

The thought rekindles the awkwardness you felt finding one of the only two clinics in London set up to provide birth control. The stigma you might have felt walking towards it through the hospital grounds, surely everyone must know that is where the heteros go? The condescending looks of the receptionist as she asks you loudly whether you have used the service before and whether you would prefer your GP not to be informed. You might find these thoughts and memories interrupting your session. Do you take this to supervision? Does your supervisor even know that you are straight? Do you know what your supervisor's personal feelings are about it? Do you fear your supervisor might be secretly pathologising you? These thoughts make you remember that you will be changing placements in a few months. You briefly hope that the next team will be more accepting.

At the end of the day people are going for a drink at the nearest gay bar on the corner. Some are bringing partners. Do you invite yours knowing that there will be staff there you are not out to? Staff whose response to your heterosexuality you cannot be sure of. Or do you go for a few hours and then leave to travel into central London and the straight ghetto of Old Brompton Street? But maybe you just want a quiet drink as you are tired and you know Old Brompton Street will be full of pumping Celine Dion and boozed pint drinkers. With no real alternative you decide to head home. Just as you have made the decision your partner texts you to say he will meet you at the tube as he is leaving for home now too. As you smile a member of staff you do not know well catches your eye and says, 'That from your girlfriend? What's her name?' Do you come out, lie or say you are much too busy to be in a relationship? You wonder what their response would be if you do come out?

Finally you reach your home tube station and as promised your boyfriend is there to meet you. You feel a flood of relief at seeing him, realising how tired you are. But do you greet him with a kiss with all these people still around? As you walk home you both have to walk down a quiet street. You start to hold hands, glad of the contact. However, unexpectedly a group of youths round the next corner and you let go. Did they see the contact? Are they going to say anything, heckle you? Worse still, is this a potentially violent situation? You both stare at the floor as you walk past.

Safe behind closed doors at last, you decide to order a pizza. Your partner is in the kitchen when the doorbell rings and does not realise you have already opened it. He shouts, 'I'll get that darling' and you notice the pizza delivery boy trying to hide a laugh as your boyfriend bounds into the hall behind you.

(C. Butler 2004: 15)

Some of the extracts in the previous section are first-hand accounts of what it is like to live in a world oriented towards the majority group. Not only talking about, but also writing an account such as 'Homoworld' from the perspective of a person of a different age, sexuality, faith, disability, social class or gender can be illuminating. Catherine Butler's account took this a step further through turning the majority group into a minority.

Concept maps and mind maps

Concept and mind maps were devised with a view to facilitating sense-making and meaningful learning through drawing diagrams that represent the current state of knowledge about a topic. It is a method for externalising concepts and propositions concerning the way that the concepts are linked. Concepts and ideas are articulated by the learner and written or drawn in boxes which are then linked together. A concept is defined as 'a perceived regularity in events or objects, or records of events or objects, designated by a label' (Novak 2008: 1). Concept maps tend to be structured hierarchically and contain multiple clusters of ideas, whereas mind maps tend to radiate from a single central point. The idea on which they are based is that knowledge is constructed in an ongoing process whereby new experiences are assimilated into existing cognitive structures or schemas (Novak and Cañas 2006). A mind map typically reflects thinking about a single topic. Such maps can be created at speed and with spontaneity as a means of focusing group brain-storming. Joseph Novak has taught primary-age children to make concept maps in response to questions such as, 'What is water?' and 'What causes the seasons?' Concept maps usually comprise nodes (key ideas that act as cata-lysts for reflection, links (lines between nodes that are not necessarily straight but represent links between concepts) and labels (words written on the links to explain the connections). The concept map shown in Figure 7.3 was constructed by faculty working together to plan instruction in veterinary medicine at Cornell University (Novak 2008).

Concept mapping has been used in the education of nurses (Caelli 1998; Carpenito-Moyet 2006) and in the planning of health services (Kane and Trochim 2007). As in many of the methods described in these chapters, accessing mental activity and representing it pictorially, diagrammatically or through recordings can aid the process of reflective practice, particularly when subject to judicious questioning and discussed with colleagues.

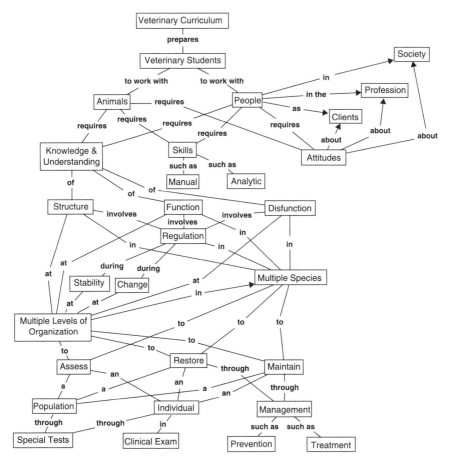

Figure 7.3 Concept map.

Six hats

Edward De Bono (2000) devised the six hats method as a process running counter to traditional Western ways of thinking by focusing on 'what can be' rather than on 'what is'. De Bono uses a metaphor to explain the purpose of the method, in which four people are each looking at a different side of a house. They offer four different descriptions of what they can see but instead of arguing about which is correct, they walk around the house and view each side in turn. In the six hats method, everyone looks at an issue simultaneously from the same perspective or in parallel, and then the view is changed with all participants shifting perspective together. After the six different views have been described, there comes a period of sifting through ideas and considering the implications while 'wearing' the blue hat. He argues that this process avoids the 'spaghetti' thinking typical in meetings or groups where people often talk to no avail at cross purposes. I have been in many such meetings. The six hats are thinking caps that act as direction indicators.

Six distinct direction indicators or 'hats' are identified:

- *Neutrality/data (White):* The white hat symbolises information which can include research findings. The hat symbolises the aspiration to separate information from opinion.
- *Feeling/emotion (Red):* From this perspective instinctive gut reactions and emotional responses are given voice without any need for justification. This hat is donned only for brief periods to avoid lengthy explanations of feelings.
- *Sombre and serious, implying caution (Black):* Wearing this hat the thinker seeks to identify possible weaknesses of ideas, potential flaws and barriers.
- *Optimism/sunshine (Yellow):* This perspective emphasises the benefits of actions or interventions and covers hope and positive thinking.
- *Creative thinking/growth (Green):* In this hat, group members seek out the potential impact of ideas in stimulating learning and development to enhance professional and/or personal wisdom.
- *Process (Blue):* The blue hat invites thinking about the thinking process as it unfolds and also about issues of control and the use of the other hats.

De Bono (2000) argues that the perspectives should always be referred to by their hats since proposing to adopt 'yellow hat' thinking would be experienced as less threatening than, for example, telling someone to be less cautious in their thinking. The hats can be used in any sequence but he advises that the discussion commence and end with the blue hat whereby the aims and a structure for the conversation are determined and conclusions drawn.

In an example provided by Jennifer York-Barr et al. (2006) group participants in a school-wide teacher planning team posed themselves the question, 'If we were to propose a bolder focus on reflective practice in our high school, what should we be thinking about in terms of implementation supports and potential issues?' The school principal led the reflective conversation wearing different-coloured hats to remind the group to stay with the specific perspective in sequence.

In their debriefing, participants shared the insight that they had a tendency to adopt a default perspective that they brought to such conversations. Some recognised a habitual caution or data-oriented way of thinking while others homed in on growth potential or wanted to move immediately to a plan for action. De Bono (2000) cautioned the importance of not seeing the hats as descriptions of people but as modes of behaviour. The process encourages participants to see strengths in approaches other than their own and to develop greater insight into the benefits of multiple 'frames'.

Sculpting

Sculpting is a method in which people or objects are placed in relation to each other to represent a person's view of a system (Lawson 1989; Lesage-Higgins 1999). A method using objects to create a sculpt was described earlier. If people are the objects to be sculpted, then sculpting becomes a group method. The sculptor is the person whose view of a system (this could be a family, a team of colleagues, a community of people living in a group home, a class of students) is represented in the sculpture. The process is guided by a facilitator who manages time, organises different contributions and invites descriptions of people's experiences in the sculpt. The designated sculptor chooses and positions people by distance, orientation, and relationship to each other. The positions may be static or moving. It is not necessary or desirable to give background information. Some sculpts can be quite graphically symbolic of interaction patterns. I recall inviting members of a family with whom I was working to create a sculpt. The father put his wife and daughter in close proximity with his son running rings round them. He took himself down the corridor, symbolic of being out of the building. The son, when it was his turn, lay his mother flat on the floor and sat on her while his father and sister looked on individually from a distance. I cite this to illustrate the evocative potential of sculpts in revealing different perspectives on the functioning of a system.

Once the sculpt is complete, participants can be asked to describe their experiences on the basis of their physical location in the sculpt – who else they could see, to whom they felt close, whether they were physically comfortable, or about the feelings that were evoked by their position. They are asked to keep to description rather than make explanatory or evaluative interpretations. The sculptor might care to experiment by asking people to change position and report the impact of the relocation.

Sculpts can be made of the past, present and future to incorporate the dimension of time or might focus specifically on a period of transition in the system. The sculptor might be encouraged to move around the sculpt to observe the system from multiple positions with a view to developing further understanding of possible conflicts and alliances. When people are the materials sculpted, they may need to de-role at the conclusion of the exercise.

Maria Marchetti-Mercer and Glenda Cleaver (2000) invited their students to sculpt their families of origin with the aims of enhancing their awareness of their functioning within their own families, and to improve cross-cultural understanding between black and white students in South Africa. The authors argued that previous negative preconceptions about each other's cultures were altered in the process of taking a role in one another's respective families.

The approach aided students in embarking on a process of breaking down a number of the prejudices and preconceived ideas that they had about each other.

The authors cautioned that the method involved self-disclosure on the part of the students and that this had implications, particularly for the few black students, in terms of feelings of vulnerability in an academic context in which evaluation has a significant part to play.

> Until 1990, the language of function at the University of Pretoria was Afrikaans, but now most undergraduate courses are also offered in English. However, a certain amount of animosity arises in postgraduate classes when Black students request English tuition. Language has long been a contentious issue in South Africa, where Afrikaans has been considered the language of the oppressor, especially by Black people ... South Africa is a country that is composed of a number of different and sharply contrasting cultural groups. Differences are apparent not only between Black and White South Africans but also between White, English speaking people and White, Afrikaans-speaking people, as well as among the different Black cultural and language groups. Given that postapartheid South Africa is still in its infancy, most students have not yet become well acquainted with the diverse cultures of their country.
>
> (Marchetti-Mercer and Cleaver 2000: 62)

This passage has served as a useful reminder to me of the desirability for supervisors and tutors of continuing to reflect on our own practices from a range of perspectives in order to respond with sensitivity to our supervisees. When we are in thrall to our own personal, and often highly charged and committed constructions of events, we can be blocked by the strength of our immersion from soaring to the 'hawk in the mind' perspective that frees us to alter how we see and hence what we do.

Chapter 8

Approaches to supervision of reflective practice (IV)

'Live' methods, recordings and groups

I am a veritable hoarder of stuff. I am sure that it will all come in useful one day. Searching through stuff about reflective practice, I have found many more ideas about methods than I had envisaged when I wrote the original book proposal. I am weaving this chapter out of the leftover stuff that did not fit in the previous three but that I think is too useful to omit. I aim to address three distinct topics. I originally conceived a chapter on group methods but I have learned that many can be adapted for use in individual supervision and I have described them earlier. Those group methods I have been unable to adapt are included here.

First in this chapter I want to describe methods that involve direct experience of another's work. These involve 'live' methods in which supervisor and supervisee work in each other's presence – an example of reflection-in-action, and the use of recordings which allow a detailed analysis of what happened then – a process of reflection-on-action.

Methods that involve 'live' supervision, recordings and technology

'Live' supervision

In some professions, live supervision is the norm. Supervision of teaching practice is built around classroom observation, pre-observation conferences and debriefing. In nursing and medicine, staff are often carrying out their work in the presence of others or working together, often on a busy ward environment. Students learn from their more experienced colleagues in the context of ward rounds, or through sitting in on patient consultations. Live supervision is widely used in counsellor education, marriage and family therapy, social work, community college, and genetic counselling training programmes in the USA (Champe and Kleist 2003). In my experience, live supervision is less commonly found when the interaction between lay person and professional is believed to require a significant degree of intimacy or confidentiality, as in the mental health professions. The presence of more than one professional may be contraindicated in work with individual clients or patients when there is a risk of them feeling outnumbered.

I have written elsewhere (Scaife 2009: Chapter 11) about the mechanics of conducting live supervision, the options available for communication between the supervisor and supervisee, and the advantages and disadvantages of the method. In this chapter I am concerned principally with the question of how live supervision might aid the development of reflective practice.

There are many advantages to live supervision (Scaife 2009), one of which is being able to change the direction of a session or procedure while it is in progress, and so the question arises as to how to preserve this possibility while working constructively together. If supervisor and supervisee are going to interact during the conduct of the work I contend that this needs to pay due respect to all parties and in particular needs to ensure that the supervisee does not feel undermined in front of a class of students or with a patient, client or family. To this end, the communication cannot consist of feedback to the supervisee, although this might be given at a later time in a debrief which takes place in private. In teaching, with the exception of issues of safety, changes of direction are only likely to occur at the instigation of the supervisee.

The following extract from Jasper (2003) is written by a student called Heidi and illustrates the sort of thing that can happen when two practitioners are working together live but the relationship between them is failing to support the process:

> Ben and I were going to the ward to help [Mrs Jones] do some exercises and reassess her progress and plans when Ben, all of a sudden, just said, 'You take the lead on this one.' Well, I had visited her by myself a couple of times, as well as with Ben, but this came as a bit of a shock. I'm used to planning interventions and really thinking about what I'm trying to achieve with a patient before I go to see them. I thought as Ben was there that he was taking the lead, especially as this was a review visit.
>
> So, I was totally unprepared really. That, and Ben being there, made me really nervous. I must have seemed a complete idiot to Mrs Jones, and usually we get on really well. I forgot loads of things on the assessment, and I could tell that Ben was getting more and more irritated with me. Things got worse when we were trying to help Mrs Jones walk alone down the ward using her frame; each thought the other was supporting her. When she stumbled neither of us was correctly positioned to steady her and she ended up on the floor. That meant that an incident form had to be filled out, and we had to use the hoist to get her back up off the ground. She was really upset, had a big bruise on her hip and was very shaken. This meant that we had to abandon trying any more work with her, and spent the time reassuring her.
>
> Ben was really angry afterwards, and said it was all my fault. He

completely ignored me when he fed back to the nurses on duty, updated
her schedule without consulting me or asking me what I thought, and
stormed off, leaving me to trot behind like a little puppy.

(Jasper 2003: 179)

In the above example the relationship between the professionals was not in a
state to support joint work. Even if it had been, a preparatory conference or
conversation in which roles and responsibilities were agreed in advance could
have helped. When working together, there may be merit in arranging scheduled breaks for consultation, providing the nature of the work supports this.

In the context of live supervision in mental health settings, the use of various
technologies such as a 'bug-in-the-ear', live video feedback or telephone call-
ins along with a one-way screen have been adopted. Live consultations during
the work have varied from the supervisor knocking on the door, phoning in
or the worker exiting at a prearranged time. In my experience, most useful of
all, and respectful to all the parties, has been the notion of a 'reflecting team',
which comprises a small group of colleagues who have been observing from
behind a screen (Andersen 1987). The team members are invited to share
their thoughts and ideas at intervals by invitation in the presence of the
supervisee and the client(s).

I began to adopt a firm structure when working together with colleagues
after having found myself on a few occasions in a process of de-consulting.
The session was not going according to the plan in my head that I thought we
had agreed in advance. The importance of clarity about structure, aims, tasks
and roles was affirmed in a study of live supervision in the training of genetic
counsellors by Hendrickson et al. (2002). Phil Kingston and Donna Smith
(Smith and Kingston 1980; Kingston and Smith 1983) pioneered a way of
working together whereby one worker takes the lead and is the only person to
communicate directly with the client or clients. The other worker supports
this structural rule by adopting a position that discourages direct communication from the client and by referential looking only towards the other
worker and not towards the client. This way of working is introduced
to clients at the outset, with an explanation that one person will take the
lead and work with them while the other will contribute by invitation at
intervals throughout the session. Reflections are tentative (I wondered if . . . ,
Perhaps . . . , I noticed . . .) and made with the intention of supporting the
work being carried out. If there are to be scheduled breaks, which I consider
to be appropriate particularly when working with a novice, this is also introduced to the client at the outset. If the supervisor has real concerns about the
direction in which the supervisee is proceeding, this can then be ironed out
between them in private in such a break. If the supervisor has a brief to assess
the performance of the supervisee then this is held in mind and carried out in
a separate consultation.

When first working in this way with students, they typically prefer initially to take the role of supervisor rather than take the lead in the interview with the client, much as I suspect would have been the case for Heidi in the earlier example. The student is reassured that it is perfectly acceptable to have nothing to contribute when invited. I have found that the method gives the supervisee as 'observer' an active role, one in which a contribution to the work in progress with supervisees' own ideas can be made, and whereby they have time and space to observe and reflect while the session is in progress. The orientation towards supporting the work being carried out through a process of reflection, rather than critiquing the practice that they are observing, models a role-relationship that can reduce anxiety when the roles are reversed. The method allows both workers to contribute and avoids the supervisor having to sit quietly while itching to change the direction of the work.

> One thing that's really hard is just keeping my mouth shut. I get very impatient when students struggle, especially with basic information, or avoid some psychosocial thing that's right in my face ... To just sit there, I can't tell you how much I squeeze my pen or pinch my leg just to bear it!
>
> (Hendrickson et al. 2002: 37)

The reflecting team approach has its origins in the field of family therapy. Apart from its use as a means of gentle introduction to live supervised work, there is evidence to support the value to clients of the multiple perspectives that may be expressed (Champe and Kleist 2003; Locke and McCollum 2001). Participants in Locke and McCollum's study reported:

> 'Different perspectives on the same problem. If the therapist can't identify, maybe someone behind the mirror will,' ... 'The team is helpful in guiding sessions. I like the idea of several heads working on the problem rather than just one. There is a greater chance of achieving a successful approach to problems,' ... 'When I would be a little confused about a question ... the team could call and reword the question ... to communicate to me in a way that I understood'.
>
> (Locke and McCollum 2001: 132)

In the family therapy tradition of the reflecting team, the aims have been to act as a springboard for new ideas and actions. The reflecting team introduces ideas that might alter the client's understanding of the problem, notices and amplifies exceptions to typical patterns of understanding and attempts to consolidate change. To give a flavour of such reflections here is a brief extract from Friedman et al. (1995). In this example the team members are basing their work on the concept of 'externalising the problem' (White and Epston 1990).

Sally: A question that just got raised for me is whether the family has come under the grip of fear and whether fear has begun to take over their lives in ways they haven't been aware of . . . I'm wondering whether there are times when the fears aren't as strong and the family doesn't get recruited into worrying so much about Nancy.

Steven: I like that idea. I think I can see how the fears have gotten a grip and what it ends up creating are detectives for the fears, trying to study and research and understand them better.

Sally: Trace their origins.

Steven: Trace their origins. And that in a way pulls people into the grip of the fears. That's part of the fears [sic] power pulling them in. In some ways it feels like the fears can take such control that they can just swallow the family up . . . yet like you were saying, there have been times where the fears haven't taken over completely and that Nancy has not cooperated with the fears. And again, are there some ways she can continue to do that and other ways her parents can help her not to cooperate. Though it is always tempting to be a detective, the fears are really so tricky and sneaky and difficult to understand that it could become a never-ending process that could further envelop them.

(Friedman et al. 1995: 186)

As a member of a reflecting team I have found that in order to contribute effectively I have to concentrate very hard and think creatively about what is going on. I then have to think about how to present my ideas in ways that stand a chance of being heard and that give clients choices about how to respond while simultaneously being respectful to my colleagues. I am not 'delivering' a directive or diagnosis but focused on understanding and offering ideas that might be useful to my colleague and client in opening up additional possibilities for change.

Supervisor reflections do not have to fulfil these aims; they can be adapted to suit the context. If Heidi and Ben had taken this approach, he might have thought it helpful to have a consultation early in the session when it became clear that Heidi was anxious and missing things from the assessment. 'I think it will be helpful to take our scheduled break now. Let's make Mrs Jones comfortable and take five minutes.' When it came to the use of the walking frame: 'I was wondering whether you would prefer to take the lead in helping Mrs Jones use her frame or whether you would like me to do that today?' In the first example the supervisor is using his authority to ensure that the patient receives proper care. In the second the supervisee has a genuine choice in which the roles and responsibilities of the parties are made clear.

I have included reflecting teams in this chapter because I think that the method provides supervisors with a means to model reflecting-in-action as a process. This can be with the aim of helping people change in relation to their mental health problems, as in the example above, or through reflecting-in-action on the process of supervision when working together with a collea-gue in the room. It provides supervisees who are taking the supporting role with time to reflect during the session since they do not have to manage the client, class or patient simultaneously, while still having the option of playing an active role in contributing to the work as it happens.

Use of recordings

With technological developments continuing apace in the twenty-first century I can foresee further extension to their application in the training of staff in education, health and social care settings. In this section I will describe just one approach to the development of skills in reflective practice using session recordings. There are many other ways of using recorded material in supervision which I describe in Scaife (2009).

Interpersonal process recall

Interpersonal process recall (IPR) is a method devised by Norman Kagan (Kagan and Krathwohl 1967; Kagan 1984; Kagan-Klein and Kagan 1997) that arose out of the development of widely available video in the 1960s. Universities invested in this technology and he decided to make recordings of visiting lecturers. They often expressed an interest in reviewing the tapes and as they did so he noticed that they tended to give a commentary concerning their experiences during their lecture. Kagan, a respectful junior academic, began to ask non-intrusive open questions which appeared to facilitate the recall and it was out of this process that the IPR method was devised. Kagan hypothesised that in any interpersonal interaction the participants are constantly experiencing a multitude of feelings, thoughts, sensations and images, and making judgements and adjustments to their communica-tion on the basis of their assessments of the reactions of the other or others. This process happens at such speed that there is no time to analyse these experiences at the time, but in reviewing recordings, the action can be slowed down and these previous reactions accessed in great detail.

IPR is a self-reflective method of learning, a process of self-discovery, enabling people to look at the way they react and interact in a relatively safe, non-threatening way (P. Allen 2004: 154). Although most often encountered in the field of counselling and psychotherapy it has been used in teaching (Lally and Scaife 1995), medicine (Bartz 1999; Winefield et al. 1994; Yaphe and Street 2003), social work (Naleppa and Reid 1998), nursing and management (Larsen et al. 2008). IPR involves supervisees in making a recording of their work which is then brought to supervision. The supervisee is the 'recaller' and the supervisor the 'enquirer' as the recording is played. Ideally, the supervisor cannot see or hear the recording, a barrier which prevents supervisors from intruding their ideas into the recall process. IPR is characterised by the following features:

- A focus on giving an account of what was happening *then* is maintained, rather than explanations or evaluations *now* in hindsight. This focus is held with a view to protecting recallers from experiencing feelings of vulnerability or threat during the recall process. Questions employing the words *was*, *did*, and *then* continually bring the interviewees' focus back to their memories of the original session.
- The replay of the recording is entirely in the hands of the recaller who is invited to stop the tape whenever experiencing a feeling, thought, picture, memory, sensation or hunch that he or she had at the time of the initial interaction and that he or she wishes to explore.
- When the recaller stops the tape, the inquirer prompts her or his recall through open questions.
- The inquirer concentrates entirely on helping recallers to develop their own understandings and insights.
- Recallers move on when they are ready.

The method aims to reduce the supervisee's fear of instruction and critical attack from the supervisor by putting the process explicitly in the control of the supervisee, and by encouraging the supervisor to avoid explanation, interpretation and advice-giving (Clarke 1997). Recallers are regarded in IPR as the ultimate experts on their innermost thoughts and feelings. The enquirer is not trying to make sense of the session being recalled. The role is to help the *recaller* to reflect on and make sense of the interaction. The enquirer's responsibility is to ask a series of open-ended questions that respond sensitively to the recaller with a view to creating freedom and openness of exploration. These questions are not leading or Socratic in style. Some types of questions are listed below.

Self-exploration
- What thoughts were going through your mind at the time?
- Any cautions on your part?
- How were you feeling then?
- Were there any pictures, memories, words going through your mind?

Own behaviour
- Was there anything you were not saying?
- What kept you from saying that?
- Was there anything that got in the way of what you wanted to say or do?
- What did you like about what was happening?

Perception of other
- What did you think the other person was feeling?
- What did you want the other person to think or feel?
- How did you think the other person experienced you?
- Was there anything about the client's appearance that you were reacting to?

Hopes and intentions
- What did you want to happen next?
- What effect did you want that to have on the other person?
- Where did you want to end up?

Previous patterns
- Have you found yourself feeling like that before?
- Did you find yourself thinking about other people in your life?
- What pictures or memories went through your mind?

Reflection
- Any idea how you came to say/do/think that?
- Did you have any hunch about what was going on?

The following is from a transcript I made of material produced by John Oates for the Open University (2005). The client is a young person and the worker is a clinical psychologist. The young man has attended a previous session with his mother. The recaller has just stopped the recording for the first time:

> I know this is early to stop (the recording) but I'm struck by how tentative I feel at that point when I had started the session and I know that Terry had not found the first session really comfortable so I was already wary of him and then I started; I just wanted to make him feel comfortable but I didn't want to gush too much so everything that came out of my mouth I could sort of hear loud into this big silence so I felt quite uncomfortable at that point but just nervous, uncomfortable and I was hoping that things would get more fluid because he was quite impassive I thought, there.
>
> So what do you think was in his mind at that point?
>
> Well, I don't know just how reluctant he was to be there, if he'd been pushed, dragged, whatever. I mean he was there, which was great. And the thing is looking at his face I was getting so very few clues that I didn't *know* so I was saying a few more sentences and watching him and he was really quite blank and I remember thinking it was a while before there was anything much of a flicker so what is strongly felt was that I didn't know.

(Oates 2005a)

This extract from the same materials is of a client presenting with severe depression, also interviewed by a clinical psychologist:

What were your thoughts at that point?

I'm aware all the time of the excruciating discomfort of the client and I sense the discomfort and agony and unhappiness. I feel that I've got to carry on. I can't sort of . . . I can't be distracted by going into some of these points and I have to allow her to tell her story and contain that discomfort but I feel it. I mean, she does look extremely uncomfortable.

What do you think she was expecting from you?

I think she's trusting. I think she's taking chances that I'm not going to be judgemental or shocked or indeed over-emotional myself. I feel as if there's a lot of trust there.

(Oates 2005b)

There is a danger, when occupying the role of enquirer, of allowing the recall to migrate into a focus on the present. Reflection-on-action is a potential second stage which may follow the recall. IPR is a protocol for relatively safe generation of experiential material. What the recaller does with the material is something to be decided in advance, if possible, by the recaller. Some IPR enquirer leads may be particularly useful in preserving the safety inherent in a focus on the past. These are of the type, 'Do you recall . . .' and 'What *did* you think were the risks you felt in saying X or doing Y'.

At the end of IPR interviews it is important for interviewers to offer to debrief with interviewees to ensure that they feel comfortable with the experience (Larsen et al. 2008). IPR can put interviewees in a sensitive and vulnerable position where they have shared not only the content of their work but also their private inner experiences.

The value of IPR in supervision and training is based on the assumption that practitioners have a wealth of information that they have not had the opportunity to acknowledge or use productively, and that sessions devoted to regenerating these important impressions and making them explicit in language help supervisees to become aware of messages that they denied, ignored or had previously not perceived. The method is viewed as helping people to improve their understanding of interpersonal processes. This might include the identification and acknowledgement of their previously un-verbalised fears and vulnerabilities in human interaction.

Penny Allen (2004) argues that IPR helps practitioners to look inside themselves when feeling 'stuck', inadequate and lacking creativity. It encourages the asking of questions such as, 'What information am I holding in my body?' and 'What can I hear, see, feel, sense?' She argues that this intrinsic knowledge is not always in conscious awareness. When practised in the method I have found it possible to replay a session in my imagination without a recording, and to metaphorically stop the tape for a process of self-enquiry. But it is difficult to remember to do this in a busy schedule and I may avoid asking myself the key questions that would uncover some of my hidden assumptions or experiences of which I am a little ashamed. Being less intimately aware of my blocks and weaknesses, my supervisor is more likely to find such questions and even if I withhold some of my reactions, I will have to face them on my way home.

Technology

Not surprisingly, developments in technology have found increasing application in learning programmes, particularly for those who live at a distance from the educational establishment or in remote rural areas. E-learning technologies (also known as 'technology enhanced learning': TEL) can offer learners control over content, learning sequence, pace of learning, time, and often media, allowing them to tailor their experiences to meet their personal learning objectives (Ruiz et al. 2006). With online and instant communication, students across the world (given time-zone constraints) can participate in e-learning initiatives which create new variables, constraints and issues that make it fundamentally different from face-to-face learning environments (Mandinach 2005). Instant messaging, chat rooms and synchronous online communication make for an immediacy of response which is sometimes enjoyed.

Asynchronous communication by email has the advantages of slowing down the communication process in ways that can be helpful, although the absence of additional cues can lead to significant misunderstandings. Face-to-face interaction is so much richer because it involves body language, the use of inflection, laughter, and variations in pace and phrasing which often carry momentum. On the other hand, in electronic methods the hidden nature of personal characteristics protects the communication from being overly influenced by visible differences such as gender, ethnicity and disability. Social relations are just as important in groups of practitioners communicating electronically as they are in face to face discussions and regular sharing of personal knowledge about individuals has been regarded as crucial for success (Carter and Walker 2008; Lee-Baldwin 2005).

Video-conferencing has been used (Marrow et al. 2002; Troster et al. 1995) for the purposes of supervision. When electronic methods of communication are adopted, clients must give full informed consent since there are many hazards which can threaten confidentiality when using the internet. Kanz (2001) advised the judicious use of initials or pseudonyms and encryption programmes in order to provide safeguards.

Using digital video, teaching sessions can be edited into shorter segments which can be made available through Virtual Learning Environments (VLEs) such as Blackboard and WebCT for online discussion. However, in my own experience of WebCT, I have found that students are often reluctant to commit their views to cyberspace, since they are unable, with reasonable certainty, to comprehend responses to their online posts without the usual accompanying cues. They are unwilling to risk destabilising relationships in which they have a long-term investment and in which the supervisor, and possibly fellow students, are perceived as occupying an evaluative role.

It has been argued that online discussion can enhance critical thinking if the dialogue is 'carefully structured to support high levels of reflection' (Whipp 2003: 331). Joan Whipp raised specific questions by email to pro-mote discussions and debates on problematic issues and inequities in urban schools. Prompted by reading Lisa Delpit's (1995) *Other people's children* she and her supervisees discussed the topic, 'Can White teachers effectively teach African American students?' This question led to a debate on the issue during which one-third of the email postings were assessed as being at higher levels of reflection than previously. Two students wrote about how email discussions concerning multicultural issues had led them to recognise the need to develop their understanding of cultures other than their own, and also to confront their own cultural heritage. MacKnight (2000) suggests that online discussion can aid the development of critically reflective prac-tice providing that staff use approaches that involve modelling, coaching, questioning, and task-structuring enacted towards specific goals.

Rhine and Bryant (2007) noted the isolation of pre-service teachers from their university-based mentors at the point at which they are most in need of assistance in developing reflective habits and linking theory to practice. As university supervisors they sought to use technology to bridge this gap between academic preparation and school-based field experiences. Their supervisees were each asked to make a digital video of one class period and select a brief clip to share with their peers on the course website. They wrote an account of the clip and posted some questions seeking feedback. The supervi-sors observed that this approach elicited reflection related to instructional and classroom management strategies, moving students from focusing primarily on self to more complex issues of teaching and learning. One of their super-visees commented: 'It was an incredibly useful method of really seeing yourself from your students' eyes. One of the best ways to really know what you do is to see yourself in action. It is incredibly revealing' (Rhine and Bryant 2007: 353). They concluded that when students sought from and provided each other with written online feedback they were encouraged to consider multiple perspectives. One of the advantages of the method was that the supervisees had time to think about their responses and this seemed to encourage contributions from those who less often expressed themselves in face-to-face groups. They cautioned that often those stu-dents who did not like or were intimidated by technology found little value in the medium as a learning tool. Those who were comfortable using technology interacted frequently and easily in the online dialogue and valued others' insights.

Many of the developments in the use of technology as an aid to reflective practice have been accomplished in university rather than practice settings and there may be limits to the suitability of such applications for supervisors in the field. Video-conferencing and email have been used with some success to support reflective practice although the findings are mixed. Some supervisees have reported that their thinking is more reflective and insightful than in traditional face-to-face approaches (Bailey and Cotlar 1994; Everett and Ahem 1994; Gilbride et al. 1996). Increased time dedicated to processing and clarifying thoughts in e-supervision was reported by Stebnicki and Glover (2001). The following is a quote from a student in a qualitative study conducted by Graf and Stebnicki (2002).

> I found the E-mail communication very helpful and effective. (It was) a good way to review what I was feeling . . . mainly my frustration. I didn't even realize that I was frustrated until I read what I wrote. The efficiency of the replies was good too . . . but it was the actual writing of the episodes that was beneficial for me. It gave me time to think about what I was learning, what I wasn't learning, how I felt about everything. I was also able to say a lot of things (mainly about how I was feeling) that I don't think I would have said during an oral supervision. Also, writing it first helped to 'say it' later. It seems that it also gave supervisors a chance to look over and think about what we had to say in writing before we talked about it orally. I think this is a practice that should be continued.
>
> (Graf and Stebnicki 2002: 12)

Graf and Stebnicki (2002) concluded that students used emails with their supervisors to reflect on many significant issues. The authors made the interesting point that unlike individual reflective journals, email enables two-way communication in addition to individualised, reflective thought-processing. I have found that email supervision can 'work', but most effectively when I have already established a trusting working relationship. At times I have interpreted emails from people I know less well as hostile on first reading. On the following day they have seemed quite innocuous. And there are advantages to the asynchronicity of text communications; there is more time to think before responding – time is expanded; and burning issues do not necessarily have to wait for the next face to face meeting – time is contracted.

John Wheeler (2007: 365) gives the following advice about email supervision:

- Do not press the send button too quickly. First thoughts may be good but they can often be improved on, and further reading may reveal ambiguities that were not obvious at first.

- Make sure that you know what the question is before giving an answer, and if necessary, ask for extra clarification to make sure.
- Do not make assumptions about skill level or professional role, which might be different from your own.
- Offer questions rather than advice where possible.
- The supervisee is the expert on the case. Your role is to facilitate and support.
- If stumped, say so, and offer to get back later.

When the purpose of supervision is to encourage reflective practice, asking questions is unlikely to go far astray. With over one billion computer users (Armstrong and Schneiders 2003) it would be surprising if the medium could not be used in ways that fostered reflection on practice online.

Electronic voting systems

Electronic voting systems (also known as audience response systems) offer a method for instantly gaining the overall view of a group about an issue. The choice of issue lies either with the presenter or can be suggested by group members. The issues to be addressed are projected onto a screen with multiple choice-type responses offered. All participants are provided with a hand-held electronic voter, or the voters can be shared. Group members select a response, send their selection to a receiver, and the facilitator can display the set of responses in the form of a bar chart, for example, using the associated computer software. The beauty of this process is that participants receive immediate feedback about the views of the group overall, and about the location of their own selections in relation to the group. Responses are private, meaning that there is no necessity for public acknowledgement of a privately held opinion.

The topics for which the voters can be used is limited only by the creativity of the facilitator and group members. I have asked people to look at examples of reflective writing, rate their confidence as assessors, predict the level of agreement in the group between markers, and award grades from A to E. I have also used the voters in conjunction with recorded material. Supervisees have watched a simulated session with a client and rated the practitioner for qualities such as degree of empathy, use of personal qualities, management of the interpersonal process and so on. What invariably emerges is difference. Although all group members have watched identical stimulus material they have constructed different meanings and are faced with this difference between them without potentially shameful public disclosure of individual views.

I have found this process to stimulate puzzlement and ongoing self-reflection, particularly for those people who find that their views on some issues are outliers to the 'average' group view, and a great deal of animated discussion can be stimulated. The method has the advantage of encouraging everyone in the group to express a view since the percentage of votes cast is displayed on screen. The presenter can wait until 100 per cent of responses has been obtained before displaying the results.

Electronic voting systems are unlikely to be within the scope of individual supervisors, and may have less relevance for well-established supervision groups in which members are confident to express their views. Steve Draper (2008) argues that the most productive application of electronic voters is in using the equipment to initiate a discussion which encourages participants to produce explanations and reasons for their views and/or for the overall aggregated results. In my experience the voters can give a full voice to quieter group members and the overall results can offer rich material for stimulating a reflective process.

Group methods

Gillie Bolton (2005: 88) holds that 'collaborative learning is deeply educative'. Some authors argue that sharing and talking with others is fundamental to reflective practice (Atkinson and Claxton 2000). A moral and political culture characterised by openness to diverse perspectives and ideologies, and a respectful acknowledgement of the importance of all contributions irrespective of status or experience is advocated by Brookfield (1995: 140).

In my working life there have been groups on whom I have relied; colleagues who value me and my work. I have also belonged to groups in which I have felt alienated, despairing, furious or picked on. Sometimes, being in a group that is not working for me, it is difficult simultaneously to participate and to work out what is going on. Brigid Proctor (2000) refers to painful stories reported by participants in 'trial and error' groups in which participants have not known what is allowed or expected and I realise that this has been a contributory factor in some of my more difficult experiences. She says of members of such a group:

> Some have struggled for months to discover how to win rewards (the approving smile), or to avoid punishment (the irritated frown). Some have spoken their minds, only to be told that what to them was their unique thought was 'parallel process', which they had never been helped to understand. One woman stayed silent and (to her initial relief) was not noticed, but when a man in the group was rebuked for not speaking, she began to imagine she must be invisible.
>
> (Proctor 2000: 42)

In my experience, groups can provide a rich tapestry for learning while at the same time being complex bodies beset by forces beyond the control of the individual. 'When a group comes together and interacts, the behaviour of everybody is modified by the "forces" present – the group dynamic. The energy present can help or hinder the learning process' (Proctor and Inskipp 2009: 152). Proctor and Inskipp (2009) provide very useful advice for anyone about to embark on supervision in a group, offering the framework in Figure 8.1 as an overall map that might guide the budding (or experienced) facilitator.

The map reminds us to attend to individual needs for belonging, acceptance, recognition, and to exercise power and influence; to clarify the task and to make sure that it remains the central focus of the group even if individuals may wish to take advantage of a 'two minute steam' (Carter and Walker 2008) to get a burning issue off their chest. Group maintenance also demands attention, with a role for the participants in creating and sustaining good group manners that uphold a positive working climate. Ögren et al. (2001) identified four categories of group climate: insecure and task oriented (the angry group), insecure and relationship oriented (the disappointed group), secure and task oriented (the sensible group) and secure and relationship oriented (the solidarity group). Factors that were found to relate to the

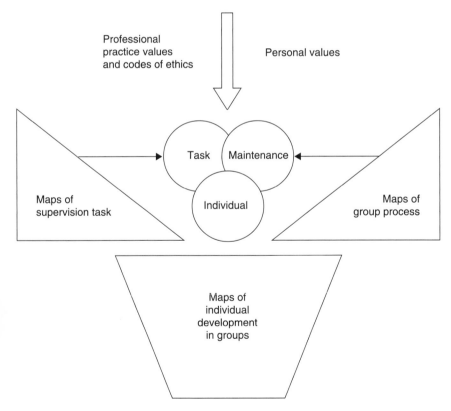

Figure 8.1 Overall map for running group supervision.

development of different climates included a high or low degree of emotional vulnerability in individual group members, and difficulties with group composition particularly where individuals felt themselves to be 'alone of one's kind' such as the only male. The experience of acceptance and support both from other group members and the supervisor were key elements in the development of effective working groups.

Inskipp and Proctor (2009: 157) argue that a group needs to have sufficient shared desire in order to work effectively together and, 'when a group engages in dysfunctional unconscious processes it is often because the task is not clear or is too difficult, or there are underlying agendas that are not voiced'.

Participation anxiety can be a dominant theme in group work, fears of appearing incompetent and of offering feedback that could harm relationships with other participants limiting contributions until trust has been established (Christensen and Kline 2001). This can be particularly salient the further on in the workers' careers:

> It's hard enough just to be sat here, let alone contemplating 'spilling all' to people you don't know well. I spend most of my days in work, trying to be a role model, leading by example and yet in this room I'm expected to peel back some of my defences and talk reflectively about my practice. That feels almost impossibly hard at the moment. I can see the point of it. I like the sound of it. But I'm not sure I'm ready for it.
>
> (Carter and Walker 2008: 148)

Despite the pitfalls that lie in wait, I have found that groups can provide one of the most satisfying and exciting routes to reflective practice. Commitment to a well-defined task has been central to the effective groups in which I have worked, and until the group is established I have found a clear, if not even rigid structure to be of benefit in order to give participants an experience of what they might be letting themselves in for.

Group supervision based on defined structures

If you decide to embark on supervision in a group, Brookfield (1995) suggests first establishing ground rules, which I would call contracting (discussed in Chapter 4 of this book). These rules help to create a structure and may be designed to ensure that everyone has the opportunity to participate in ways that suit them, to ensure that ideas and not people are critiqued, and that all contributions are treated respectfully. He suggests a structure entitled 'the circular response discussion exercise' which is designed to encourage attentive listening. A theme is determined by the group and a volunteer speaks for two minutes about the theme. The next person in the circle paraphrases the contribution and then makes her or his own contribution, explaining how it is grounded in the comments of the first contributor. After two minutes the turn moves to the next person in the circle. When all have spoken, the floor is opened for general reactions. My only difficulty with such a structure is the sense of impending 'doom' as my turn approaches. I have found random turn taking less tense although it can still be a struggle to be first and last.

Brookfield (1995) proposes that in such structured critical conversations, people consider taking one of three roles: storyteller, detective or umpire. The storyteller describes an incident from practice that may have been particularly fulfilling, frustrating or puzzling. The detectives (all other group members bar the umpire) try to identify explicit and implicit assumptions about teaching and learning as the story unfolds. They try to imagine themselves as the other characters in the storyteller's account. When the storyteller has finished speaking the detectives ask questions designed further to develop understanding from different perspectives. They are bound by a rule that they must only request information for the purposes of clarification and must not pass judgement, give opinions or make suggestions. The umpire bans any questions that imply that there was a better way to deal with the story told; such questions might begin, 'Didn't you think to . . .' or 'Did you really believe that . . .' When all of the questions have been answered the detectives report back to the storyteller what they have constructed as the underlying assumptions revealed by the account. They are asked to state these tentatively and to ground their reporting in their own experiences. The umpire continues to block anything with a judgemental bent. The detectives then present possible alternative interpretations that are plausible and consistent with the reported facts, the umpire again blocking any contributions that suggest a 'right' way of seeing. After listening to the contributions the storyteller can give additional information that may shed further light on the different perspectives. In the final phase the storyteller and detectives assess the significance of the conversation for their work. Everyone states what they have learned and how it may impact on their future actions. This takes the reflection into the domain of reflective practice. The umpire gives a summary concerning adherence to the rules in terms of group members being respectful listeners and talkers.

A specific Structured Group Supervision model was described by Wilbur et al. (1994) in which six steps are followed involving a 'plea for help', question period, feedback/consultation, pause for 10–15 minutes for reflection, response statement by the presenter and a final discussion which might involve the supervisee in summarising what has been helpful or in which group dynamics may be processed. Techniques for establishing, clarifying and deepening the focus of supervision groups were described by Nathalie Kees and Nancy Leech (2002). After an initial short presentation of an issue for supervision by one of the group members, the rest of the group respond in turn starting with a sentence stem, 'I am [presenter's name] and what I am struggling with most is . . .'. After listening to all the responses, the presenter chooses the most helpful contributions in order to narrow the focus for effective use of the group's time. In the next stage each of the group members asks questions of the presenter. In order to deepen the focus the presenter then listens to a discussion between the rest of the group members, sitting outside the group before rejoining in order to share her or his reactions.

A number of structures for organising group supervision derive from specific theoretical approaches (such as solution-focused or narrative). These can be adapted to more general contexts. I have encountered these structures when participating in groups of practitioners from a range of different disciplines. Never having met the other group members before, but trusting in the structures and adhering closely to the instructions, I have been supported in reflecting on my practice in what I have experienced as very constructive small group settings.

In a structure based on a solution-focused approach (Visser and Norman 2004) the session is divided into six sections. In the *Preparing* phase each participant takes a few minutes to think of, or ideally has prepared in advance, a topic, issue or case that they wish to discuss. In the second phase, *Presenting*, one member of the group describes an issue or situation and specifies what kind of input would help. The other group members listen without interruption until the presenter has finished. In the next phase, *Clarifying*, the group members each take turns to ask open questions that invite clarification. They are particularly interested in recognised and unrecognised assets: what the case presenter is already doing that is supporting progress. 'Why' questions are discouraged as they can invite defensiveness. The group members speak in any order. In the *Affirming* stage each member of the group tells the presenter what has most impressed them, taking the opportunity to compliment personal qualities, resourcefulness and skills. The presenter remains silent. In the *Reflecting* stage the group members take it in turns to say one thing at a time in response to the presentation. Anyone who wishes may 'pass' and the cycle continues until everyone has said all that they wish or the time allocated has expired. The input in this stage may be varied and could include reflections, metaphors, rhetorical questions for later consideration or technical input. In the final *Closing* stage the presenter responds briefly to the group's contributions. When this approach was adopted by a group of managers, the topics presented included finding an employee difficult to manage, improving skills of delegation, improving cooperation between departments and managing highly experienced team members.

Harry Norman (personal communication 2007) suggests that groups of about five people work well and when I completed the exercise each stage was restricted by time. Presenting was allocated five minutes, Clarifying six minutes, Affirming three minutes per person, Reflecting twelve minutes and Closing five minutes. In a group of five people this approximates to forty-five minutes.

Lincoln Simons (2008) described a peer supervision group based on ideas derived from narrative therapy. The aim of the structure was to give voice to diverse explanations and understandings of the work being carried out. The format was designed to make space to challenge taken-for-granted ideas, to listen respectfully to all views, to value differences in knowledge and experience and to place clients at the centre of the discussions.

The structure involved a presenter bringing an aspect of her or his work to the group and being interviewed by another member of the group about this issue. The interview was witnessed by the other group members. Following the interview, the interviewer would join the witness group and discuss their responses in the manner of a reflecting team. The interviewer then talked further with the presenter, picking up on points made by what was termed the 'outsider witness group'. There was a final discussion by all.

Michael White (2000) is very specific about the purposes of outsider witness groups whose members are engaged in the retelling of the story that they have experienced in the original telling. They are meant to contrast with taken-for-granted ways of speaking about people's lives in forums such as case conferences. He argues that such ways of speaking often reduce and pathologise people's lives through processes of normalising judgement. In contrast, the purpose of the reflecting team as a witness group is to show interest, curiosity, and make links with one's own experiences. Team members ask questions of each other about how what they have heard has aroused their interest and captured their imagination, what images have been evoked, how these images connect with the history of their own work and lives, and the potential effects of being touched by what they have heard. The aim is to encourage thoughts and ideas outside usual routines and to extend the limits of understanding.

I am struck by a significant commonality between these approaches to group supervision although they derive from different traditions. The commonality is in the prohibition of judgement, in the sense of ensuring that the task does not involve making an assessment of the work being presented or of the worker doing the presenting. White (2000) expressly introduces the reflecting team by saying that it is not their place to engage in acts of judgements on the lives of others. However this non-judgemental climate is created, I would contend that it is conducive to the development of deeply reflective practice and reduces the likelihood of participants rolling into a ball, spines outwards.

Action learning sets

Before embarking on this book I had heard of but not experienced action learning sets. I have been surprised to learn how widespread this way of promoting learning has become. I have found examples of its use in industry and in the private and public sectors of health and education. The founding of the approach in the 1940s is attributed to Reginald Revans, who worked with the Coal Board and in hospitals in the UK. Since its original conception action learning has come to mean different things to different people and various schools of practice have been identified (Marsick and O'Neil 1999). These have spawned different definitions and described different processes while some features are common. Common features include a focus on work-based problems which do not have a single correct answer, and while initially usually involving a facilitator, the learning sets are intended to consist of participants who perceive themselves to be on an equal footing without any sense of expert input which might be seen as definitive. McGill and Brockbank (2004) define action learning as follows:

> Action learning is a continuous process of learning and reflection that happens with the support of a group or 'set' of colleagues working on real issues, with the intention of getting things done.'
>
> (McGill and Brockbank 2004: 11)

Four schools of action learning were proposed by Judy O'Neil (1999, cited in Marsick and O'Neil 1999): Scientific, Experiential, Critical Reflection and Tacit. The experiential school is based on Kolb's (1984) experiential learning cycle. The critical reflection school holds that the kind of reflection found in the experiential school is useful but insufficient unless it includes the underlying beliefs and assumptions that shape practice. This kind of reflection can go beyond exploration of individual participants' assumptions, to an examination of organisational imperatives. Action learning sets typically comprise four to six people, possibly from different backgrounds or disciplines, who are of roughly equivalent status (Dixon 1998) ideally encompassing a diversity of background and experience (Marquardt 2004).

From my reading I have extracted the following characteristics of action learning that I believe can make it well suited to a process of reflective practice.

- The method is learner-centred, with the aim of building on knowledge derived from experience at work and oriented towards action.
- Authority and expertise belong to the participants, providing a contrast with traditional didactic approaches to teaching and learning.
- Life experience is brought into the foreground as the single most important resource for learning.
- Learning takes place through shared social activity in a cooperative climate, contrasting with a traditional orientation involving competition with other individuals.
- The conditions necessary for collaborative work need to be created, perhaps initially with the support of a facilitator, but with the aim of becoming autonomous.
- The focus of the sets is reflection on practice, moving forward into action.

- Reflection is regarded as a necessary precursor to effective action.
- Ground rules, including frequency, duration, confidentiality and a process for running the sessions, ensure that the meetings are formal and take place in protected time.
- Learning sets are typically closed groups that work on the problems and issues brought by individual members or on a collective task.
- Membership is voluntary.
- The focus may be technical and/or personal matters.

McGill and Brockbank (2004) suggest that the kind of dialogue that takes place in an action learning set is of a type termed 'connected knowing', which 'values a dialogue that relies on relationship as one enters meaningful conversations that connect one's ideas with others' and establish "rapport"' (Goldberger et al. 1996: 277). This contrasts with 'separated knowing' in which pronouncing or reporting one's ideas is valued. Connected knowing is characterised by an orientation towards standing in the shoes of the other person in order to try and know with them.

In an action learning set undertaken in this spirit a number of stages delineate the process (McGill and Brockbank 2004). A member of the group presents her or his issue or problem. The other group members listen with full attention, attempting to suspend pre-emptive judgements, conversations with themselves or other distractions. The key as a member of the audience is to try and listen from the presenter's standpoint without interruption. This includes allowing silences while the presenter takes time to think and reflect. Members then attempt to reflect or restate and clarify what the presenter has said with the aim of developing coherent understanding of the presenter's position. These tentative developing understandings are offered in a questioning mode: 'What I think you said was . . .', 'If I have understood you . . .'. This process continues until there is assent between the presenter and the rest of the group. At this point the members of the set give a résumé of the presenter's issue for the benefit of the presenter.

Throughout this process there is an emphasis on empathy, imagining the experienced reality of the presenter and trying to discern the emotional component which may be expressed directly or need to be read between the lines. The reflection involves expressing understanding and thereby affirming the presenter's experience while not implying agreement.

Next follows a period in which group members use their local knowledge to ask Socratic questions which probe and encourage exploration of the issue. 'Why' questions are avoided since these can be experienced as attacking. Sheila Stark (2006) argues that by actively participating in a questioning and reflective process with others, new ideas and insights emerge from which a course of action can be developed and implemented. In later meetings set members critically review the outcome of the action agreed and taken as a result of which further refinement may emerge.

It has been argued that the organisation in which set members are working must be conducive to individuals trying things out and taking risks in a non-threatening environment (Peters and Waterman 1982). In Stark's research this was not typically the case. She states:

> both cultures (of nursing and teaching) are in a constant state of flux with new structures, demands and targets being imposed on professionals relentlessly. The experiences of the nursing sets highlighted that this led to sustained role disruption, involving movement of either themselves or their colleagues or both. Such an organisational climate is not conducive to affording the time and continuity necessary for effective action learning. Not only are these workforces experiencing acute shortages, the professionals are under increasing pressure to be 'all things to all people'. Further, as the 'audit culture' (Power 1996; Strathern 2000) expands, many public professions are being held accountable by external systems of monitoring and centrally established performance targets and indicators (McDonald and Harrison 2004). An unintended effect of these processes of inspection, control, and 'continuous improvement' is that innovation and empowerment are squeezed, in favour of proficiency in achieving measurable outputs.
>
> (Stark 2006: 38)

In her research she found that participants talked about having experienced a deep level of reflection resulting from questioning their actions, beliefs and traditions and those of others, and from learning how to ask insightful questions. In the following example, participating in the action learning set led to questioning of a controlling management style:

> Having to be clear about the problems in relation to the communication patterns in my workplace was difficult. You know they are not good and you can give some vague reasons as to why, but when really probed, it is hard! I had to really think. Their question got me to ask more questions. I began to see *I* used really controlling language . . . it is really easy to criticise others and not see it in yourself.
>
> (Stark 2006: 32)

'Action learning seeks to throw a net around slippery experiences and capture them as learning, i.e. replicable behaviour in similar and, indeed, differing contexts' (P. Smith 2001: 36). This metaphor brings to my mind two kinds of slipperiness: experiences that are elusive and those that risk setting me off on a slippery slope. As I have learned more about action learning sets, I cannot help but see many similarities with what, in my profession, I would call peer supervision groups. When working well and in a climate of trust with peers I have experienced groups that have helped me to get a grip and stopped me from skidding out of control, illuminating my practice in the present and for the future.

Inquiry-based learning

> What emerges are physicians without enquiring minds, physicians who bring to the bedside *not* curiosity and a desire to understand, but a set of reflexes that allows them to earn a handsome living.
>
> (Bishop 1983, cited in Boud and Feletti 1997: 18)

It was this kind of view that led to the introduction into universities of problem-based learning (PBL) which is generally credited to the medical faculty at McMaster University, Canada. Staff there restructured an entire curriculum in order to promote student-centred interprofessional education as a basis for lifelong learning in professional practice (Neufeld and Barrows 1974). Traditional curricula were thought to serve as poor preparation for the skills that were required of health practitioners at the completion of the course (Morales-Mann and Kaitell 2001; Price 2003). The idea of PBL is for students to

> learn from and build upon each others' questions, show openness to different points of view, listen to and respect others' ideas and work collaboratively towards reasonable conclusions. It is a way of challenging students to become deeply involved in a quest for knowledge – a search for answers to their own questions.
>
> (Barell 2007: 3)

Such learning with understanding 'is more likely to promote transfer than simply memorizing information from a text or lecture' (Bransford et al. 2000: 236).

The effects are regarded as revitalisation of classroom learning, and the development of student learning that involves both independent and cooperative problem-solving of true-to-life problems (Boud and Feletti 1997). PBL has been found to have a large and potentially long-lasting impact on self-directed learning skills and on transfer of learning to new problems (G. Norman and Schmidt 1992). These authors found that problem-discussion activated prior knowledge which is elaborated upon and subsequently used for the comprehension of new information. Inquiry-based (or enquiry-based) learning (IBL/EBL) seems to follow a similar process but does not necessarily take as its starting point a 'problem' but rather a topic or issue which could be framed as a problem. In nursing it is argued that 'clients have needs that must be met rather than problems that need to be solved' (Long et al. 1999: 1744). EBL encompasses PBL, small-scale investigations and research (University of Manchester 2008). These approaches are essentially student-centred, with an emphasis on group work and use of the library, web and other information resources. Lecturers become facilitators, providing encouragement and support to enable the students to take responsibility for what and how they learn. It is argued that students learn not only to investigate questions posed by others, but also to formulate their own topics from which derives useful learning, that they gain a deeper understanding of the subject-matter and the capability to tackle complex problems that they will encounter in the real world (University of Manchester 2008). The nursing profession in particular anticipated that PBL would bridge theory–practice gaps, would produce critical and reflective thinkers, good communicators, problem solvers and lifelong learners (Rees 2004). The approach has begun to incorporate theories of humanistic psychology and adult learning, experiential learning and deep learning theories (Mantzoukas 2007; Quinn 2000; Suhre and Harskamp 2001).

In this section there is space to consider only how such approaches might be relevant to reflective practice in the context of supervision. The following characteristics of IBL suit the approach to small groups of peers supported by light-touch supervision:

- Supervisees work in small groups on real-life issues from a practice setting.
- Supervisees are expected to manage their own direction, choice of topics to investigate, the process of cooperation and report production, the group process and their own contributions to the process and outcomes.
- The supervisor 'nudges' them in potentially useful directions and may constrain the choice of theme in order to ensure relevance.
- The learning that takes place is 'just in time' rather than 'just in case'.
- The emphasis is on peer support.
- Supervisees are encouraged to notice how they are learning (metacognition) especially by being asked to report on their learning process.
- There is greater emphasis than in traditional approaches on learning and less on knowledge (i.e. process over content).

The aims of IBL are to develop transferable process skills, to encourage cooperative and self-directed learning involving information retrieval, information management, evaluation of information, division of labour, meeting of deadlines, constructive social processes and orientation towards professional norms. Because they are group members supervisees will almost inevitably bang up against different opinions and need to engage with a process for resolution. It seems to me that this process, introduced in pre-registration training, almost forces supervisees to examine their own thoughts, feelings and behaviour in such groups and this can be encouraged by the supervisor when supervisees show tendencies to attribute fault to others. The very process of inquiry invites reflection which can also be encouraged by the assessment process and marking criteria if formal coursework is required.

I think that this approach shares most of its features with action learning sets although IBL is typically found in the context of preregistration education and in consequence is oriented towards a curriculum that has predetermined elements. Unlike action learning sets, the facilitator continues to be involved, albeit with a light touch throughout. IBL groups tend to produce written reports and these often form part of the assessment process. It is not so clear that written output is expected from action learning sets. Maggi Savin-Baden (2003: 19) argues that, 'Action learning sets are more individualized, freer flowing and centred upon personal learning and reflection to achieve effective action'.

Despite this she has suggested that for many tutors:

> problem-based learning is used as a means of helping students to challenge borders, construct knowledge and to evaluate critically both personal knowledge and propositional knowledge on their own terms. Thus students are expected to develop qualities of moral and intellectual as well as emotional independence, and are required to set their own goals and delineate their own processes for learning . . . The idea that students learn to deal with conflict in learning, in teams and between themselves and tutors, will help them to develop a criticality that they are unlikely to need to engage with if they are undertaking more traditional lecture-based forms of learning.
>
> (Savin-Baden 2003: 23)

Although the facilitator, or for the purposes of this text, the supervisor, adopts a relatively hands-off posture, I can see many challenges to the role, not least because the facilitator in preregistration training has a clear and potent assessment role. While many tutors consider the approach to result in professionally relevant deeper authentic learning it requires them to cede control over the curriculum, and to have the skills to help groups of students to negotiate difficulties such as when one of the group members is seen as failing to fit in or to pull their weight. Prevention seems to offer a key and it can be helpful to make it clear that the supervisor's task is to offer assistance. Weekly anonymous feedback sheets from each participant, containing ratings of their own contributions and those of their peers, made to the group (an early warning system) can help to flag up difficulties before they have become entrenched (Jon Scaife, personal communication 2009).

Throughout the IBL process the facilitator has to make decisions about if, when and how to intervene and how to monitor the group's progress without intruding. This takes much reflection and can be seen as encouraging such a stance among facilitators, not only group members. For readers who are interested to learn more there are many excellent texts by authors from a range of disciplines, for example John Barell (2007), who comes from the discipline of teaching, Dankay Cleverly (2003), Bob Price (2003) and Kay Wilkie and Iain Burns (2002) from nursing, Tim French and Terry Wardle (2007) from the perspective of medicine and surgery, Anthony Guerrero and Melissa Piasecki (2008) from psychiatry and Maria Napoli (2006) about working with families.

Chapter 9

Reflective writing

When Tony Ghaye was the editor of the journal *Reflective Practice* between 2004 and 2006 he received more papers about reflective portfolios than any other kind of reflective account (Ghaye 2007). Because of the widespread use of reflective journals as a course requirement, students may be more likely to experience or anticipate reflective writing as being part of their academic rather than practical experience. But reflective coursework assignments themselves are typically addressed to descriptions of and reflections about practical experience. They are often a place where practice and theory connect. I will come to them later, but writing can be a very helpful method for encouraging, not only assessing, critically reflective practice and there are excellent sources available to which I will provide signposts.

In some approaches to therapy, metaphorical stories and letters are written to or by clients (G. Burns 2001; Mahoney 2003). In Cognitive Analytic Psychotherapy (CAT) the therapist presents the patient with a written Reformulation (Ryle 2004). This includes a description of the client's life so far, the difficulties they have struggled with, how they have survived the difficulties, and a reformulation of their presenting complaints as Target Problem Procedures to be worked on. Imagining receiving such letters can help supervisees to work out the way in which they want to communicate such ideas. Letters have been written by teachers to their students with a view to encouraging further reflection and development of their ideas (Murphy and Smith 1991). Val Wosket (1999) describes work in which she and her client wrote and shared separate accounts of each session. Val says that from her experience with Rachel she has come to ask herself whether mistakes and errors are to be welcomed, rather than regarded as something to be avoided. She highlights the extent of the learning that resulted for her from this process of exchanging writing.

In this chapter I will describe different kinds of writing that can be used in preparation for supervision, to share in supervision, and that connect practical experience with academic requirements. Supervisors are very well placed to assist supervisees not only in developing their critically reflective professional self through different kinds of writing in and about their practice, but also in shaping their reflective writing for the purposes of their learning and to meet coursework requirements.

Writing can present special challenges to people who are blind or have visual impairments. Many adjustments are possible, best made in individual consultation. These include Braille note-takers, powerful magnifying glasses, felt-tip pen written large, personal shorthand, laptops with screen readers, Dictaphones, and the provision of a scribe. The challenges are particularly acute where confidentiality is at stake and the approach needs to take account of individual preferences.

When I was thinking about this chapter I was very taken by the account of 'my first kiss' written by Francie Choy, a Year Nine student (13 and 14 year olds).

My First Kiss

'You have to do it sometime,' I thought for at least the 500th time.

My heart was pounding louder than a drum, playing with the utmost strength.

'Oh my god!' I chided with myself. 'Just press your lips against his and hold on till you lose your breath. Then pull back. You can do it.'

Another voice in my scrambled brain said, 'Your mother would never approve!!'

'So?', said another voice in my silly brain, 'So what. Who cares what mom thinks? It's my life!'

'Hi!' said my boyfriend, interrupting my thoughts.

'Hi!' I said listlessly.

'Is anything wrong?' He asked.

'What? Oh, nothing's wrong. Oh come on! Let's get it over with!'

'Gee, you're SOOOOO enthusiastic!!' he said in this really, I repeat really sarcastic way.

I felt as though I was talking to an enemy. 'Listen, I want it. You want it. So let's get it over with, OKAY??!!'

'Okay!!,' he said, mad. Then he said gently, 'Let's not fight.'

'Okay.' I whispered.

He drew closer and closer to me. We were just a teeny inch from kissing. I drew back while he fell back, startled.

'What?' he stammered, 'Why?'

'I'm scared . . .' I said shaking.

'Scared!?,' he said surprised.

'Yeah, I've never done it before,' I said close to tears.

'You haven't! Gosh, well . . . uh,' he fumbled.

'But I want to, okay?', I said weakly.

'Allright . . .!', he said, smiling, his brilliant eyes dancing.

He pulled closer to me, and I wrapped my arms around his neck.

While his lips were just a millimetre from mine, I shivered.

Finally, he put his lips tenderly on mine. I held on, just swept away, as he was. Then we pulled back. We breathed.
I'll always remember my first kiss.
The End.

(Murphy and Smith 1991: 59)

It reminded me not of my first kiss (the details of which I have thankfully forgotten) but of the first time doing many things at work that have involved being scared. Sometimes I'm still scared, years after the first time. It reminded me of the way that fear and anger intertwine and of how different could have been the outcome if Francie had not confessed her inexperience. It reminded me of how students and trainees have to face so many first times during their training and that this does not miraculously cease upon qualification.

Gillie Bolton (2005) champions a reflective process that involves focusing on detailed stories or narratives of practice, imaginative creations drawn from experience, rather than 'factual' descriptions of 'what actually happened'. She states:

The use of the aesthetic imagination in creating this material provides a screen as wide as life itself, drawing upon all of a practitioner's faculties. Attempting to reflect only upon 'what actually happened' and then to subject such an account to rational questions such as 'how might I have done better?' unnecessarily restricts what might be explored.

(Bolton 2005: 18)

Jerome Bruner (1990) argues that creating stories is a human and natural response for making meaning or comprehending the events in our lives. Story-making can connect what appear to be independent and disconnected elements of an experience to make it into a whole (Polkinghorne 1988). It can help to engage supervisees' 'moral imagination' (Rath 2002) and can give writers an opportunity to empathise, particularly when they are in potential positions of power, such as in the doctor–patient relationship explored by Coles (1989).

Purposes of reflective writing

Like other methods for encouraging the development of reflective practice, I see reflective writing as primarily for the purpose of learning through widening and deepening the writer's individual starting perspective. We vary in our capability to express ourselves orally. Reflective writing is likely to suit some of us as a more effective way to think, reflect and link ideas than discussion with our peers and supervisors. Writing gives us an opportunity to speak with a different 'voice'.

The purposes of reflective writing have been described as: to open up new perspectives or windows on experience, to externalise implicit values which can then be examined through text, to facilitate access to tacit knowledge (Chambers 2003), to teach empathy (DasGupta and Charon 2004) and to create informative, descriptive material from the mass of ideas, hopes, anxieties, fears, memories and images provoked by everyday working life (Bolton 2005). Bolton argues that writing for reflective practice is a first-order activity in that it *is* the reflective mode. Osterman and Kottkamp (1993) suggest that the written form seems to interject another level of reflection beyond expressing thoughts orally. The writing process involves pausing, cycling back, rereading and reflecting on the ideas that we are formulating and the record made allows us to return to the product. Writers are shapers and creators of their own texts, whether these be journal entries, fictions, poems, screenplays or shopping lists. Given these purposes, I have come to the tentative view that all writing for reflection best starts off unfettered.

In a brave experiment with portfolio writing in the secondary school classroom, Sandra Murphy and Mary Ann Smith (1991), in consultation with a group of colleagues, categorised the overall purposes of portfolios as student purposes and teacher purposes. The former included empowerment and motivation of students as writers and self-assessors, and the latter, learning about teaching strategies and student performance. Since it has become mandatory in many professions to demonstrate reflective practice in order to graduate, the requirement to keep journals, logs and diaries has become ubiquitous and I wonder if this does not place undue emphasis on teacher purposes. Murphy and Smith (1991) argue that purposes have a nasty habit of becoming contradictory. Are practitioners writing for themselves, to aid them in developing as a reflective practitioner, or are they writing for their educators, in order to pass the course?

> As students we are expected to fill our portfolios with reflections on our nursing experiences, this includes writing about things that upset us, reflecting upon possible triggers and how we felt afterwards. I remember leaning against the door of the sluice with my fingers in my ears to drown out the sound of an elderly patient calling again and again for her dead mother, who she swore had just gone to the corner shop. I remember becoming nauseated when entering the room of a dying patient and being transported back to the age of 11 when I had experienced the same smell in my father's room at the hospice . . . My husband and best friend are the only two people I wish to confide in. My feelings are private – yet I am expected to frame them in prose and submit them to my university.
>
> I don't know my lecturers or personal tutor intimately. What right has anyone to ask for such personal information, let alone ask that it be graded by a faceless lecturer? As nurses we respect patients' rights not to disclose their personal feelings. Yet no such right is afforded to students.

I have had reflections returned with requests for more details about my feelings. I comply but deeply resent being asked to do so.

(Sinclair-Penwarden 2006: 12)

Student portfolios have been defined as 'a purposeful collection of student work' that tells the story of students' efforts, progress or achievement in a given area or areas: 'This collection must include student participation in selection of portfolio content; the guidelines for selection; the criteria for judging merit; and evidence of student self-reflection' (Arter and Spandel 1991). These authors give very useful advice for anyone planning to design portfolio assignments, emphasising the centrality of purpose and student participation.

Types of writing

Many different types of writing have been advocated for the purposes of reflective practice. These include anecdotes, descriptions of a scene, poems, letters, free writing, fictional stories, and journal, log or diary entries. The act of writing, particularly in educational and professional settings, is often in response to the demands of others (Jasper 2003). We have written coursework assignments, case notes, reports, emails, policy documents, letters, our curriculum vitae. In my working life, this writing has not been accompanied by joyfulness. Much of it has been for others in a style that fits the purpose. It can be quite difficult to let go of an externally imposed structure to write more freely and from the imagination in order to write-to-learn. Melanie Jasper (2003) argues that writing-to-learn rather than learning-to-write requires a major shift in perception for most people and that it is difficult to shrug off years of prior conditioning in order to write for ourselves.

Some authors (Rolfe et al. 2001) divide reflective writing into two categories termed analytical and creative. Analytical strategies incorporate analysis and/ or synthesis in the writing process and methods include learning journals, critical incident analysis, dialogical writing (in which a hypothetical conversation between self and other is constructed) and making a case (creating a persuasive argument as for the purposes of a debate). Creative strategies include writing a letter, email or memo (either unsent or with an imaginary recipient), writing from the position of another character in an event, writing as a journalist or outside observer, storytelling and poetry (Jasper 2003). Some overlap of methods between types or strategies of writing seems probable.

Creative strategies

Supervisors who wish to encourage the development of reflective practice are often in a good position to encourage creative writing as a reflective act. I find that it is rare for supervisees spontaneously to bring examples of their writing to supervision. They are busy people who have plenty of formal writing to complete every day. There is, though, no reason why a supervision session could not be given over to one of the methods described in this section. In my experience supervision tends to fall into a regular pattern and when I become aware of this I may suggest trying something different to see what emerges. Writing is one option. The resultant text can be private; the issues it raises material for supervision.

Free reflective writing

Gillie Bolton (2005) argues that while still anchored to the experiencer's perspective, a free writing process can harness buried memories, allows entry into the life of another through the creation of a character on the page, and can take what is known into the unknown through writing a fiction. This kind of writing comes from imagination and the author's intuitive knowledge of relationships, motives, cause and effect, ethical issues and values. This kind of writing is not about facts, it is about outwitting the inner police-officer editor and writing whatever comes to mind. In one of Gillie's workshops I found myself unchained gleefully to write a fierce tirade against a distant colleague. It wasn't really about her but gave vent to my frustration about presenteeism. It made me consider when, as a worker, I might decide to draw a line and refuse to be budged.

Here is a piece from Chris Banks, a participant in Gillie's workshops, reflecting on the thought police:

> It's happening – that thing where I dismiss my own thoughts: *No, not that. You'll get stuck if you go with that. That's so dull, you'll bore yourself stupid. Not that, not that, not that.* It makes it so impossible to get started and then to follow through. It's the Thought Police, as Gillie said Ted Hughes said. I have a whole battalion of them – bobbies on the beat, sergeants in the office, sharp-eyed interrogating inspectors – loads of them. And then there's the Crown Persecution Service complete with judge and jury and some hopeless, depressed woman from Victim Support as my only ally.
>
> Is it experience that tells me, *Don't go there, it'll be dull?* Not just dull – something more like, *It won't get born. It'll be a messy miscarriage, a deformed foetus that'll die shortly after it slips into the world.* Is it experience? In fact, experience tells me, *Focus, write, give yourself over to it and whatever comes out will be healthy, with full lungs and kicking limbs.*
>
> (Bolton 2005: 49)

Fictional writing for learning

Jasper (2003) advocates that if you are suffering from a block in getting started on your writing, the only thing to do is to start writing! She suggests beginning by talking with someone else and I have found it helpful to record then transcribe such conversations with supervisees. Private writing can be about anything at all, but that puts me in mind of a rabbit in headlights. The scope for choice of content and direction is huge and it is easy to freeze. I have found it helpful to have someone else define the parameters. Supervisors are ideally placed to take this role for supervisees, and to sit down with them while they write, irrespective of whether the content of the writing is shared. This can impose a kind of discipline whereby the writing happens because it has been prescribed and space provided. In a 'stories at work' group Bolton (1994) invited participants, after a very brief introduction, to begin by picking up their pens and writing whatever came to mind, however disjointed and rambling, for six minutes. Since it was not for sharing they could write a list, a rant, about a dream, a fairy story, or just words. The only 'rule' was that the pen was not to stop during the six-minute period, even if this meant repeating the last word over again until another idea surfaced.

At the conclusion of the six-minute period participants were asked to write a piece for ten to fifteen minutes entitled 'A time when something vital was learnt'. They were again asked to write without stopping or thinking. The focus could be on something long gone, like learning to swim or cross the road, or could be more recent and more intimate. At the end of the writing period, all the participants realised that they could write; something had surfaced for each of them. They were invited to look through their two pieces of writing and to make connections, writing another piece if they wished or sharing what they had written with others in the group. Before reading, group ground rules were discussed and agreed.

A similar process can be followed when writing alone. The first stage can be regarded as 'dumping mind-clutter' onto the paper. Some of what turns up may be important while some people prefer to screw up and throw away the product of the six-minute 'splurge'. The main issues are to write uncensored, without stopping to think and without reference to spelling, punctuation or grammar. The second piece of writing is similar and Bolton (1994) suggests:

- Write with a focus; the story of a vital occasion but without questioning the selection process.
- Choose the first event that comes to mind rather than anxiously trying to reason why you may have chosen this topic.
- Only allow twenty to forty minutes in which to write so as not to waste writing time in thinking.
- Recreate the situation as memory gives it, with as many details as possible.
- Consider it fiction in order to relieve fears of embarrassment. Allow elements into the story that are at the hazy edge of memory or that embroider the text.
- Ignore spelling, syntax, grammar and repetitions which can be amended later if need be.

- The writing does not need good form; there is no need for clear beginnings and structure. Musings can be incorporated and tidied later; disclosures can be edited in future drafts.
- Include: details, tone of voice, the way someone is dressed, what is said, incidentals and divergences are all included.
- Reactions, emotional responses and feelings can be penned.
- Judgements are for later.

Bolton (2005) goes on to suggest a third stage, in which the products of the writing splurge are examined with an open mind, seeking connections and fresh understandings, making additions, deletions and alterations. She suggests filling out the narrative with as much detail as possible and asking oneself questions. The result might be shared with a peer and additional pieces might be developed in which other perspectives are explored. Bolton makes many suggestions for development that include rewriting the story from the viewpoint of a different character, giving the story a title, changing the age, gender, sexuality, ethnicity of the lead character, or rewriting in a different genre; as a newspaper article, advertisement, romance, science fiction or a children's story. Be a reporter and write an interview with a protagonist from the story, or write a letter to yourself from one of the characters. The list could keep you writing for the rest of the month. She goes on to suggest further topics: about your name; one truth, one wish and one outright lie about yourself; the story of a favourite set of work clothes; entering your work space or that of a colleague; describing a character from work who you know well; or writing as an object you use at work (desk, pen, mug).

To me this kind of writing feels very freeing and different from my conception of a journal, diary or log, although I could see myself including such pieces of writing in a private record. While maintaining their privacy, supervisees can be encouraged to undertake such writing and to bring the products of their reflection to supervision.

Richard Winter et al. (1999) argue that journals, portfolios and diaries often employ a fragmentary and chronological structure that does not help writers to become aware of the way that they shape their experiences through a process of selection and interpretation. If reflective writing is conceived as a form of fictional shaping, journal entries can be potential components of what they call a 'patchwork' text in which disparate elements are consciously placed side by side in order to raise issues, heighten ambiguity and highlight alternatives that may benefit from clarification. Like Bolton, they argue the benefits to reflective practice of fictional stories which provide protection for their authors and a richness in which implicit meanings are embedded. These creative writing methods are intended to go beyond the rational, tapping into imaginative resources and generating different perspectives on an experience. I have wondered whether it is helpful to keep in mind the idea of an audience when writing a fiction or whether this would serve to constrain.

What follows are two extracts from pieces of writing by Bernadette Saharoy, written as variations on a theme – part of her patchwork text.

Through the eyes of a child

Jimmy wasn't keen to put a dress on anyway, to go to the operating theatre, but couldn't understand it at all when the nurse insisted he put it on what appeared to be 'back to front'. His back felt cold as he tried to pull it around him tightly to keep it closed. His Mum always had to pester Jimmy to eat his food at home. He'd promised to be good in hospital and eat everything the nurses gave him, but today the nurses did not give Jimmy any food at all. It was his favourite for lunch as well, corned beef. Jimmy wondered whether it was a punishment for not eating his meals at home. He asked his Mum whether he would not be able to have corned beef after he'd had his tonsils out either. He didn't really understand everything that was happening and wondered when he would be able to eat again.

A nurse began to put a sticky white cream on Jimmy's hands and plasters over the top of it. He told her over and over that he hadn't fallen or cut himself, but she didn't listen to him. Suddenly a man arrived at Jimmy's bedside and lifted him over onto another bed which he then began to push. Jimmy wondered why HIS bed was moving and no one else's was. He felt quite special. Jimmy's Mum and a nurse followed him out of the ward. When they arrived at the operating theatre, everyone had masks on covering most of their faces; it was difficult for Jimmy to hear what they were saying. They had looked at Jimmy's plastic bracelets with his name on: Jimmy had thought he could have told them his name and his address and telephone number, if they had asked him. He was nine years old after all. As he was pushed down the corridor, he peered in though windows. In one room he saw people washing their hands and getting dressed in green clothes. He thought they must have just woken up.

(Saharoy, in Winter et al. 1999: 78)

Your mother v my mother

As I began with my routine explanation of pre-operative checks, I was
   interrupted by her rather abrupt question:
'But what will this surgery really mean for me?'
Total abdominal hysterectomy – intravenous infusions, skin clips or stitches,
   patient-controlled analgesia . . .
'and surely my womanhood is being taken away from me?'
A very complex issue . . .
'Yes but think of the discomfort and pain you've had for so many years.
   Anyway, about your intravenous infusion . . .'
'Have you any particular worries about tomorrow's surgery?'

Probably nausea, wound healing, chest infections . . .

'It's my family you see, I'm terrified of never seeing them again, I'm terrified of dying,' she replied with obvious fear in her voice.

Why didn't I think of that? Yes, losing her home and family. Of course, wouldn't my own Mother be just as afraid? And then I surprise myself by saying

'Your fears are the fears of any caring Mother. I'm sure your children would be proud to know that they are your priority, even during this very stressful time in your life.'

The look in her eyes told me that my simple reassurance had been of some help to her. As I turned to leave, she said:

'You see motherhood means everything to me.'

(Saharoy, in Winter et al. 1999: 79)

The author used a variety of formats to explore her role in preparing patients pre-operatively and in the process discovered the value of involving herself and her personhood in her professional work. Fictional characters have a habit of taking on a life of their own, writing their own story though the pen of the author. It seems to me that this kind of writing stands a good chance of taking the writer far beyond any originally conceived plot and plan, revealing amoebic thoughts and ideas that reside somewhere out of reach of the conscious mind.

Winter et al. (1999) suggest that the process of assembling a patchwork text can be aided through questions, especially if people are writing in the context of a small group. Group members (or a supervisor) may suggest ways of developing the work by portraying the topic from a different point of view or by highlighting something missing. Stories can act as a metaphor for aspects of practice or may take shape as an expression of empathy with the 'other' in a professional encounter.

Peter Ovens (2003) describes an assignment entitled 'Becoming a science specialist primary teacher' which also involves the weaving of patches into a text. The students have a great deal of control over the content of the six different kinds of writing that are required. One kind takes the form of personally reflective notes about the progress of students' learning in a 'jotter' to which he regularly responds. Others involve much freedom of choice in that they may encompass thoughts on a television programme or the kinds of learning about science that might be encouraged when taking children out on school visits. He says:

As the module progresses, each patch is read and discussed in a small group seminar of critical friends, including me as the tutor, all of us giving formative comment, before it is 'published' electronically to the whole group of students. So the module develops its own growing resource base of diverse and stimulating student writing. In stitching their patches together at the end of the module, a student is encouraged to reappraise her/his patches, review personal learning with reference to their own Jotter and in conversation with the critical friends group, so as to clarify an emergent pattern of themes or of chronological development to structure the Patchwork Text.

(Ovens 2003: 547)

Writing and discussion are placed at the centre of the learning process and students are tasked with making a distinctive personal enquiry into the meaning of the learning process as they become professionals. Ovens (2003) argues that the text combines openness and flexibility with reflexivity and rigour.

Cartoon strips

Cartoon strip characters offer alternative personalities with whom supervisees might usefully try to identify. In a group setting I ask individuals to write a first-person account of a scene from the perspective of one of four characters in an episode. Four accounts are written by individuals or small groups so that each of the characters in the scenario has a voice. The participants take it in turns to read out the first-person account to the rest of the group. This can be particularly stimulating when the characters differ in age, gender and so on. The process can have the effect of bringing home the multiplicity of perspectives likely to be taken whenever there are several participants in an event. I have a particular fondness for the Posy Simmonds cartoon reproduced in Figure 9.1 because of the voices that have been given by participants to both of the children and Trish's friend.

Personal illness narratives

In the medical profession, 'the physician is not only the witness to the patient's story but also oftentimes an agent within the story and even a co-creator of the patient's story' (Hunter 1993). Thus, through conversation in professional encounters new meanings may emerge. Empathy is an espoused virtue for medical practitioners though it has been argued that traditional medical training tends to teach students that what lies beneath their white coats is irrelevant to their work. Little attention is paid to the fact that physicians' bodies, not only those of their patients, experience 'normal' health variations such as pregnancy, let alone illness. Sayantani DasGupta and Rita Charon (2004) describe how writing personal illness narratives may enhance medical students' empathy with their patients by thrusting the hitherto 'mind-defined physicians' into their 'very real bodies' through role-reversal. 'In the process of witnessing, interpreting and translating their own illness experiences, these physicians become better able to listen empathically for the stories of their patients' (DasGupta and Charon 2004: 353). They asked their

Figure 9.1 Bittersweets.

students to develop a personal illness narrative concerning an illness experienced either by themselves or by a family member. The students were asked to write as follows:

- Bring to class an idea for your illness narrative which you will begin writing during the session.
- Try writing your narrative from the point of view of the ill person's body.
- Try writing your narrative in a different form – prose, poetry or dramatic dialogue.
- Try writing about the familial, cultural or ethnic context of your narrative's ill body.
- Write about how the ill person's body is perceived or represented by others – consider writing from the physician's point of view (if there is one in your narrative).
- Address the issue of bodily integration into self.

Students described positive reactions to writing their own and listening to others' illness stories. They valued the rare opportunity to share emotional and physical vulnerability, to examine their feelings and thoughts about the bodily nature of illness, health and selfhood. Students made the following comments:

> 'I wanted to get all my thoughts out before I get it confused with all the intellectualizing I'm prone to doing.' 'The women in our group were so outwardly strong so it was interesting to hear their vulnerabilities expressed in their pieces.' 'I felt vulnerable yet detached from the experience [of illness]. I suppose the latter defence mechanism comes in handy when you realize that little separates you from your patients.' 'It was frightening, enlightening, uncomfortable, and ultimately very healing.'
> (DasGupta and Charon 2004: 354)

Other writing exercises can also encourage an empathetic shift in perspective. These include the composition of letters to patients met in early physical diagnosis courses or autobiographical sketches of students' anatomy cadavers. Exercises in writing a clinical story from the patient's point of view, particularly when written in the first person (Marshall and O'Keefe 1995), encourage students to reduce the emotional distance between themselves and their patients.

Unsent letters

Unsent written communications have been advocated as good vehicles for the expression of strong emotions. They are advised 'when we are angry with someone else or feel the situation is out of our control, or that we are disempowered in some way' (Jasper 2003: 161). The writing is intended to serve as a powerful way of bringing order to chaos and freeing up the intellect to manage the situation. It is intended to provide distance while preserving intensity. In the example that follows, the author clarifies her needs and while deciding to continue her scheduled day, might later use the material more deeply to reflect on her life path and her future direction.

Sample letter from Dana Ecelberger, Mendocino, California

To whom it may concern,

   I'm thinking of yesterday; how I felt so permeable, penetrable. How the madness of the civilized world stood at my door in a self-righteous fit and demanded to be let in. My door seemed to be blown off its hinges, and I had no way of keeping anything out. The cars speeding bumper to bumper along the freeway, each with a solitary driver shuttered away – not unlike turtles hiding in their shells with a false sense of security. The shopping center that has been growing like a disease upon the belly of what used to be wetlands. The cellular phones, lines of fast-food restaurants, fast oil changes, fast checking, fast lanes. They all made me wonder if it were me who had gone crazy or everyone else. I wanted to park the truck in the parking lot of one of the many, many, obscenely many shopping malls, take a company check and write myself a few thousand dollars, and catch a plane to someplace far away where no one knows me, where no one has heard of America, and where they have a kind of reverence and cautiousness around the insane. I wanted to stop and call someone to drive down to get me, to feed me, to rock me back to sanity, but I didn't want to bother anyone I knew. I wanted to call my boss in that moment of hysteria and say, 'Listen, I want you to understand I have hit the wall. I've come undone and I need a break now. Today. Please help me.' I needed to give up. I needed to fall without breaking anything. I wanted to disappear behind my eyes, draw the shades and never again leave the house. I wanted to eat real food. But, there was no time for that. Instead I spoke in a very firm voice to the disintegrating woman and to the truthful eye, and I warned them and cajoled them and told them to just keep driving. And I cried because I'm so strong I cannot give up, even when continuing on is destroying me.

(L. Smith 2002: 35)

Writing as a character or object

This kind of writing is designed to encourage an observer perspective. While it is impossible to 'be' the other, attempts to imagine an event from a different perspective may be enhanced by the act of writing with the voice of another. It is a way of attempting to 'decentre', a process discussed in Chapter 7. I have found that voices given to inanimate objects can be particularly useful in unchaining the pen, and in generating new ways of seeing. This piece was prompted by a suggestion to write a story entitled 'A clean sheet':

> Here I am again on the laundry shelf, and it's lovely and warm in here with all my companions. Light goes on – just when I was feeling drowsy too – someone is picking me up – what rough hands she has got – I wish she wouldn't hold me close like that. Am being carried along – what's that tune she's humming. I'm sure I've heard it before . . .
>
> Hours have passed and now someone is coming into the room – three people in fact but one of them is very frail. She is being undressed by the other two – now she is being washed – they are doing their best to converse with this old lady but she does not appear to understand what they are saying to her. They lose interest in talking to her and start to talk to each other about the day's happenings. What a pity that they have not time to talk to this old lady.
>
> Now she is lying on top of me and is being covered by the duvet, one of them has at least taken the time to make sure that she is comfortable and has kissed her goodnight.
>
> All is quiet now, her breathing is slowing down and I can feel her relaxing and she is getting warm. What's that she is saying – she is now talking about bygone days – as though she is young again – and talking to a young soldier. She is walking with him down sunny lanes and is feeling really happy – now a tear falls from her cheek and lands on me – a salty stain spreads, albeit a small one – I am touched by this emotion – what can I do – what is she thinking about now?
>
> She moves slowly with a slight moan, and then goes quiet – she is sleeping now.
>
> (Bolton 2005: 94)

This text prompted many discussions about staff relationships with residents, and the concern for their work to be carried out with grace and loving care.

Joy Jarvis et al. (2004) asked pre-service teachers to create fictional stories to help them learn more about the experience of living with a disability in school. The students were asked to combine their existing knowledge of schools and children with newly researched information about a specific special need in order to create a story told in the first person by a child. The quality of work produced, and the expressed changes in attitude suggested that story form not only engaged and motivated students but also resulted in deepened understanding and a clear link with practice. Beth's story was written from the perspective of a deaf teenager. She reported that writing her story increased her awareness of the inequity faced in everyday situations that a hearing person might take for granted, such as a cancelled train, a changed platform, an emergency siren, or a fire alarm. The following is an extract from 'Deaf People Don't Dance' by Beth.

I got on the train at Hatch End Station but after two stops the train just stopped and the doors stayed open for ages. I was all on my own.

Eventually a man came along in a British Rail Uniform and put his head into the carriage and said something, I couldn't tell what he had said but I saw him mouth 'Get off.' Now there was no one on the platform, no train and no information on the announcement boards.

'Where has everybody gone?' I thought to myself. I give up, I'm not asking, there's no point, I might as well walk from here.'

(Jarvis et al. 2004: 8)

These creative writing strategies connect closely with practical experience; they derive from actual experiences at work.

Poetry

Bolton (2005: 127) says that, 'Poetry strips away cloaking veneers, lays bare thoughts, ideas, feelings, values, dilemmas about identity, etc., through image, metaphor and other poetic devices'. Poems are capable of communicating messages subtly and in a manner that is capable of creeping behind defences. Sometimes they are capable of revealing thoughts of which the author was formerly unaware.

The poetic mind knows better than the cognitive: A medical course member wrote, 'I like poetry because I can't make it do what I want it to do, it will only do what *it* wants. I didn't want to write the poem I did write; I wanted to write a nice glowing poem about being a mother'.

(Bolton 2005: 127)

I am very grateful to Robin Waller for sharing with me the two poems that follow. The first was written many years after the experience and shows just how very difficult and emotionally taxing can be work with our fellow humans, especially when we allow ourselves to be involved and care.

The birth of humility

Diabetic woman
On a long stay ward.
She's not my patient,
Not really.
But at night
On duty
She's mine.
For I'm the new doctor
Who can do anything.

In pain,
Rotting buttocks
Maggot deep bedsores
Moaning, forever moaning
Her suffering invades.
The nurses are silenced.

I push morphine
Into her body.
More and more and more.
How much will it take?

Sweet Jesus
It shouldn't be like this.
Her pain
And my pain
Now Siamese twinned.

Die, please die.
End our suffering
End my suffering.
Murderous thoughts
Scab inside.
It's the birth of humility.
    (Robin Waller, in Bolton 2001: 54)[1]

The second poem concerns the impact of work culture on staff morale. While expressing the author's feelings, the poem could serve as a communication to colleagues and staff in management roles. The poetic device may provide an acceptable channel through which authority may be challenged, the message being expressed through an indirect route.

A view from the trenches

In war time
Generals issue orders
Soldiers obey
Or get shot

In the Directorate
Must staff obey
Managers memos
Or be disciplined?

1 'The Birth of Humility' by Robin Waller published 2001 in *Medical Humanities*, 27, 53–54. Reproduced with permission from the BMJ Publishing Group.

The real battle is outside
With frightened children and families
Then why
Fight amongst ourselves?

(Waller 2000: 4)

Analytical strategies

Analytical writing approaches are often among the methods of choice adopted by professional training courses because they tend to sit comfortably with structures and frameworks for supporting and assessing reflective practice. These methods can lend themselves to formally assessed written coursework assignments intended to demonstrate competence as a reflective practitioner. This does not make them more effective than creative strategies as approaches to the development of reflective practice but may give them an edge in helping writers to get started if a structure is provided. David Boud (2001) emphasises the value of a clear separation between writing for learning and writing for assessment purposes: 'The exploration of the self that reflection involves requires a relatively protected environment in which one is not continually preoccupied by defending oneself from the scrutiny of others' (Boud 2001: 15).

Dialogical writing and 'making a case'

These approaches involve writing a hypothetical conversation between self and other. Jasper (2003) suggests that frameworks providing a set of cues in the form of questions are particularly useful for supporting this kind of writing. She recommends Borton's (1970) developmental framework as a relatively simple model that can be used whatever your experience of reflective practice. The basic structure involves three questions: 'What?' 'So what?' and 'Now what?' The first question encourages identification and detailed description of an experience. The second involves analysis of the experience and the construction of a personal theory or formulation with hypothetical explanations drawing on a range of sources including previous experience, literature and the views of others. The final stage involves planning intervention and action. In the hypothetical dialogue the enquirer might ask, 'What is your previous experience?' 'Why is this relevant?' 'What happened?' 'What does that mean?' 'So what did you do?' 'So, what was the problem?' 'Now what sense do you make of it?' and 'What have you learned?' These questions are versions of what we ask each other when holding an ordinary everyday conversation, when we say such things as 'Just a minute – what were you thinking about then?' or 'What made you do that?'

Dialogical writing involves asking myself questions of this type and responding to them on the page in response to a simulated 'other' who challenges my current perspective and extends my viewpoint. Making a case is similar to dialogical writing while close to an academic writing style in which a problem is analysed and an argument presented to support proposed actions.

Getting ready for supervision

I like to be prepared for supervision, often bringing to my supervisor a dilemma that I have been unable to satisfy by reflecting alone. I have to confess that I rarely bring written material with me although it is through my writing that material for supervision sometimes emerges. Michael Carroll and Maria Gilbert (2005) have created an exercise that can help to support supervisees in their preparation for supervision:

> Have your notebook beside you. Relax, take some deep breaths and allow yourself to concentrate on your breathing for a minute or two. Then let your mind drift back over your recent work . . .
>
> What surfaces for you immediately? Notice and let it go (you might want to make a note of it in your supervision notebook). Let your mind wander over the following questions:
>
> 1   What interactions/sessions/clients/interventions were you pleased with?
> 2   What was difficult for you?
> 3   What were you/are you uncertain about?
> 4   What are you looking forward to in your next working session?
> 5   Are there any anxieties about the way you are working with a par-ticular client/group/programme?
> 6   Are there any anxieties about your relationship with clients/other tutors/managers/team members etc?
> 7   Are there some doubts/anxieties/feelings just 'out of view' which you would rather keep out of view? Identify the feelings as well as the items.
> 8   What interactions have you enjoyed most? What were the feelings?
>
> Jot down a list of what has surfaced for you as a result of this reverie.
>
> (Carroll and Gilbert 2005: 29)

They describe further strategies to identify suitable material for supervision which they suggest adding to the list. The items may then be tentatively prioritised and sorted by significance and willingness to discuss. Such detailed preparation for supervision might form the basis of a good habit – developing the 'internal supervisor' proposed by Patrick Casement (1985).

Learning journals

Where reflective practice is concerned, learning journals often appear as course requirements across a range of professional training courses. David Boud (2001) suggests that we write journals for many different reasons: to capture an experience, record an event, explore our feelings or make sense of what we know. Sometimes this writing is purely for ourselves and sometimes for others. It can be a medium of self-expression, a record of events, a form of therapy or an approach to learning. A number of terms have been used to refer to *regular* writing for reflective purposes which include learning logs, reflective journals, portfolios, and diaries. Gillie Bolton (2005) suggests that a log straightforwardly records events and that its usefulness lies in its capability to act as an *aide mémoire*. Diaries are at the other extreme in that they can contain anything at all. Portfolios typically contain examples of someone's work, sometimes accompanied by a reflective commentary. Journals are records of events, thoughts and feelings relating to a particular domain and/ or with a particular structure. 'A reflective practice journal is like a diary of practice but in addition includes deliberate thought and analysis related to practice' (Bolton 2005: 164). In Jennifer Moon's (2006) definition, learning journals contain an accumulation of material over time (rather than being completed 'in one go') that is largely based on the author's reflections. The overall intention is that learning should be enhanced. 'Dialogue journals' contain written conversations between two or more people responding to each other's entries.

Learning journals have been described as serving a number of purposes for their authors and often these coincide with the overall purposes of critically reflective practice (Moon 1999). I am interested here in the qualities that are specific to *regular written* reflection in the context of supervision.

RECONSTRUCTING KNOWLEDGE

Reflective journals have been reported to show evidence of their authors relating ideas introduced by the teacher or supervisor to their own experience. The journals that were most valuable to students in Margaret Roberts' (1989) study were those in which there was a constant looking backwards to their authors' experience as learners, and forwards to being beginner teachers, showing a continuous attempt to make sense of new knowledge in terms of past and imagined future experiences. This process of looking back and forwards may be assisted by the compilation of a written record. A journal can also provide a place for disjointed ideas, which currently do not appear to fit, to be parked in the journal lot so that they do not become lost for good. All students interviewed in a study by Jeannie Wright (2005) used their journals for clarifying and developing thoughts and ideas, sometimes by slowing down the thinking process.

RECORDING AND CLARIFYING IDEAS THAT EMERGED IN THE
SUPERVISORY CONVERSATION

Supervision often leads, through conversation, to the identification of new ideas. Learning journals can be used as an *aide mémoire* and time can be set aside at the end of the supervision session for together summarising and making a note of what has emerged in the conversation. These can be reviewed in the process of planning the next piece of work. Used in this way they may have the characteristic of a log rather than a reflective journal. However, if ideas emerge spontaneously during a later incubation period when the attention of the thinker has been elsewhere then the ideas arising in supervision can continue to be developed and clarified both spontaneously and through further deliberate consideration. Sometimes journals may be used when people think that there has been a misunderstanding that needs to be cleared up later. An example from Roberts (1989) is, 'I think I may have given the impression in this session that I am a raving fascist . . . I would hope this is not the case.'

Supervision conversations, even those of apparent significance at the time, can readily evaporate into the ether. Making written notes afterwards can help to 'fix' or capture key fleeting ideas and experiences. Because writing is creating, it is likely to be of greater benefit if the supervisee makes the notes, rather than leaving critical judgement to the supervisor. If written notes are mandated, as may be the case for preregistration students, then the status of the notes as part of the case record needs first to be established in order to honour commitments to confidentiality.

EXPRESSING FEELINGS

Journals can be a useful place privately to express feelings, perhaps with a view to bringing them to supervision at the next opportunity. Such an outlet can offer a safe repository for unwelcome feelings elicited by work and can stop excessive rumination through a process of disengagement in which an internal process is externalised. By writing about positive emotions, supervisees can reaffirm their commitment to the work and revisit their written triumphs at a point where their motivation has taken a dip. The value of learning journals in providing an opportunity to express strong emotions on the page has been shown to be in itself a helpful therapeutic process (Bolton 1999; Lepore and Smyth 2002; Wright 2005).

CHARTING CHANGE OVER TIME

Sometimes, particularly when feeling disheartened, it is easy to lose track of positive progress and recall what it was like to be a beginner. I kept a journal when my children were little and I was learning how to be a mother. Although

I knew intellectually that the difficulties that I was experiencing at the time would change as they grew older – what 10-year-old wants constant nursing? – it served as a good practical reminder that all things must pass and while I may continue to struggle, the source of my anguish would change. A material record can serve as a useful reminder.

For Jeannie Wright's participants, rereading was sometimes experienced as an integral part of the reflective process. Her participants all gave examples of personal and professional changes that they had recorded in their journals:

> it feels much more like a stream of consciousness rather than kind of delving too far back, having said that there is one thing I've written this year which relates to changes in my attitude. I've written probably a page and a half on how I've done this dysfunctional scale recently and how . . . I remember reflecting on the fact that if I was to do a dysfunctional attitude scale when I was say 18, and compare it with one I've done fairly recently you'd have thought you were looking at two completely different characters, so huge chunks of myself have changed.
>
> (Wright 2005: 516)

The keeping of a journal as a barrier to reflection

While there may be many good reasons to keep a learning journal, there are also many barriers that can hinder the process. Rita Newton (1996) found that 'getting to grips' with reflective writing was a long and painful process. This is what she has to say:

> My initial difficulty was that it is not easy to just pick up a pen and to start writing. My background means that I deal with facts and figures and judgements are based on these, not on feelings or thoughts which you may just happen to have at the time. Writing about personal experience was profoundly difficult. Boud et al. (1993) suggest a possible reason for this in that the culture of academic and professional writing has always devalued personal experience in the 'quest for objectivity and generality'. So we can see two instant barriers that restrict personal writing, namely previous experience and the traditional nature of academic writing.
>
> I did find that once I overcame the initial barrier of putting pen to paper, I struggled further because I did not have a focus. I was so used to someone telling me what to write about that I felt as though I was writing about nothing – I could not cope with this literary freedom. Also I struggled with the time management skills required in writing a journal – the heart was half willing but the time management was weak! I continued discussing my difficulties with the Set members.
>
> . . . *Jayne commented on the amount of 'reflecting in the mind' which I had done. She said that it was far in excess of the reflecting that she had*

done, despite the fact that she had written a journal for that week . . . We agreed that perhaps I thoroughly participated in the process of reflection and probably enjoyed and benefited from it. Perhaps what I was sceptical about was the process of journal writing. (Journal entry from Action Learning Set on Reflection, Week 4, 1994)

This proved a major breakthrough in my attempts to overcome my internal barriers to reflection, and it was an external source which had assisted in the process. By forcing myself to keep a journal which I disliked, on a subject I disliked, I found that it was not the subject at all that was at the centre of my aversion, but the process of journal writing itself. Walker (1985) refers to one of his students who had made a poignant comment when filling in an evaluation form,

but I also thought it [keeping a journal] was a scary experience as I pushed away the overcoat of defences that had kept a lot of strong feelings or hard thoughts at bay. Working through this was hard, damned hard at times.

(Newton 1996: 144)

To the obstacles identified by Newton (1996) may be added fear of negative evaluation resulting from open-ended writing requirements, privacy issues and the hierarchical role positions of supervisor and supervisee in educational contexts. Willingness and ability to write reflectively has been shown to be affected by the developmental level of the supervisee, perception of the trustworthiness of the supervisor, clarity and nature of the expectations regarding the journal and the quality of the feedback from the supervisor (Kerka 1996).

Newton (1996) suggests that barriers to writing reflective journals are often attributable to factors internal to the learner, but with work they can be overcome. In order to do so the following conditions may help:

- Recognition, acknowledgement and identification of the barriers.
- Gaining clarity about the task and its purposes.
- Finding a focus and/or structure within which to write.
- Making a commitment to overcome barriers, possibly through learning together with others in a group.
- Working with effective facilitators who are able to create conditions in which authentic dialogue, support and challenge can occur.

There is one more barrier to reflective writing that I have encountered and this concerns the first languages of the writer and reader. If supervisees are to draw on their reflective writing in order to illustrate coursework assignments, this is complicated without a common first language. In my experience, students for whom English was a second language offered to provide a translation of their first-language writing, acknowledging that some meaning would be lost or distorted in translation. This meant that the task became more demanding than for students for whom English was their first language. A related issue is described by Harris (2008), whose South African students found ease of expression in English very challenging.

In a study of Hong Kong Chinese, supervisees tended to take the view that the supervisor was responsible for decision-making, and often became frustrated if no clear instructions were given. The authors argued that the Chinese attitude towards hierarchical relationships and the practice of subordination to authority influenced the supervisor–supervisee relationship (Tsui et al. 2005). Tamara Brown et al. (2006) drew attention to the difference between 'low context' cultures in which communication tends to be informal and direct, relying less on non-verbal communication than 'high context' cultures in which communication is more relational and contemplative. Miscommunication is easy when supervisor and supervisee are used to contrasting forms of talking and writing.

Types of learning journals

PRIVATE RECORDS

Learning journals written as a personal aid to thinking and critical reflection can be completed as a private exercise. Varying degrees of structure are possible. Musings committed to the page can help me to know more about what I feel and think. The material included can be unbounded since no one else will see the document. When used in this way, I, the author, need to see the exercise as useful and worthy of the time commitment involved. In their study Snadden et al. (1996) found some resistance to the idea of reflective writing even though the journals served no formal assessment purpose. The enthusiasm of educators was essential to engaging the commitment of learners. These kinds of journals can be used for self-evaluation and for reviewing progress. While private, this type of journal could be regarded as interactive since authors conduct a dialogue with themselves, taking the role of both learner and educator.

INTERACTIVE JOURNALS

Journals can be used interactively between supervisees and supervisors and/or between peers. The interaction may be through exchanged written comments, or supervisees may use their journals to inform their verbal contributions to the next supervision session. This kind of journal has also been described as 'conversing in writing' (Drevdahl and Dorcy 2002). Such journals are regarded as lending themselves to conversations via the Internet through email, focused chat rooms (Jasper 2004) and instant messaging. Journalling sites such as 'Blogger' have been used (Stiler and Philleo 2003) with a view to trying to ameliorate some students' frustration with the com-position process in a more traditional format. The medium may encourage the adoption of a more casual voice than would a formal assignment. The availability of online diaries and websites, and their openness to worldwide feedback in response to posts suggests that people can be comfortable with this medium. The site designer is able to decide who will be given permission to view or make comments on the postings.

When used interactively and when both parties write in the journal, the contributions may be very influential each upon the other. Margaret Roberts (1989) reports the use of learning logs by student teachers with school children. Analysis of the entries made by the pupils showed three categories of response: 'descriptive' – statements of what had happened in the lesson; 'evaluative' – in which judgements were made about aspects of the lesson; and 'reflective' – in which the pupils explored their ideas. Initial results were disappointing in that very few pupils used the latter category, rarely recorded any of their thinking and almost never used them to explore their thinking further. An analysis of the teacher's contributions produced the categories 'evaluative positive', 'evaluative negative', 'questions', 'expressing feelings' and 'replying to an entry'. Within these categories the evaluative dominated. Following the analysis the teacher changed his contributions so that the cat-egory of 'questions' dominated. Subsequently some of the questions were answered briefly by pupils in their journals, some were discussed orally, and the questions generally were regarded as opening up the pupils' thinking. From this point the journals were seen as being more communicative, as including more reflection and argument, and of more use to both student and student teacher.

In a post-registration nurse training context in South Africa, Maureen Harris (2008) gives an account of the introduction of an interactive learning journal. She described how students found reflective writing difficult, and although they were willing to accept its value and engage in the process, they benefited from a regular, specific and sensitive critical response from their writer-responder and follow-up supportive contact. Self-evaluation for the purposes of 'owning' their own ideas was also difficult, and required ongoing support and validation. Questions in journals were answered with further questions to encourage students to think more deeply and, where possible, to encourage them to make connections between concepts. Reflec-tions were treated as thoughts that would benefit from further development and elaboration.

In this study guidance was provided not only for the students in order to complete their journals, but also for the responders:

- This is a personal experience. The relationship between the student and the writer-responder needs to be assessed by the student. Students are to share only what they feel safe about sharing and are free to question or challenge the role of the writer-responder within the terms of reference.

- The role of the writer-responder is not that of an evaluator, but rather to guide, promote and challenge critical reflective thinking.
- Confidentiality between student and writer-responder will be maintained.
- The journals remain private between student and writer-responder [and moderator]. Students, however, are encouraged to share and discuss chosen entries with peers in class or tutorials.
- The focus of the response will be on the process and not on the content per se.
- The response will be non-judgemental and focus on supporting, motivating and guiding student reflections and critical thinking. Students may question any evidence to the contrary.
- The writer-responder will accept the student's entry as 'their truth' and will read all entries for the purpose of supporting critical reflective thinking.
- In the reflective section, the student is encouraged to write using 'her own voice' and style. The purpose is to focus on the thinking process and not the academic merit of the writing per se. Therefore, writing style will not be corrected.
- The writer-responder will undertake to respond with timeliness and respect to each student.
- The writer-responder will be conscious of the ethical nature of the engagement and will not penalise students in any way for weaknesses or lapses shared in the reflections.

(Harris 2008: 318)

Despite the above guidance, responses were perceived in different ways according to the quality of the relationship that had been established between students and responders. Students who had established a safe relationship with their writer-responder through shared expectations were enabled to describe and critically examine a situation, respond to questions about the motive behind actions, seek alternatives to what happened and by reflecting on the situation, learn from it and so grow in knowledge. Other students questioned the authority or value of the 'faceless' writer- responder and felt misunderstood: 'She always criticise but not correct you. She don't criticise in a positive way/constructive way. She don't care' (Harris 2008: 324). The lack of personal contact allows the journal writer to create an imaginary responder who may be regarded as insensitive to the learning needs of the writer. If this is the case when the task is explicitly not about assessment, how much more of a dominant role may the reader play when assessment is at issue?

Julie Hughes, a teacher educator reported in Bolton (2005: 177), engaged in journal dialogue with all new teachers individually from induction. Early in the course, some group members were uncomfortable with in-depth self-disclosure and self-analysis, particularly when this was in written form. Hughes responded to journals with comments, questions, thoughts, supportive statements and disclosures written in the margins, in the text and at the end of the entries. All of the dialogue was hand-written, personal and dated, sometimes with different coloured gel pens, stickers and illustrative sketches. She reported that this led to the emergence of a sense of expectancy and trust such that in the second semester students were excited about sharing their journals with each other. The students tended to follow the example modelled by the tutor and this led to 'dynamic conflict and contestations' and growing self-awareness. Hughes concluded that sensitivity is vital to encourage honest reflection and risk-taking for all dialogue turn-takers.

Drevdahl and Dorcy (2002) similarly emphasise the importance of trust between the parties contributing to an interactive journal, in this case concerning the processes experienced in group work. They highlight the need for students' thoughts and journal entries to be respected and kept confidential. The educator is regarded as a co-traveller who is slightly removed from the group: a mentor who can facilitate from the position of a more experienced traveller. The journals are treated as private conversations between student and faculty members. They are used both to encourage and challenge. The authors state, 'Even students with extensive group practice invariably gain new insights about themselves and about how to work in partnership with others. Nearly every student mentions the importance of paying more attention to group processes' (Drevdahl and Dorcy 2002: 257). One student wrote:

> Some things I learned were very life changing to me. The main item that I learned . . . is that I need to believe in myself more. I have good qualities and need to recognize these and not devalue myself for qualities that yet need to be developed . . . making mistakes does not make me less of a person, rather they are learning opportunities for me.
>
> (Drevdahl and Dorcy 2002: 258)

Interactive journals offer opportunities for learning and development of both writer and reader. Providing personalised feedback on journals in the context of trusting relationships with educators was found by Spalding and Wilson (2002) to be the most important strategy in promoting reflective thinking and in encouraging growth. Reflection upon the process of supervision itself might be included in an interactive journal, and enable the supervisor to learn more about what is helpful and what is unhelpful to the supervisee. But, if I am to show my reflective writing to my supervisors I need to know that they are trustworthy. I want them to model openness through their own preparedness to reflect, to write about their confusions and uncertainties and to ask questions about the usefulness of their interventions.

Guidance for writing a reflective journal

Authors vary in their opinions regarding the amount of guidance that best facilitates the keeping of a learning journal. Sarah Burns (1994) found that students wanted guidelines but educators showed some reluctance to provide these, fearing they may lead to a uniformity that suppresses the student's own approach. A specific structure was seen as a definite disadvantage by some students who were training as counsellors (Daniels and Feltham 2004). On the other hand, Jennifer Moon (2006) notes that many students struggle to warm to free writing. She suggests asking appropriate focused questions, designed to connect academic texts with explorations of professional practice. These might be based on the structures discussed in Chapter 2. The author of the following piece was a student who initially struggled with the open-ended task of writing for oneself:

> For me, in beginning a reflective learning journal, I had to make a conscious effort to recognise my own learning experiences; to make a normally subconscious process much more deliberate. My initial reaction to the task of writing a reflective learning journal was 'Blast!' Well, perhaps that wasn't the exact word that I used but it was certainly a curse of some sort. I was overwhelmed by the thought that reflecting upon all my learning experiences and matching these to theory would be a chore, would be time consuming. I didn't recognise it as a beneficial piece of work.
>
> My feelings towards a reflective learning journal were in themselves a developing process. When I began writing the first few entries into the journal my feelings were a confused mixture. I could not determine whether reflecting upon my learning felt a natural process that I went through on an everyday basis but was now putting onto paper or whether it was a forced process that I was adhering to as a requirement of the course. I think at the outset I was forcing myself to think about my learning in a way I had not knowingly done before.
>
> (Christey 2006)

Moon (2006) argues for the place of both structured and free-writing approaches. Free writing allows the journal to act as a 'friend', somewhere uninhibitedly to vent feelings, express enthusiasm, and to park dilemmas and difficulties while continuing to try and sort them out. Structured journals can help writers to get started, to make sense of experiences and support practice. A highly structured variant is Ira Progoff's (1992) 'intensive journal' which comprises multiple sections with recommended methods for its completion. Sections include the Daily Log, Stepping Stones, which are the meaningful transitions in our lives from birth onwards, and Intersections, which involve the roads not taken and their effects on our subsequent life paths. Other sections allow recording of dreams, meditations and dialogues with people, our bodies, society, and with events and circumstances. Progoff (1992) saw journalling as a way to create expressions of the human spirit and for individuals to gain awareness of the meanings of life. The intensive journaling process is specifically non-analytic in approach. Progoff (1992) argues that it is particularly valuable when people focus on particular areas of experience at a critical time in their lives. The impact results from the process of journal completion itself, which is supported by the highly specific structure.

Jasper (2003) suggests a structure based on topic headings such as a reflective write-up of each day, a reflective review of learning from practice encounters, specific critical incident analyses, planning for the future and responses to activities designed to encourage reflection. Bolton (2005) lists a range of suitable subjects including the relative status of therapist–client, physician–patient and supervisor–student; the effect of such hierarchies on work; the balance of responsibility between practitioners and the propensity for related feelings of shame or guilt; progress with personal objectives; the effects of the forces of anger, compassion, denial, conflict, and uncertainty; and changes and developments in professional practice.

Margaret Roberts' (1989) headings include comments on ideas that seem useful; comments on ideas that you would like to try out for yourself; any confusion or puzzlement; ideas that emerge spontaneously; what most helpfully prompted ideas; comments on what you have found irrelevant, impractical or demotivating; details of what you found difficult to understand or do; fears, hopes and anxieties; successes and what pleased you.

The journals used by Roberts (1989) in initial teacher education were a course requirement but were not formally assessed. In my view, where the journal is assessed, supervisees are likely to develop more confidence in writing about their doubts and confusions once they have experienced the style in which the supervisor responds to their writing. A manner of response which encourages further reflection and questioning, rather than making judgements about the content of the journal, is desirable.

Formats

A variety of formats for writing a reflective journal has been proposed. Bolton (2005) suggests that the journal is best regarded as a prized possession and pleasurable investment. She keeps a loose-leaf folder which can hold all shapes and sizes of material from A4 sheets to newspaper cuttings and back-of-the-envelope jottings. Some authors suggest a physical structure for the journal such as starting a new page for each entry and using one page for a description with the facing page for reflective analysis (Berthoff 1978; Jasper 2003). It is argued that this double entry approach is useful because it allows space to record continued reflections that later follow the initial experience (Heath 1998).

Another option is to adopt three headings of 'Description', 'Reflection' and 'Action'. This is proposed by Woodward (1998), who suggests that journal authors note something, reflect on it and then propose action in order to give added purpose to the reflection. Woodward (1998) sees it as essential that the requirement to propose action does not drive the entries to the journal.

Jasper (2004) describes the double entry approach as 'the open-page technique'. Alternatives include adopting a framework which can be used to demonstrate learning outcomes. This might involve ruling columns or spacing out headings. Sections of a journal can address focused topic areas. This might be aided by the use of file dividers.

A major consideration is whether the journal is completely private or to be shared. If it is to be kept for the purpose of completing formal assignments, guidance is likely to be issued by tutors. I see sharing as a possible constraint which might usefully be addressed by a loose-leaf format. This would allow the submission of parts of the journal and the retention of privacy for material felt to be inappropriate for the eyes of others.

Summary

In conclusion, engagement in a process of reflective writing has been shown to contribute to the development of 'a deeper sense of knowing' (Bennett-Levy et al. 2003: 145). The success of such a venture relies on the enthusiasm of supervisors and may benefit from their participation with the supervisee in an interactive writing process. Journal entries that are freely, self-critically or spontaneously written are most likely to result in new insights. If we are lucky and we have created a safe and trusting relationship with the supervisee, we may have the privilege of such writing being shared.

> Small marks on paper, the 'little bugs' that baffled Tarzan in Edgar Rice Burroughs' classic story (1912), have the most extraordinary power to move us. Within a few lines of a well written piece of fiction these small black imprints on paper can lead us rapidly to imagine whole worlds, and even be concerned about imaginary characters and what might happen to them. The magic is no less in the reading than in the writing . . . But the written word on paper has a status, autonomy and visible accessibility of its own; you can go back to it. Yet there is also something tentative and provisional about it.
>
> Writing, then, is different. It isn't freeze-dried speech, but something else.
>
> (Steinberg 2004: 47)

Chapter 10

Assessment of reflective practice and the supervisor's role in coursework assignments

This chapter has two main sections; the first is addressed to the assessment of reflective practice and the second to the supervisor's role in relation to supervisees' coursework assignments.

Assessment of reflective practice

> Tell me how you will measure me and I will tell you how I behave.
>
> (Goldratt 1997: 109)

I hope that this book so far has shown that critical reflection can be a powerful means for enabling practitioners, irrespective of their level of experience, to learn and develop their knowledge and skills through a reflective process capable of revealing implicit values, beliefs and cultural assumptions that may otherwise go unseen and unchallenged, and that supervisors can have a significant role to play in this process. However, can the skill of reflecting on practice be an intended and assessed learning outcome of formal education, while allowing learners the freedom to engage in a genuine and authentic reflective process? David Boud (2001) argues that the usual conventions of assessment demand that people display their best work. He advocates the separation of writing for learning and writing for assessment because purpose constrains form. The imperative to do well academically may discourage students from engaging in honest and open reflection (J. Hargreaves 2004; Snadden et al. 1996). There is an argument that reflection has no place in assessed written work (Rai 2006).

For supervisors, it is supervisees' practice that is at issue. How they represent their practice in their coursework is a different but related matter. The fieldwork supervisor may both support supervisees in developing their reflective practice and help them to represent this in their coursework assignments. I have felt a vested interest in supervisee assignments both in terms of ensuring that they reflect the knowledge and skills that I have observed in practice, and because they are, to some extent, a reflection on my own skills as a supervisor. I want the assignments to achieve a pass mark and in this spirit have insisted on seeing and responding to written assignments prior to sub-mission. This has sometimes proved a challenge to supervisees who prefer to work 'just in time' to deadlines.

Reflection is about exploration, understanding, questioning, probing dis-crepancies and examining what can be very personal material. 'There is always a danger that assessment will obliterate the very practices of reflection which courses aim to promote' (Boud 1999: 123). Other authors also suggest that assessment of reflective practice constrains the process (V. Hobbs 2007; J. Roberts 1998; Pecheone et al. 2005; K. Smith and Lev-Ari 2005). Handing in honest writing about inner thoughts and feelings may be construed as danger-ous. Four out of the six interviewees in a study by Jeannie Wright (2005) had previously kept a learning journal. Views about having to hand in the reflective writing varied over time. The same student said: 'it's like giving away a bit of me; I wanted it back as soon as I'd handed it in' and later in the course:

> I don't know how difficult other people find it to write about their per-sonal things, because I'm aware the first one I wrote, I was much less honest about my feelings. I didn't say things that I might have said or I said them in a kind of coded abbreviated form 'cause I thought some-body else is going to read this and I don't want them to read everything about me. But as I went on through the year it seemed to matter less that somebody else was reading and mattered more to me to get down a complete and accurate description of the way I felt.
>
> (Wright 2005: 514)

At times I have had great difficulty as a supervisor in persuading supervisees that I regard 'mistakes', uncertain or imperfect practice as inevitable and that my interest lies in their capability to learn by identifying their own points for development. How much more difficult it may be to persuade supervisees of the value of putting these in writing and submitting them to a supervisor or tutor, particularly a faceless assessor who may determine their right to prac-tise. Writing in order to produce what the imagined assessor wants may be particularly salient for students from minority groups. Students in a study by Lillis (2001) felt the need to disguise their Black bilingual selves because of the risk they experienced in revealing themselves both in terms of anticipated marks and how they expected to be viewed by the tutor.

Valerie Hobbs (2007) argues that when students are asked to reflect on their strengths and weaknesses as part of a required, graded course assignment, it seems that genuine examination of self is already a lost cause. It means going against the instinct to accentuate strengths when being assessed. A dilemma for course tutors and supervisors is that professional training courses now frequently demand the demonstration of reflective practice (National Occu-pational Standards, undated). If this is to be accomplished through written work it has been argued that the writing will need to demonstrate academic rigour while not necessarily being consistent with established conventions of academic writing (Rai 2006). How can written tasks involving summative assessment of students' developing ability to reflect on their practice avoid penalising them for exposing doubtful practice? What guidance can be provided that will encourage exploration, uncertain understanding, questioning, and probing of discrepancies? Are the requirements of reflective practice compatible with formal assessment?

The issue of extrinsic and intrinsic motivation

By definition, reflective practice is reliant upon self-motivation. If it were dependent on extrinsic motivation (passing examinations), professional practitioners would be like the radiography student cited at the beginning of this book who managed to 'pass' reflective practice but did not understand what it was about and gave up worrying about it at the earliest opportunity on qualification. Learners who are motivated by interest and satisfaction associated with the learning process itself (intrinsic motivation) are more likely to take responsibility for their own learning as a lifelong process. 'High stakes testing' – when the results of summative assessment have important consequences for learners – has been shown to have a number of negative consequences. These include lowering the self-esteem of students with relatively poor attainments, increasing student anxiety and encouraging teachers to take a 'transmission' or 'telling' approach to teaching (Harlen 2003). Research in schools has shown that students not only judge the quality of their work by the grades that they are awarded, but that this influences how they judge their own worth as people (Leonard and Davey 2001; Reay and Wiliam 1999). Thus individuals may bring to supervision a long history of experience and implicit values about education and assessment that are incompatible with the central tenets of reflective practice. In the worst case, summative assessment may have trapped some students in, 'the vise of a self-fulfilling prophecy of failure' (Bloom et al. 1971: 88). Having said all that, I have also found that when particular aspects of a course are not formally assessed, students tend not to take them seriously. Crème (2005) argues that what is assessed sends signals to students about what teachers believe is important and Graham Gibbs (1999: 41) says, 'Assessment is the most powerful lever teachers have to influence the way students respond to courses and behave as learners'.

Considering whether assessment and reflective practice can be, albeit uneasy, bedfellows leads me to a discussion of the purposes of assessment.

Purposes of assessment

My experience of pre-registration students suggests that there is often an understandable preoccupation with passing the placement with me, passing the course, passing assignments and obtaining high grades. This may be peculiar to my profession. I have also encountered an attitude of, 'What is the minimum that I need to do in order to pass the course?' If the latter view leaves more space for greater experimentation and the development of learning for understanding within the discipline then I thoroughly approve. I have been hard pressed to convince students of this though.

Diagnostic assessment

Assessment has multiple possible purposes. First of all, as a supervisor or teacher I need to gain a perspective on the current knowledge and skills of supervisees. This is often known as 'diagnostic' assessment although I would prefer the term 'formulatory' since it implies less certainty and multiple hypotheses about the state of current knowledge. This purpose is for my benefit as a supervisor, in order to inform the process of designing a suitable learning environment and learning experiences. Diagnostic assessment operates through an attitude of curiosity, and 'attunedness' on the part of the supervisor to the supervisee's inferred knowledge and ways of learning. In practice this requires the supervisor to explore the supervisee's current knowledge through conversation, through reference to intended learning outcomes, observation and discussion of the supervisee's practice and so on. It is not an easy process in my experience because the questions I ask can too often seem like interrogations designed to find out how the supervisee's knowledge is wanting.

A second purpose of assessment that benefits the supervisor is that of finding out if my supervision strategies are being successful in bringing about desired learning. This could be learning desired by the supervisee and/or the intended learning outcomes for a course leading to qualification. Diagnostic assessment may lead me to revise my supervisory strategies and methods, and the learning aims for this supervisee. Otherwise, I am reliant on habit and guesswork. My habitual ways of working may not suit this individual. If I fail to take account of the supervisee's specific learning needs we are unlikely to enjoy a productive time together.

Effective teachers emerged from a study by John Hattie (2009) as highly dedicated people who continuously sought feedback from their students in order to improve their teaching. They also made their ideas, goals and their approaches to assessment open to students, including their own uncertainties and errors, thus serving as a model to their students. The classrooms that they managed were crucibles in which students could feel safe to make mistakes and learn from, rather than be punished for them. This was no small scale study: it involved an analysis of 800 meta-analyses of 50,000 studies relating to achievement. What emerged was a crucial orientation towards diagnostic and self-assessment in which effective teachers modelled effective reflective practice. This finding is congruent with innovations in approaches to assessment which have derived from a holistic view whereby assessment is integrated with an overall approach to learning and teaching (McDowell and Sambell 1999).

Formative assessment

When the purpose of assessment is to encourage supervisee learning and development, it is typically know as 'formative' assessment, also known as 'assessment *for* learning' (AfL) which contrasts with 'assessment *of* learning'. Sandra Murphy and Mary Ann Smith (1991), in a discussion of the use of portfolios for teaching and learning, listed the following as examples of the aims of formative assessment:

- To motivate and empower students, encouraging a sense of ownership and accomplishment.
- To help students to learn how to evaluate their own progress and to assess their own learning and growth.
- To allow students to identify and document skills and knowledge acquired through life experiences.
- To encourage a process of systematic analysis through ongoing review and revision of work.
- To examine reflective practice as a process.
- To provide an avenue for reflection and the setting of personal goals.
- To provide a focus for conferring with students about their reflective skills.

There is extensive research evidence documenting the benefits of formative assessment in improving learning, particularly when formative feedback is given at a time that students can respond to it by improving their work (Black and Wiliam 1998; Harlen 2009). Despite overwhelming evidence for the benefits of formative assessment, it has been argued that responding to this message presents a major challenge for higher education, given an increasing concern with attainment standards, increasing student/staff ratios, greater unitisation of curricula and the demands on staff to be research active and generate funding (Yorke 2003).

Studies show that feedback in the form of comments rather than grades or marks has a greater positive effect on student achievement and interest (R. Butler 1988; Scaife and Wellington 2008). The key features of assessment that promote learning have been described by the Assessment Reform Group (1999):

- It is embedded in a view of teaching and learning of which it is an essential part.
- It involves sharing learning goals with students.
- It aims to help students to know and recognise the standards they are aiming for.

- It involves students in self-assessment.
- It provides feedback that leads to students recognising their next steps and how to take them.
- It is underpinned by confidence that every student can improve and involves both teacher and student reviewing and reflecting on assessment data.

(Assessment Reform Group 1999: 7)

The final point in the list emphasises the affective – that assessment for learning involves how teachers and learners feel, and values – that formative assessment is underpinned by a belief in the possibility of improvement. Feelings and values are legitimate foci of assessment when learning is at stake. Because self-esteem is involved there is a need for care in providing formative feedback, not only because feelings can be hurt but also because the pre-existing level of self-esteem is thought to condition how supervisees will receive the feedback (Young 2000). Formative assessment can be particularly salient in the development of skills in reflective practice because the supervisor can have a significant role in sensitively orienting the supervisee to matters that would benefit from thoughtful analysis and to useful methods for tackling these. Recursive cycles in which supervisees respond to formative assessment with revisions to their work have led to a reconceptualisation of 'feedback' as 'feedforward' (Hounsell 2007).

There are many possible approaches to formative assessment. Supervisees will have their own views about how they are progressing and self-assessment is at the heart not only of reflective practice but also of developing and maintaining competence (Falender and Shafranske 2007). These authors drew attention to the notion of meta-competence; the use of available skills and knowledge to solve problems or tasks and to determine which skills or knowledge are missing, how to acquire these, and whether they are essential to success. Meta-competence is dependent on self-reflection and self-awareness (Weinert 2001) and is achieved through self-assessment. 'Learning to learn, or the development of learning power, is getting better at knowing when, how and what to do when you don't know what to do' (Claxton 1999: 11).

SELF-ASSESSMENT

Self-assessment involves learners in asking themselves questions and making judgements about their own work. I see it as a relatively informal and frequent experience that takes place spontaneously across life domains. I find myself constantly self-assessing not only in formal academic or practice settings but also around day-to-day issues such as how much seasoning to put in the soup, whether the email I just sent could be misinterpreted, how angry it is reasonable for me to feel about my missing luggage, whether my spontaneously given hug was suited to the circumstance, whether jumping the amber light was wise. The process is often rapid or else it would impede me in acting. 'Drawing on our intuition we do what feels right. It is an emotional response that complements our knowledge and what we understand about a subject, and which enables us to act in a situation' (UK Centre for Legal Education 2008: 1). I am an individual knower, the only person who can make these personal connections, drawing on and questioning what I know already and working out how to think and act now and in the future.

The kind of assessment often discussed in formal texts under the heading of self-assessment is summative; in one variant, students might be invited to grade their own work (Race 2001). Phil Race (2001) argues that self-assessment has many advantages and in particular can deepen students' learning experiences by helping them link their work to intended learning outcomes and by 'applying assessment criteria themselves on their own evidence' (Race 2001: 6). He notes that when tutors also assess the work and the grade given is lower than that awarded by students themselves, there is a risk of them losing faith in the value of the exercise. I agree that this is a risk and I am not convinced that self-*grading* is a reliable method for achieving the purpose of enhancing learning.

It has been argued that 'all acts of assessment, whether by teachers, subject matter experts, peers or the individual learner, involve these two stages: establishing criteria and judging work in the light of them' (Boud 1995: 12). For many purposes I agree, but since I also believe that self-assessment is implicit in most of what we do, as a supervisor I can encourage supervisees to verbalise some of this internal dialogue. Guy Claxton (1999) argues that opening up a dialogue about the nature of quality in their work enables students better to monitor and manage their own learning and that this is of crucial importance where professional judgement is the key to good practice.

Standards or desired learning outcomes in the domain of reflective practice tend to be specified in broad terms. For example the British Psychological Society demands that clinical psychology trainees demonstrate 'high level skills in managing a personal learning agenda and self-care, and in critical reflection and self-awareness that enable transfer of knowledge and skills to new settings and problems' (British Psychological Society 2008). This does allow free rein to supervisors and supervisees regarding the design of more specific criteria that would satisfy them both about the capability to engage in reflective practice, or to use a more intuitive and informal approach to assessment in regard to this broad criterion.

Even in formal academic settings and subjects, it has been shown that performance is enhanced through individuals and their peers taking an active part in the assessment process. In a review of the impact of self-assessment and peer assessment on students in secondary schools, Sebba et al. (2008) reported positive outcomes in terms of improved attainment, enhanced self-esteem and improved 'learning to learn'. The classroom culture was an important variable with the teacher needing to be committed to learners having control over the assessment process, and to involving students in co-designing assessment criteria. I would argue that supervisors are well placed to encourage such forms through the use of methods described in earlier chapters.

PEER ASSESSMENT

It has been said that 'Students can learn a great deal about their own attempt at a task by assessing two or three other students' attempts at the same task' (Race 2001: 6). The learning derives from a comparison of their own judgements with those of fellow students. However, David Boud (1995) cautions that the process of comparison needs careful design in order to avoid the generation of defensiveness. He suggests that:

> when peer assessment is used to provide rich and detailed comments from other students about their reaction to the presentation, then students may be more able to take this, along with their own perceptions and whatever other information is available, and form a judgement that will influence future learning, rather than having to defend themselves and assess the validity of judgements from others which may not be supported by information and which allow for no opportunity to respond.
>
> (Boud 1995: 16)

Boud criticises the use of peer marking which can undermine group cooperation and focus away from the purpose of assessment for learning. I agree with him that it is only the learners themselves who will decide what to do with feedback and with their marks. All the grades in the world will only make an impact on learning if the learner so chooses.

I think that peer assessment needs very cautious and careful handling if it is to serve the function of enhancing learning. One approach is through limitation to descriptive rather than prescriptive feedback. This still involves assessment. Osterman and Kottkamp (1993) propose what they term 'I-messages' which connect a description with a feeling and consequences. These can be used to address issues about which the assessor feels critical. They illustrate I-messages with the example of a parent conveying to a child with an untidy room (description) the health hazard that may arise from the presence of unwashed dishes (consequence). As a result of the health hazard, the parent feels upset (feeling). These authors also advocate the use of active listening and of non-judgemental, non-critical, accepting and supporting questions. Later in this chapter I give some examples of the kinds of responses that might be given by peers or supervisors with the aim of enhancing learning.

SUPERVISOR ASSESSMENT

What can a supervisor usefully do through formative assessment to encourage the development of critically reflective skills? Modelling reflection of my own practice seems like a good starting point, showing that formative assessment through questioning is a lifelong process. I have written previously about the use of constructive challenge as a way to foster development and growth through an invitation to test one's capabilities to the full (Scaife 2009). Supervisors can motivate supervisees to take their learning forward and to gain in confidence. Feedback from clients, colleagues, managers and tutors can undermine confidence. A focus on what a supervisee *can* do provides affirmation and combats downheartedness. While a supervisor's identification and naming of strengths may offer a boost to confidence, prompts that encourage supervisees to engage in this process for themselves may foster a lifelong professional orientation more fitting with the idea of reflective practice. If the aim is to encourage noticing growth over time, it would be appropriate to reflect on examples of practice over a timescale – from the beginning to the end of a placement or practicum, to focus on initial approaches to the work and later revisions. A written record such as an informal journal can be reviewed together for evidence of progress. The focus may be not only on the products of reflection in terms of impact on practice, but also on progress in developing the process of reflection itself.

I regard self-assessment, peer assessment, diagnostic and formative assessment as having much to offer in encouraging the development of reflective practitioners. Supervisors are in a key position to encourage and model self-assessment and peer assessment. There is much to be said for supervisors sharing with supervisees their reflections on the assessment process itself and the issues and dilemmas with which they are faced, particularly when making a final judgement in the role of gatekeeper to the profession.

Summative assessment

Examiner

The routine trickery of the examination
Baffles these hot and discouraged youths.
Driven by they know not what external pressure
They pour their hated self-analysis
Through the nib of confession, onto the accusatory page.

I, who have plotted their immediate downfall,
I am entrusted with the divine categories,
ABCD and the hell of E,
The parade of prize and the backdoor of pass.

(F.R. Scott (1899–1985) 1966)

> I hate the moment when papers are passed back. I hate getting the dreaded C. I always get Cs.
>
> (Murphy and Smith 1991: 10)

Particularly in training contexts, supervisors are required to make summative judgements about a practitioner's competence, and this will usually include the skills of reflective practice as specified (either explicitly and/or implied) by professional licensing bodies and institutions of higher education. I continually struggle with some of the issues concerning summative assessment and I am not alone. What follows are some of those that vex me.

Issues in the summative assessment of reflective practice

Content and process

Engaging in reflective practice is a process. While the outcome of the reflection will have important implications for practice, in my view it is the process which is central. The content of reflection is determined by the reflector. Practitioners may be able to describe frameworks for reflection, and in their reflection draw on relevant information and theories, but may it be possible to do so without having developed the qualities that define reflective practice? I have seen examples of assignments where facts and theories have been used to justify rather than reflect on practice.

The content of coursework assignments designed summatively to assess the skills of reflective practice is likely to be determined by supervisees themselves. It is unlikely that they will be given a standard question unless it is in a form that begins by inviting them to choose an example from their own practice. They could be invited to reflect on the description of a critical incident provided by a tutor or supervisor, but this would not demonstrate their capability to recognise examples from their own practice where there is no predefined set of instances.

I find assessing evidence of a process more challenging than assessing knowledge of facts. No easy box-ticking and crossing in such assignments. At least written assignments allow me to confer with colleagues when in doubt, but as a supervisor I am faced with assessment on the basis of unrecorded conversations that have often taken place one-to-one. It doesn't surprise me that there are no widely accepted methods of assessing reflective practice (Stewart and Richardson 2000).

Reflecting and writing about reflecting

Supervisors are in a key position to judge the reflective skills of supervisees as they are exemplified in clinical work and in verbal interchanges in supervision. Written accounts of reflection on practice and the practice itself are both presented in coursework assignments. I have experienced dilemmas in assessing this kind of assignment when the written account is of a high standard but the work described has serious flaws in terms of ethical or professional issues. The written account cannot be awarded a satisfactory grade because of the unsound practice it describes. In contrast, supervisees who are highly skilled at reflection may lack the capability adequately to demonstrate this in their written work. The supervisor can have a key role for such individuals both in validating their skills and in helping them to demonstrate their skill in their writing.

The issue of fairness

I doubt there would be much argument that assessment processes need to be fair and equitable and I have learned that this does not mean treating everybody the same. At the same time there is a need to justify decisions against standard formal criteria or requirements. The issue of fairness is encapsulated in formal requirements and in such processes as moderation of marking. Fairness is helped by transparency so that supervisees are aware of the matters that will be concerning me when I am assessing their practice, and by a continuous assessment process in which formative assessment has provided supervisees with information and ideas with which to develop their practice. Fairness can be of particular salience when cultural differences pertain. What adjustments am I to make when assessing the practice of supervisees of ethnicities, genders, ages, faiths and disabilities that differ from my own? Fleming (1999: 88) states, 'The greatest bias in marking comes from the "like me" effect'.

Although 'Birdy' in the following quote is not training as a practitioner, he is, from prison, undertaking a course of academic study in political ideology supported by his tutor Michael Lenney. I have included this as an example of the need for those engaged in supporting learners to be open to the impact of culture on the means of expression and the selected focus of reflections made by supervisees.

> I asked Birdy to reflect upon our first meeting, and to construct the image he had of me as an academic prior to our first meeting. Birdy writes:
> I have been socialized by prison officers and prisoners alike that most academics working in the system are egotistical wankers' (stet) who can't find their arses with both hands. Academics have been constantly portrayed as being people who journey through life with heads full of theories, which are not applicable to the reality of life, or at least, the harsh reality of prison life. My specific criticism of academics in general, however, is how can people who spend years at university studying areas like psychology, education and management then turn out to be so

insensitive, judgemental, inflexible, untrusting and act in ways that would seem to undermine the very fields of study that they have been trained in?

(Lenney 2006: 185)

Frame (2001) makes a case for the importance of raising supervisees' awareness of their own spiritual attitudes and faith beliefs. Differences in faith beliefs impact on assessment because strong faith-based opposition to matters such as abortion, homosexuality or contraception may make these 'no go' topics for reflection for the supervisor, supervisee or both parties. Effort may be needed to bring these commitments into the reflective practice arena and the supervisor may be faced with making a judgement about a student who refuses to work with clients who are facing one of these issues.

As Western universities extend their courses to a wider range of international students, teachers are challenged to respond to cultural expectations regarding education. In courses that require reflection on experience and the articulation of new insights with implications for practice, assignment requirements may be characterised by levels of ambiguity outside the experience of international students. This could be likened to being good at soccer and then suddenly required to play with an oval ball. Janet Sayers and Trish Franklin (2008) reported that large numbers of students increasingly sought help in understanding assignment requirements:

the spirit in which the tests are conducted (valuing both process and outcome) is increasingly being eclipsed by the need to perform and get the correct answer. A growing number of students appear to make little or no attempt to work with the questions on their own, identify the gaps in their knowledge, and seek understanding of how and why an answer is correct. Instead, there seems to be an expectation that other students will simply give them the answer. Additionally, when tests are marked in class, it is clear that answers have been altered.

(Sayers and Franklin 2008: 84)

In their article they describe how they have had to work hard in reflecting on course design in order to take account of these cultural differences while retaining the philosophy and spirit in which the course was conceived. How challenging is the balance between retention of the spirit of reflective practice while making reasonable adjustments that ensure equity when assessing the work of diverse student groups?

The issues of consistency between assessors and marking criteria

I share the experience of Martin Talbot (2002) in reading evaluation sheets completed by delegates after I have given talks or led workshops only to find that while the majority of them have usually given favourable ratings and comments, a few outliers have found the event unhelpful or my style not to their liking. These comments have a much greater impact on me than those of the delegates who expressed satisfaction. In Talbot's case he was described by two respondents as 'patronising' and 'condescending'. This set him off on the path of reflection. I find that there is a temptation to write off those who are 'out of line' but this is unlikely to lead to further learning and development. Talbot used the responses as a stimulus to critical reflection and argued that this had greater potential to enhance his teaching than would a process of mulling over the issue in a more leisurely and less purposeful fashion.

It is all very well for registered practitioners to have the luxury of reflecting on differences of view between assessors of our work, but I have known of supervisors losing sleep, ruminating on their capability fairly to assess the practice of supervisees. And supervisees have railed months later about what they regarded as unfair assessments made of their work by supervisors.

Even when there is the opportunity for collating the views of multiple assessors, there is no guarantee of consistency in the assessment process. The art work of twins entered for A levels with two different examination boards obtained grades of A from one and B and C from the other (Curtis et al. 2000). Grades awarded by different tutors to their tutorial groups showed very large disparities between assessors in a study reported by Fleming (1999). John awarded fifteen A+ grades (twenty-two students) with the lowest graded B. Jim awarded no A+ grades, four Cs and five Ds (twenty students). It has even been shown that a single examiner may award widely differing marks for the same essay when assessed at different times (Jones 1986). Despite huge amounts of institutional time and effort devoted to making assessment criteria explicit and 'objective' in order to assure quality and eliminate error, Peter Ovens (2003) found that his colleagues used a largely tacit process to assess students' work, the formal criteria being used post hoc for the purposes of justification. Similar findings were reported by Binch and Robertson (1994). I think that this approach is common, other than among staff new to the assessment role who are seeking guidance to assist them in an unfamiliar task. Ovens (2003) introduced a new kind of assessment, called Patchwork Texts, designed to challenge his students' image of science which he viewed as deeply rooted in assumptions about its authority, rationalism and certainty. A similar conclusion regarding detailed assessment criteria was reached by Murphy and Smith (1991) when introducing portfolios to replace more traditional assessment methods in the context of secondary school English teaching:

> during the first year we developed some marathon scoring systems for portfolios that left us with enough numbers to start a stock exchange, but not much else in the way of analysis or even satisfaction.
>
> (Murphy and Smith 1991: 8)

It is worth bearing in mind that every grade boundary is a site of potential contention. Error can be minimised and potential injustices avoided by using only one – pass and fail. As far as I can see, most if not all other functions of grades in professional education can be accomplished using qualitative feedback. The assessor is a proxy for the community of practice. My assessment is based on inference from what I observe. The inferences are mine which means that my own assessment practices are appropriately subjected to critical reflection which might involve consultation with the peers whom I represent.

One approach to the issue of assessment criteria is described by Kathryn Pavlovich (2007). Her aim was to learn more about how the course purpose might have changed student perceptions of who they were, why they were studying in the management school and what was their purpose. The final assignment was to respond to the question, 'How did you understand reflective practice at the beginning of the course and how do you understand it now?' The marking criteria were developed together with the students at the end of the semester with the aims of providing greater ownership, engaging with the assignment at a deeper level, and encouraging more reflection. The student-developed criteria were: exploration of individual learning process (journey of learning); process of learning; examples and applications (appropriateness and relevance); depth of probing of ideas; scope of content addressed (classes, readings, experiences); richness of engagement; and overall synthesis. Pavlovich (2007) struggled with the task of adapting her preconceptions of grading to the student-developed criteria. She experienced this as resulting in a highly qualitative process, the challenge being to justify a grade through a standardised format. She concluded that the criteria developed were well grounded in pedagogy, and that they enabled clear differentiation between students in terms of conceptualisation of their learning. Supervisors are in a good position to negotiate criteria for assessing reflective practice with their supervisees, ideally through the contracting process undertaken at the beginning of the placement, reviewed as the placement progresses.

The issue of levels of skill

Government and professional bodies and institutions of higher education generally specify intended learning outcomes or standards which must be achieved in order to gain professional status. Judgements are referred to these criteria rather than to a norm for a particular population. But are we to judge someone's average, best or worst performance against these criteria? What if the skill is demonstrable within one context but not in another; on one occasion but not on another? Because supervisors are not basing their judgements on a formally submitted assignment, these questions are particularly pertinent. I might be bowled over by the extent of reflection shown by a supervisee in relation to a specific issue, but amazed by her or his apparent lack of critical reflection in relation to another. I have also found that supervisees vary enormously in their starting knowledge and skills, even those at the same stage of their training or education. Some will be more skilled at the outset than will others at the completion of their course. For this reason I have tended to judge performance in relation to broader issues such as openness to learning and evidence of progress being made. I do have a baseline below which I would be too concerned to have the confidence to award a pass grade but within that I accept significant variation.

Criteria for summatively assessing reflective practice

The literature cited at the beginning of this chapter problematised the assessment of reflective practice and I also believe that there is a danger of suppressing the very qualities I wish to encourage by emphasising my summative role. In reality, in my profession, failure of a practice placement is a relatively rare event and by half-way through, unless supervisees engage in unethical or highly dangerous practice, they are going to pass. I have used this as a focus of discussion. What will you do in the rest of the placement that might be more experimental now that you know that you have already passed the placement? Postman and Weingartner (1971) advocate an express stance assuming from the outset that the student will pass the practicum since this opens the door more widely to using the experience for learning.

After raising all these issues, the reader may well ask, but where does that leave me in the task of assessing reflective practice? For a start the emphasis can be on self-assessment, self-identification of criteria by which to judge competence on this dimension, and formative assessment. After all, there is a question as to whether I have created the conditions and learning environment in which this supervisee has been able to develop as a reflective practitioner. At the same time I believe that it would be irresponsible to pretend to give up the supervisor role as gatekeeper. It would be dishonest to invite supervisees to self-assess their final 'mark' for their placement. Together we might challenge the assessment process and work to enhance the student's learning but the final judgement, however imperfect, is mine. When the award of a final grade is ostensibly handed over, there is a danger of being left to ask questions like, 'Do you really deserve the mark you have given yourself?' (R. Edwards 1989: 7) which for me is not really a question. How could students award themselves a grade that would exclude them from their chosen profession, lengthen the period of their training or otherwise lead to serious negative professional or economic consequences?

In deciding a final grade I would return to the characteristics of reflective practice described in the introductory chapter and ask myself if these have been shown during supervision. Tom Bourner (n.d.) states, 'Reflection is the process of turning experience into learning and that learning is *emergent* rather than *planned*. It is difficult to specify, *a priori*, planned learning outcomes for a process that yields emergent learning outcomes' (italics in original). He suggests a solution to the problem of assessing reflective learning by basing it on evidence of the capacity to interrogate experience with searching questions. Jeannie Wright (2005) offers some criteria which she uses to assess reflective journals:

- Demonstrating a further understanding and appreciation of self.
- Identifying personal strengths.
- Identifying personal blocks and blind spots and suggesting ways these may be overcome.
- Demonstrating an understanding of personal assumptions, values and beliefs and how they may influence their interactions with others.
- Demonstrating an awareness of cultural/gendered and socio-economic influences on their values attitudes and beliefs and suggesting ways to attempt to overcome their effect in practice.
- Demonstrating their ability to apply theory into the practice environment.

(Wright 2005: 509)

It seems to me that both holistic and analytical approaches are relevant to the assessment. I find it helpful to operate a 'bottom line' which is something like, 'Is this person skilled enough or open enough to learning that I would be happy for her or him to work with a loved one upon qualification?' While I regard this as a good starting point, there are dangers that I will be looking for someone to be just like me. The selection literature tells us that selection bias can easily lead to discrimination against those who are perfectly competent but not like me. The values of assessors inevitably play a part in their judgements so a system of checks and balances is also needed. What I trust is a holistic, self-critiqued, invariably subjective judgement weighed against others made independently by experienced members of the community of practice.

The supervisor's role in coursework assignments

This section is about the work of supervisees who are completing courses, either for registration purposes or as part of their continuing professional development. Supervisory help with coursework requirements is not usually mandated or disbarred, but I have often found myself approached for such help and in some cases my input has been required by the training course. Supervisors may also be tasked with providing work for supervisees that serves as material for their coursework.

Issues in regard to coursework assignments

Providing suitable experiences

Assignments set by courses with a view to illustrating reflective practice are likely to be based on the student's clinical experience. There is widespread reporting in the literature of the use of reflective journals and portfolios for such purposes. The supervisee may need to carry out a particular project or report on their experiences with clients. I have found that advance knowledge of such requirements allows me to forward plan. If we wait until the placement begins, it may be too late to obtain ethical approval or find suitable work. The supervisee needs to be alerted early if suitable work cannot be found so that alternative arrangements can be made by the course.

The supervisor's knowledge of the service, the nature of its policies and practices, and the supervisor's established relationships with staff can help to smooth the way for supervisees. Permission to carry out the work within the service may be needed. There may be a need for access to the employer's policy documents or data about the local population served. The supervisor is often in a good position to know key people from whom this can be obtained.

Confidentiality

Where assignments involve clients, students or services, supervisors and managers will have concerns regarding the confidentiality of material written up or of the sources from which information may be extracted. Employing organisations will have policies governing such matters. Although the educational institution will probably insist on the removal of all identifiers from work submitted for assignments, in my experience supervisees are not always adequately vigilant about this, and it is quite easy involuntarily to leave in an occasional name. Supervisees benefit from clarity about the supervisor's concerns and the employer's policies. I regard it as prudent for supervisors to read assignments prior to submission and this means setting a timely deadline that deters last-minute-ism.

Supervisors have a responsibility to safeguard participants. Published work requires informed consent and it is ethical and respectful to extend this requirement to coursework assignments that are going to sit on a shelf in a university. Informing clients and other participants may affect the way in which the work is written up and may constrain the nature of the writing or even the way in which the work is conducted. Liza Monaghan (personal communication, 2000) suggested to me that while clinical work shapes assignments, assignments may also shape the clinical work since the supervisee may have the write-up in mind during the work. Resolving the tension between offering a service to clients and meeting the students' needs for their coursework is an issue with which supervisors may need to engage (Evans 1997).

Obtaining informed consent may constrain the write-up of an assignment but not necessarily to its disadvantage. There are potentially creative ways of involving participants in writing about the work. In the context of a counselling relationship, Val Wosket (1999) agreed with a client that each would write up their own account of the sessions and these were used both to inform the work and for publication. Some clinicians write joint notes of sessions together with their clients and this method could be adapted for the purpose of a reflective practice assignment. In my experience these approaches are not always included in assignment guidelines.

The effects of the assignment on the tripartite arrangement

Coursework assignments represent a visible presence of the training institution in the fieldwork placement. This is likely to make a greater impact where the assignment draws on work carried out on the placement but can have an indirect effect even if the coursework is not connected with the practicum. The levels of energy that the supervisee brings to the practical work can be adversely affected by the demands of assignments, particularly as deadlines approach. Supervisors may experience themselves in a three-way relationship with the supervisee and the supervisee's assignments in which the supervisee's practice appears to have lowest priority. This can be frustrating and disappointing.

Ideally the demands of coursework assignments and the nature of the practical work dovetail but this is not necessarily the case. The potential for conflicts and irritations is likely to be lessened by exploration in supervision, possibly involving staff from the educational institution when resolution seems difficult. Supervisors do not want to feel that they are overburdening supervisees with practical work when assignments dominate because the spectre of course failure can loom large in the supervisee's consciousness.

The supervisee's coursework assignments have the capability to evoke memories of the supervisor's own professional education. Lack of confidence may encourage the supervisor to remain distant from the assignment for fear of providing misleading input or being unhelpful. Instead, this prior experience could be treated as material for reflection together with the supervisee on the impact of coursework requirements on practice and on confidence. Mutual denigration of the nature of the assignment is unlikely to benefit the supervisee's progress and development. Ideally, supervisors and course staff work together to create a coherent approach to supporting trainees' assignment work, rather than leaving students to sort out any incompatibilities themselves.

The potential for conflicting input

Supervisors' roles in relation to the practical work completed on the placement are usually much clearer than their role in coursework. In the former, the supervisor has defined responsibilities whereas in the latter, course staff are also likely to be involved and may be the 'official' supervisors of the work. Where more than one supervisor is involved in the same piece of work there is potential for conflicting input and advice, although this in itself may provide material for reflection providing it is not too confusing. Multiple consulting is a strategy sometimes adopted by supervisees experiencing anxiety about assignments. It can also lead to an implicit invitation to the supervisor to do the reflecting for them. In this case a focus on the anxiety may be a fruitful topic for reflection.

Types of coursework assignment adopted for the assessment of reflective practice

The literature abounds with examples of assignments designed for the purpose of summatively assessing reflective practice (Varner and Peck 2003). There has been recognition that conventional essays and projects are not suited to this purpose. Instead, learning journals, patchwork texts and portfolios have been developed as a way to allow greater freedom from the usual academic constraints of writing. Portfolios are a *selection* of student writing for a purpose (Murphy and Smith 1991: 8).

The development of journals (also logs and diaries) for the purpose of coursework assignments arose from the shift in higher education to the notion of authentic or performance assessment. This is intended to allow learners to demonstrate application of knowledge, skills and attitudes using situations that reflect or simulate actual life experience (Woodward 1998). Issues identified as arising from the use of journals for the purposes of summative assessment include the following:

- In order to encourage greater freedom to take risks and engage in meaningful reflection, it is helpful to create both a private and public version of reflection (Schutz et al. 2004).
- Portfolios contain a selection of pieces. 'The benefits of portfolios lie as much in the decision-making processes they initiate as in the range of products they contain' (Murphy and Smith 1991: 14).
- The selection of entries and justification of meeting the assessment criteria can be in the hands of the author.
- Evidence of reflection is encouraged by the application of broad assessment criteria which may be constructed in conjunction with students.
- Some courses employ journals in group work in order to provide opportunities for students to practise the skills of communication and collaboration that are essential to professions such as community health nursing (Drevdahl and Dorcy 2002). These authors argue that while not designed for the purpose of diagnostic assessment, such assignments may also provide serendipitous learning opportunities for assessors about the

suitability of the learning environment that has been provided. Assessment of the assignments also provides opportunities for faculty members to learn about communication and cooperation.

Martin Hays (2004) draws attention to the problem of student balking. He found that they often grumbled at the initial prospect of journal writing, and that some were openly sceptical. These views usually shifted through exposure and increasing confidence as they began to see the benefits themselves:

> At first I couldn't believe that you were asking us to write journals and pass them in each week. I really didn't understand what you were looking for, and didn't see any learning value in it for me. In fact, I thought it all a bit childish and maybe just 'make work.' Over the course of the term, however, I came to value journal writing a lot. It was interesting to see how my views changed over time. I honestly believe that I have become a more effective Team Leader at work as a result of exploring what was happening at work in my journal, thinking about it in the context of our readings and class discussions, and 'listening' to your suggestions and questions [written feedback to journal entries].
>
> (Hays 2004: 3)

Purpose usefully governs what goes into a portfolio or selection from a learning journal. If the purpose is to show engagement with reflective practice across contexts students may be advised to include a range of pieces including their best or most representative piece, a piece about learning something they didn't know before and reflections on the process of reflection, writing, selecting and self-assessing. If the purpose is to explore learning to reflect in a professional community, students may refer to responses from others, and consider what helped and hindered their learning.

Formative assessment of journals and portfolios

To grade or not to grade? Murphy and Smith (1991) describe different ways to assess students' portfolios: assessors describe, analyse, moderate, discuss, annotate and interview. They write letters to their students. They think in terms of what they want their students to learn. They emphasise process by calling the portfolios a 'culminating activity'.

> When teachers make portfolios primarily a tool for teaching and learning, they do not get carried away with the final judgement day.
>
> (Murphy and Smith 1991: 77)

Not getting carried away with the final judgement day means responding to student writing en route and this is labour intensive for assessors or supervisors whose aim is to encourage the development of reflective skills (Hays 2004). But personalised feedback on journals in the context of an effective working alliance with tutors was found to be the most important factor in enhancing reflective skills by Spalding and Wilson (2002). The process of engaging in an evolving written dialogue helped to build the relationship between student and tutor and proved a rewarding experience for both parties.

Pavlovich (2007) quotes a Chinese student and I have reproduced her journal entry here because it highlights a contrast between the experience of conventional methods of assessment and of completing a reflective journal, a discrimination that students need to make as they encounter such coursework assignments for the first time:

> Reflective journals were strange to me and none of my three journals has a good mark. When I first did the journal, I just thought this was an assessment to ensure the students would do the readings, and then write a summary about it. So I did the journals in my own way.
>
> However, one day I was really shocked by a classmate's journal! Having the girl's permission, the teacher read out her reflective journal to the class. I suddenly noticed the difference between hers and mine. She did the journal by her heart, she did not see the journal as an assessment, and the journal was from her deep voice. She related the reflective journal together with her feeling, her life experience and her spirit together.
>
> I suddenly noticed I am too little and small. I understand that study is not only gaining skills and knowledge; the purpose of study is to learn from one's own heart and to improve one's shortcomings. Therefore, I decided to change myself, change my attitude to the study. I decided to try my best to learn how to use spirituality to change my life. Now, I know that reflective journals is a useful tool which help people to go back to their own heart and to see what is their deep voice and feeling. I try to link the study with my daily life. I observe and feel everything happens to me and people around. Every night, when I lay on my bed, I can hear my inner voice and I can sum up important things to my brain. As long as I study this course, I can feel my heart and my spirit is light [Liu NN].

(Pavlovich 2007: 289)

Types of response to assignments that might be useful for formative purposes

There are many possibilities for responding to assignments, determined by the supervisor's purpose. It has been argued that imperatives and assertions emphasise expert power and that when feedback is 'terse' the tone of statements made appears categorical (Mutch 2003). Alistair Mutch (2003) examined written comments on student assignments provided by lecturers in the categories 'factual', 'comment', 'developmental', 'implied developmental', 'conversation' and 'neutral'. If the purpose of feedback is the development and enhancement of learning, then developmental and implied developmental comments might reasonably be expected better to fulfil the purpose, providing that the assignments involve a two-stage submission process whereby students have an opportunity to respond to such comments.

Invite students to ask questions in their text to which the reader might respond

I have come to the view that feedback from a supervisor is of limited value unless it connects with the issues and needs of the supervisee. In order to accomplish this, it is probably helpful if the feedback is invited rather than unsolicited. This allows recipients to have a degree of control, enables them to protect their vulnerabilities, and enhances the possibility that the feedback will connect with their learning needs. It also gives some protection to supervisors, preventing them from inadvertently undermining rather than enhancing the confidence of the supervisee.

Supervisees can be invited to pose questions in their text to which the supervisor agrees to attempt to provide a response. These may concern gaps in knowledge or take a more general form:

- 'Is this section too long?'
- 'Do I need a more punchy beginning?'
- 'Do I need to give more detail?'

I regard this as a relatively safe way for supervisees to obtain formative feedback and for supervisors to respond to the conscious learning needs of supervisees.

Questions (curious ones)

Supervisors may draw on the typology of questions described in Chapter 5 which may be just as useful or challenging when asked in the context of a written assignment as in conversation during supervision.

- 'I would be interested to know how the interviewees were selected. How did you record data? Were there any ethical issues to consider? Were they individual or group interviews?'
- 'What has your portfolio shown you about yourself as a practitioner? When were you impressed by your own voice and surprised to find what you thought? Were there times when you wanted to challenge the opinions that you found yourself expressing?'

- 'You asked yourself: "What assumptions am I making?" What answers were forthcoming?'
- 'Would you wish to say any more now about your feelings of having been placed in a bind by conflicting advice?'
- 'If another colleague told you this same personal story, how might you respond?'

Notes of strengths and affirmative comments

When I have sent manuscripts to academic journals for publication or to colleagues for comment I have often been struck by my resistance or willingness to accept feedback according to the particular comment made or to the style in which they are framed. I am particularly appreciative of comments that affirm my writing and I have been surprised how uplifted I have felt on the rare occasions that they have been presented in bright colours and super-large bold text. Boud (1995) argues that useful feedback affirms the worth of a person while offering reactions to content. He cautions that praise directed towards the person rather than the work can be experienced as patronising or controlling and that contrived praise in particular can be counter-productive. I would also caution against the use of the word 'but' following an affirmative comment which I experience as taking away from what went before. Some examples of such comments follow:

- 'I have come to expect original and unusual writing and thinking from you and I was not disappointed here. I welcome your own voice in the essay, even though I don't always find it easy to follow. I have found your ideas expressed here, and in your special interest session presentation, engaging and imaginative.'
- 'The abstract does its job well: it is clear and informative.'
- 'This is a very long excerpt to include in the main body of the text but I think it works. It fits with your commentaries before and after it.'

• 'This is a brilliant idea!'

Suggestions for development

Here, affirmative statements are paired with suggestions for further development and I have found that these can be particularly useful when trying to encourage supervisees to make developments to which they are resistant.

- 'You've referred to a "topic guide" several times, without saying what it is. I think it could help to add a brief early explanation.'
- 'I appreciated the depth and extent of your reflections which has helped you to write an assignment which really engaged me. The outstanding quality of your work demands a bibliography that meets the standards of

the Harvard system (see British Psychological Society Style Guide). I know that making this accurate can be a tedious job but your work deserves this in order to enhance its academic credibility.'

- 'Paragraphs like the last two look relevant but they seem rather isolated where they are. I think it could help if you expanded the Introduction to include some commentary, perhaps along this sort of line: 'In this assignment I will first describe/outline/set out etc. . . . After this I will . . . and then . . .'

- 'I am not sure what you mean here. Are you able to rephrase this?'

- 'This is a concise, well-organised case in support of WebCT, at least in the context that you have explored it here. I am left wondering, though, if it is so good why aren't more tutors using it? Could it be that not everyone feels as positively as you do about virtual learning environments? Perhaps you could acknowledge that there are some reservations about their use, even if you think that they are not justified.'

Letters

Letters to students can encompass each of the kinds or response outlined above. This is an extract from a letter from a teacher to a student in secondary education who is studying English (Murphy and Smith 1991):

> Dear Ron
> Your portfolio is a delight! It showed that you are aware of your reader and you take care of your reader. For example, your presentation of the portfolio worked well: table of contents, introductory letter, short introduction to each piece, dated papers. I found the collection easy to follow and I felt you were guiding me to the features of your writing that pleased and concerned you.
>   The outstanding feature of your writing for me is the imagery. The way you described your feelings of boredom – 'like a rainy Sunday morning with no electricity at all while your friends are out' is anything but boring! You observe closely, Ron, and often you find the irony in things.
>   How much do you revise your work? I know I have to write several drafts before I'm satisfied. My impression from looking at the draft you included in your portfolio is that you've made few changes. I'd like to see you dig in next year and tackle revision. For example, the piece on your mother deserves a second or third round. You want to add examples and incidents for statements like, 'She stands strong when troubles occur.'
>   (Murphy and Smith 1991: 54)

This feedback has the benefit of including a question, identification of specific strengths with examples, suggestions for further development and self-disclosure: 'This is what I do when I write'.

Possible roles of the supervisor in relation to coursework

Knowledge about the coursework in which supervisees are engaged provides information about the global demands to which they are subject and about implications for the nature of the work carried out on the placement. Supervisors have a legitimate interest because the coursework may reflect on their own practice, and in order to ensure that the requirements of their employing agency have been honoured.

Normaliser

Either through their own professional education or through previous involvement in coursework, supervisors may have developed a good knowledge of course requirements and of appropriate standards for the work. They are also likely to have supervised other students who have experienced similar worries and practical difficulties with their coursework. A supervisee sometimes can feel that he or she is the only person who is experiencing difficulties. A supervisor's knowledge can serve to reassure, as can the early construction of back-up plans in the event of false starts.

In my experience student practitioners usually take their professional education very seriously. I regard this as right and proper unless this attitude impedes learning. If seriousness is wearing them down, the supervisor's use of humour can bring a sense of proportion and lightness to the burden of the assignment. Strategies described elsewhere in this book can be employed such as asking the supervisee to role reverse with the assignment. Questions like, 'If the assignment had a voice, what would it be saying to you about how much more time to spend?' 'Would it prefer you to work harder for longer and go for an outstanding mark, or would it want you to get finished and go for adequate?' may be useful. Genograms of the supervisee's current interests and commitments can be used to map relationships between the assignment and other factors such as family, socialising, holidays, clinical skills, hobbies and so on, the aim being to put the assignment into perspective against the other facets of the supervisee's life.

Thought-organising assistant

A significant way in which supervisors can use their skills is in helping students to clarify and focus their ideas about coursework. Organisation and structuring of thoughts can be achieved through judicious questioning and possibly by sketching out the responses in a diagram which links key concepts and ideas, as in knowledge mapping. It is not necessary for the supervisor to have detailed knowledge of the topic. Supervisees may have masses of information from multiple sources but have reached a position in which they cannot 'see the wood for the trees'. Diagrams allow large amounts of data to be presented within a confined space and linked together to develop understanding and critical questioning. Questions which address the assignment requirements such as 'What question are you trying to answer?', 'Who are the key characters?', 'How does X link with Y?' can help in the organising process.

Theory provider

The course on which the supervisee is registered has a role as theory-provider for the practice placement but supervisors themselves may be an equally good source. Courses cannot address all relevant theory and supervisees may look to the supervisor to help narrow down their literature searches or to help link theory and practice. Supervisors may also have their own areas of expertise through which supervisees' experience may be enriched.

Reassurer-encourager

Supervisees beset by doubts about their capability to complete an assignment can be reassured by a supervisor who shows genuine confidence in their ability to be successful. Uncertainty about capability can lead supervisees to avoid starting an assignment and the supervisor can have a useful role in co-constructing a timetable and encouraging the supervisee to stick to it.

When it is unclear what form the encouragement might helpfully take, a dialogue may be of use. This might involve helping supervisees to think about how they have successfully completed previous assignments, and what has helped them to learn and progress with the task. Someone with a block about writing might be encouraged to write a time-constrained 'splurge' or begin with an audio-recorded dialogue explaining her or his work and reflections to the supervisor, a friend or colleague. The transcript of such a dialogue can be edited into a first draft of an assignment. Beginning with a first draft is alien to supervisees who equate first and final attempts. Encouragement to write anything at all as a starting point can serve to unblock the writing process. The supervisor may also agree to help in the tidying process as each redraft is made.

Boundary setter

There are a number of ways in which supervisors can usefully set boundaries for supervisees in relation to their coursework. Not least is to help the supervisee to select a 'do-able' topic. Supervisees sometimes aspire to produce a startlingly original or very extensive piece of work. While laudable, it is probably unrealistic in the context of a professional training course. The supervisor may be able to offer reassurance that the successful completion of a more modest piece may be more valuable than an ambitious unfulfilled work, providing that the supervisor can be confident about having an accurate picture of course requirements by consultation with course staff and coursework guidelines.

The role of boundary setter can also be of help to supervisees who have become engaged in unhelpful multiple consulting. A discussion regarding the inputs of the different consultants and the effects of the inputs on the progress of the assignment might help the supervisee to give up the idea of finding the 'right' helper. Such a conversation might employ questions about the future; for how long and with how many consultants will the supervisee persist, and how many times will he or she face disappointment before changing perspective on how to progress the work.

Motivator

The role of motivator may be of help to supervisees who appear to have lost their way during their professional education, a process which itself can contribute to the experience of reduced or fluctuating motivation (Stoltenberg and McNeill 2009). It may help supervisees who are suffering in this way to understand that they are not alone in their reactions.

In psychodrama, the concept of 'warming up' describes the process of establishing a state of motivation that renders tasks exciting and enjoyable. The development of this state is facilitated by participation in warm-up exercises. Such exercises may be related only indirectly to the subsequently enacted drama. If it is taking hours or weeks for supervisees to progress a coursework assignment then they are probably not warmed up to the task. Supervisors might help by exploring with them the types of activity that have been effective as warm up exercises in their past experience.

Supervisees can experience feelings of being infantilised by the demands of assignments and take a passive position in relation to the work. This can create an urge in supervisors to take over. I have learned that this is unlikely to help in the long run, since it is the supervisees' capabilities that are at issue. By keeping in mind the long-term goals of my interventions rather than a short-term solution to an immediate problem, I am likely to be more useful to the student's overall development. I have to remind myself that my creativity is best oriented towards devising questions and more questions, and to communicating my firm belief in the capability of the supervisee to become an effective lifelong reflective practitioner.

Outcomes of reflective practice

In this chapter I have referred many times to the complexities of assessment. David Tripp (1993) has pointed out that all too often the fate of an idea is determined by the success of a project when first attempted. He cites Flynn (1972), who asks what would have been the 'right' method to evaluate the idea that aircraft should replace other means of transport as a safe and relatively cheap method of long distance passenger travel. Would it have been at the time of the Wright brothers' first flight? At many points in the development of commercial aircraft, outcome and effectiveness studies would have concluded that the project was too expensive, time consuming and dangerous to proceed further. Tripp (1993) argues that flying developed not as a result of a single endeavour or based on the results of a study using formal 'gold standard' research evaluation methods but because many different people liked flying and the idea of flying. Learning arose from each attempt to develop a flying machine and the process took place over a long time scale. Developments are still occurring.

This is my experience of many developments in my own profession. For it to have become so ubiquitous, many professionals must like the idea of reflective practice and believe in its capability to enhance professional practice.

It has been argued that reflection is 'a behavioural scientist's nightmare – almost impossible to define tightly, and well nigh uncontrollable' (Bennett-Levy 2003: 16) and that there is very little empirical research in the psychology literature to suggest its value. His own research showed that reflection had an impact on practice in the domains of enhanced therapeutic understanding, the development of therapeutic skills (Bennett-Levy et al. 2003), enhanced self-concept and greater confidence in the role of clinician (Bennett-Levy et al. 2001). The capacity to mentally represent past, present or future events, and to reanalyse, re-evaluate, and find new meanings in them at one day, five years, or fifty years' distance from the original event, is one of the cognitive skills that almost certainly distinguishes humans from the rest of the animal world (M. Wheeler et al. 1997).

I want to finish this book with a story from a book by Malcolm Gladwell that unites my interests in psychology and, through my family, music. It also represents my experience of being a woman growing up in the twentieth century when doors have been opened to me that were closed to earlier generations. It illustrates why we need to learn more about ourselves and our inevitable assumptions and prejudices the better to challenge our routine practices so as to enhance the possibility of enriching the lives of the people with whom we have the privilege of working.

> When Julie Landsman auditioned for the role of principal French horn at the Met, the screens had just gone up in the practice hall. At the time, there were no women in the brass section of the orchestra, because everyone 'knew' that women could not play the horn as well as men. But Landsman came and sat down and played – and she played well. 'I knew in my last round that I had won before they told me,' she says. 'It was because of the way I performed the last piece. I held on to the last high C for a very long time, just to leave no doubt in their minds. And they started to laugh, because it was above and beyond the call of

duty.' But when they declared her the winner and she stepped out from behind the screen, there was a gasp. It wasn't just that she was a woman, and female horn players were rare, as had been the case with Conant. And it wasn't just the bold, extended high C, which was the kind of macho sound that they expected from a man only. It was because they *knew* her. Landsman had played for the Met before as a substitute. Until they listened to her with just their ears, however, they had no idea she was so good.

(Gladwell 2005: 254)

Carper's model of reflective practice

1 **Description**

 1.1 Write a description of the experience.
 1.2 What are the key issues within this description that I need to pay attention to?

2 **Reflection**

 2.1 What was I trying to achieve?
 2.2 Why did I act as I did?
 2.3 What were the consequences of my actions?

 • For the patient and family?
 • For myself?
 • For the people I work with?

 2.4 How did I feel about this experience when it was happening?
 2.5 How did the patient feel about it?
 2.6 How do I know how the patient felt about it?

3 **Influencing factors**

 3.1 What internal factors influenced my decision making and actions?
 3.2 What external factors influenced my decision making and actions?
 3.3 What sources of knowledge did or should have influenced my decision making and actions?

4 **Alternative strategies**

 4.1 Could I have dealt better with the situation?
 4.2 What other choices did I have?
 4.3 What would be the consequences of these other choices?

5 **Learning**

 5.1 How can I make sense of this experience in light of past experience and future practice?

5.2 How do I *now* feel about this experience?

5.3 Have I taken effective action to support myself and others as a result of this experience?

5.4 How has this experience changed my ways of knowing in practice?

- Empirics
- Ethics
- Personal
- Aesthetics

Bransford and Johnson (1972) illustration

If the balloons popped . . .

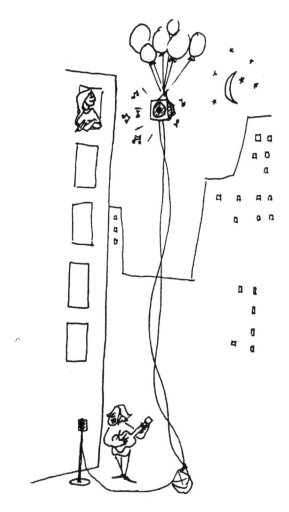

References

Adamson, F. (2008). Working with image and metaphor in coaching supervision. *Coaching Supervision Academy.* Retrieved 28 December 2008 from: www.coachingsupervisionacademy.com/our_approach/working_with_image_and_metaphor_in_coaching_supervision.phtml

Allen, G.J., Szollas, S.J. and Williams, B.E. (1986). Doctoral students' comparative evaluations of best and worst psychotherapy supervision. *Professional Psychology Research and Practice, 17,* 91–99.

Allen, P. (2004). The use of interpersonal process recall (IPR) in person-centred supervision. In K. Tudor and M. Worrall (eds) *Freedom to practise: person-centred approaches to supervision.* Ross-on-Wye, Herefordshire: PCCS Books.

Allen, R. (2009). Psychological care in physical health settings: the role of reflective practice with healthcare staff. *Clinical Psychology Forum, 199,* 24–28.

Althusser, L. (1971). *Lenin and philosophy.* New York: Monthly Review Press.

Amundson, N.W. (1988). The use of metaphor and drawings in case conceptualisation. *Journal of Counseling and Development, 66,* 391–393.

Andersen, T. (1987). The reflecting team: dialogue and meta-dialogue in clinical work. *Family Process, 26,* 415–428.

Anderson, J.R. (1980). *Cognitive psychology and its implications,* San Francisco, CA: W.H. Freeman.

Anderton, K. (2004). *Student nurse.* Retrieved 24 August 2008 from: www.studentnurse.org.uk/reflection.html

Argyris, C. (1976). *Increasing leadership effectiveness.* New York: Wiley.

Argyris, C. and Schön, D. (1974). *Theory in practice: increasing personal effectiveness.* San Francisco, CA: Jossey-Bass.

Armstrong, P. and Schneiders, I. (2003). Video and telephone technology in supervision and supervision training. In S. Goss and K. Anthony (eds) *Technology in counselling and psychotherapy: a practitioner's guide.* Basingstoke: Palgrave.

Arter, J.A. and Spandel, V. (1991). *Using portfolios of student work in instruction and assessment.* Portland, OR: Northwest Region Educational Laboratory. Retrieved 24 August 2009 from: www.literacynet.org/icans/chapter02/portfolios.html

Assessment Reform Group (1999). *Assessment for learning: beyond the black box.* Retrieved 28 May 2009 from: www.assessment-reformgroup.org

Aten, J.D. and Hernandez, B.C. (2004). Addressing religion in clinical supervision: a model. *Psychotherapy: Theory, Research, Practice, Training, 41*(2), 152–160.

Atkins, S. and Murphy, K. (1994). Reflective practice. *Nursing Standard, 8*(39), 49–56.

Atkinson, T. and Claxton, G. (2000). *The intuitive practitioner: on the value of not always knowing what one is doing.* Buckingham: Open University Press.

Bailey, E.K. and Cotlar, M. (1994). Teaching via the Internet. *Communication Education, 43*, 184–193.

Ballard, S. (2000). Experiences of supervision in a pre-registration nursing degree course. In J. Spouse and L. Redfern (eds) *Successful supervision in health care practice.* Oxford: Blackwell.

Barell, J. (2007). *Problem-based learning: an inquiry approach*, 2nd edn. Thousand Oaks, CA: Corwin Press.

Barnat, M.R. (1977). Spontaneous supervisory metaphor in the resolution of trainee anxiety. *Professional Psychology, 8*, 307–315.

Barry, S. (2008). *The secret scripture.* London: Faber & Faber.

Bartz, R. (1999). Beyond the biopsychosocial model: new approaches to doctor-patient interactions. *Journal of Family Practice, 48*, 601–607.

Bateson, G. (1972). *Steps to an ecology of mind.* New York: Chandler.

Battino, R. (2005). *Metaphoria: metaphor and guided metaphor for psychotherapy and healing.* Carmarthen, Wales: Crown House.

Beattie, A. (1987). Making a curriculum work. In P. Allen and M. Jolley (eds) *The curriculum in nursing education.* London: Croom Helm.

Beglin, S. and Bassra, P. (2007). Managing complex eating disorder cases using a Cognitive Analytical Therapy (CAT) approach. Retrieved from: www.bps.org.uk/down loadfile.cfm?file_uuid=26D76984-1143-DFD0-7E8B-80F0BD2968EF&ext=ppt

Beinart, H. (2004). Models of supervision and the supervisory relationship and their evidence base. In I. Fleming and L. Steen (eds) *Supervision and clinical psychology.* Hove: Brunner-Routledge.

Benner, P. (2001). *From novice to expert: excellence and power in clinical nursing practice.* Upper Saddle River, NJ: Prentice Hall Health.

Bennett, S., Plint, A. and Clifford, T.J. (2005). Burnout, psychological morbidity, job satisfaction, and stress: a survey of Canadian hospital based child protection professionals. *Archives of Diseases in Childhood, 90*, 1112–1116.

Bennett-Levy, J. (2003). Reflection: a blind spot in psychology? *Clinical Psychology, 27*, 16–19.

Bennett-Levy, J., Turner, F., Beaty, T., Smith, M., Paterson, B. and Farmer, S. (2001). The value of self-practice of cognitive therapy techniques and self-reflection in the training of cognitive therapists. *Behavioural and Cognitive Psychotherapy, 29*, 203–220.

Bennett-Levy, J., Lee, N., Travers, K., Pohlman, S. and Hamernik, E. (2003). Cognitive therapy from the in-side: enhancing therapist skills through practising what we preach. *Behavioural and Cognitive Psychotherapy, 31*, 143–158.

Benrud-Larson, L. (2000). Reflecting on practice in supervision. In J. Spouse and L. Redfern (eds) *Successful supervision in health care practice.* Oxford: Blackwell.

Bernard, J.M. and Goodyear, R.K. (1992). *Fundamentals of clinical supervision.* Boston, MA: Allyn & Bacon.

Bernard, J.M. and Goodyear, R.K. (1998). *Fundamentals of clinical supervision*, 2nd edn. Boston, MA: Allyn & Bacon.

Bernard, J.M. and Goodyear, R.K. (2008). *Fundamentals of clinical supervision*, 4th edn. Columbus, OH: Pearson.

Berthoff, A. (1978). *Forming, thinking, writing: the composing imagination.* Rochelle Park, NJ: Hayden.

Bhugra, D. and De Silva, P. (2007). The silver screen, printed page and cultural competence. *The Psychologist, 20*(9), 528–540.

Binch, N. and Robertson, L. (1994). *Resourcing and assessing art, craft and design.* Corsham, Wilts: National Society for Education in Art and Design.

Binder, J.L. and Strupp, H.H. (1997). Supervision of psychodynamic psychotherapies. In C.E. Watkins, Jr. (ed.) *Handbook of psychotherapy supervision.* New York: Wiley.

Bishop, J.M. (1983). Speech delivered at the Annual Meeting, American Association of Medical Colleges, 8 November.

Black, P.J. and Wiliam, D. (1998). Assessment and classroom learning. *Assessment in Education, 5*(1), 7–74.

Bloom, B.S., Hastings, J.T. and Madaus, G.F. (1971). *Handbook on formative and summative evaluation of student learning.* New York: McGraw-Hill.

Bogo, M. and McKnight, K. (2005). Clinical supervision in social work: a review of the research literature. *Clinical Supervisor, 24*(1–2), 49–67.

Bolen, J.S. (1984). *Goddesses in everywoman: a new psychology of women.* New York: Harper & Row.

Bolton, G. (1994). Stories at work: fictional-critical writing as a means of professional development. *British Educational Research Journal, 20*(1), 55–68.

Bolton, G. (1999). *The therapeutic potential of creative writing: writing myself.* London: Jessica Kingsley.

Bolton, G. (2001). Bird, woman's wardrobe and the birth of humility. *Journal of Medical Humanities, 27*, 53–54.

Bolton, G. (2005). *Reflective practice*, 2nd edn. London: Sage.

Borton, T. (1970). *Reach, touch and teach.* London: Hutchinson.

Boud, D. (1995). *Enhancing learning through self assessment.* London: Kogan Page.

Boud, D. (1999). Avoiding the traps: seeking good practice in the use of self assessment and reflection in professional courses. *Social Work Education, 18*, 121–132.

Boud, D. (2001). Using journal writing to enhance reflective practice. In L.M. English and M.A. Gillen (eds) *Promoting journal writing in adult education.* San Francisco, CA: Jossey-Bass.

Boud, D. and Feletti, G.I. (eds) (1997). *The challenge of problem-based learning*, 2nd edn. London: Kogan Page.

Boud, D., Keogh, R. and Walker, D. (eds) (1985). *Reflection: turning experience into learning.* London: Kogan Page.

Boud, D., Cohen, R. and Walker, D. (1993). Understanding learning from experience. In D. Boud, R. Cohen and D. Walker (eds) *Using experience for learning.* Milton Keynes: Society for Research into Higher Education and Open University Press.

Bourner, T. (n.d.). *Assessing reflective learning.* Retrieved 13 August 2009 from: www.brighton.ac.uk/cupp/resources/assessment.htm

Bradshaw Tauvon, K. (1998). Principles of psychodrama. In M. Karp, P. Holmes and K. Bradshaw Tauvon (eds) *The handbook of psychodrama.* New York: Routledge.

Bransford, J.D. and Johnson, M.K. (1972). Contextual prerequisites for understanding: some investigations of comprehension and recall. *Journal of Verbal Learning and Verbal Behaviour, 11*, 717–726.

Bransford, J.D. and Johnson, M.K. (1973). Consideration of some problems of comprehension. In W.G. Chase (ed.) *Visual information processes*. New York: Academic Press.

Bransford, J.D., Brown, A. and Cocking, R.R. (eds) (2000). *How people learn – brain, mind, experience, and school*. Washington, DC: National Academy Press.

British Psychological Society (2008). *Criteria for the accreditation of postgraduate training courses in clinical psychology*. Leicester: British Psychological Society. Retrieved 19 July 2009 from: www.bps.org.uk/document-download-area/ document-download$.cfm?file_uuid=9B2B3F2E-1143-DFD0-7EC6-DF42DDE42 A1A&ext=pdf

Brookfield, S.D. (1986). *Understanding and facilitating adult learning*. Buckingham: Open University Press.

Brookfield, S.D. (1987). *Developing critical thinkers: challenging adults to explore alternative ways of thinking and acting*. Milton Keynes: Open University Press.

Brookfield, S.D. (1992). Uncovering assumptions: the key to reflective practice. *Adult Learning, 3*(4), 13–18.

Brookfield, S.D. (1995). *Becoming a critically reflective teacher*. San Francisco, CA: Jossey-Bass.

Brookfield, S.D. (2001). Repositioning ideology critique in a critical theory of adult learning. *Adult Education Quarterly, 52*(1), 7–22.

Brookfield, S.D. (2005). *The power of critical theory for adult learning and teaching*. Milton Keynes: Open University Press.

Brown, J. (1997). Circular questioning: an introductory guide. *Australian and New Zealand Journal of Family Therapy, 18*(2), 109–114.

Brown, T.L., Acevedo-Polakovich, I.D. and Smith, A.M. (2006). Cross-cultural issues affecting the supervisory relationship in counseling children and families. In T. Kerby-Neill (ed.) *Helping others help children*. Washington, DC: American Psychological Association.

Bruner, J. (1990). *Acts of meaning*. Cambridge, MA: Harvard University Press.

Burnham, J. (1993). Systemic supervision: the evolution of reflexivity in the context of the supervisor relationship. *Human Systems, 4*, 349–381.

Burnham, J. (2000). Internalised other interviewing: evaluating and enhancing empathy. *Clinical Psychology Forum, 140*, 16–20.

Burnham, J. (2005). Relational reflexivity: a tool for socially constructing therapeutic relationships. In C. Flaskas, B. Mason and A. Perlesz (eds) *The space between: experience, context and process in the therapeutic relationship*. London: Karnac.

Burns, G.W. (2001). *101 healing stories: using metaphors in therapy*. New York: Wiley.

Burns, S. (1994). Assessing reflective learning. In A. Palmer, S. Burns and C. Bulman (eds) *Reflective practice in nursing: the growth of the professional practitioner*. Oxford: Blackwell Scientific.

Burroughs, E.R. (1912). *Tarzan of the apes. All-Story Magazine*.

Butler, C. (2004). An awareness-raising tool addressing lesbian and gay lives. *Clinical Psychology, 36*, 15–17.

Butler, R. (1988). Enhancing and undermining intrinsic motivation: the effects of task-involving and ego-involving evaluation on interest and performance. *British Journal of Education Psychology, 58*, 1–14.

Butterfield, L.D., Borgen, W.A., Amundson, N.E. and Maglio, A-S.T. (2005). Fifty years of the critical incident technique: 1954–2004 and beyond. *Qualitative Research, 5,* 475–497.

Butterworth, T., Cutcliffe, J.R. and Proctor, B. (2001). *Fundamental themes in clinical supervision.* London: Routledge.

Byng-Hall, J. (1995). *Rewriting family scripts.* New York: Guilford Press.

Caelli, K. (1998). Shared understandings: negotiating the meanings of health via concept mapping. *Nurse Education Today, 18,* 317–321.

Campbell, D. and Grøenbæk, M. (2006). *Taking positions in the organization.* London: Karnac.

Candy, P.C. (1990). Repertory grids: playing verbal chess. In J. Mezirow (ed.) *Fostering critical reflection in adulthood.* San Franciso, CA: Jossey-Bass.

Carey, M. and Russell, S. (2002). Externalising – commonly asked questions. *International Journal of Narrative Therapy and Community Work, 2.* Retrieved 29 November 2008 from: www.dulwichcentre.com.au/externalising.htm

Carpenito-Moyet, L.J. (2006). *Understanding the nursing process: concept mapping and care planning for students.* Philadelphia, PA: Lippincott Williams & Wilkins.

Carper, B. (1978). Fundamental patterns of knowing in nursing. *Advances in Nursing Science, 3,* 71–75.

Carroll, M. and Gilbert, M.C. (2005). *On being a supervisee: creating learning partnerships.* London: Vukani.

Carter, B. and Walker, B. (2008). Using group approaches to underpin learning, supervision and reflection. In C. Bulmer and S. Schutz (eds) *Reflective practice in nursing,* 4th edn. Oxford: Blackwell.

Casement, P. (1985). *On learning from the patient.* London: Routledge.

Chambers, P. (2003). Narrative and reflective practice recording and understanding experience. *Education Action Research, 11*(3), 403–414.

Champe, J. and Kleist, D.M. (2003). Live supervision: a review of the research. *The Family Journal,* 11, 268–275.

Chapman, V. (2000). A caring moment with Rachel. In T. Ghaye and S. Lillyman (eds) *Caring moments: the discourse of reflective practice.* Dinton, Wilts: Quay Books, Mark Allen.

Christensen, T.M. and Kline, W.B. (2001). Anxiety as a condition for learning in group supervision. *Journal for Specialists in Group Work, 26,* 385–396.

Christey, K. (2006). Writing a reflective learning journal. *CPD Update* (online). Retrieved 31 March 2009 from: www.teachingexpertise.com/articles/writing-reflective-learning-journal-642

Clarke, P. (1997). Interpersonal process recall in supervision. In G. Shipton (ed.) *Supervision of psychotherapy and counselling.* Buckingham: Open University Press.

Claxton, G. (1998). *Hare brain, tortoise mind.* London: Fourth Estate.

Claxton, G. (1999). *Wise up: learning to live the learning life.* Stafford: Network Educational Press.

Cleverly, D. (2003). *Implementing inquiry-based learning in nursing.* London: Routledge.

Coles, R. (1989). *The call of stories: teaching and the moral imagination.* Boston, MA: Houghton Mifflin.

Collins, N.M. and Pieterse, A.L. (2007). Critical incident analysis based training: an approach for developing active racial/cultural awareness. *Journal of Counseling and Development, 85*(1), 14–24.

Combs, G. and Freedman, J. (1990). *Symbol story and ceremony: using metaphor in individual and family therapy*. New York: Norton.

Constantine, M.G. (1997). Facilitating multicultural competency in counseling supervision. In D.B. Pope-Davis and H.L.K. Coleman (eds) *Multicultural counseling competencies*. Thousand Oaks, CA: Sage.

Conway, P.F. (2001). Anticipatory reflection while learning to teach: from a temporally truncated to a temporally distributed model of reflection in teacher education. *Teaching and Teacher Education, 17*(1), 89–106.

Cormier, L.S. (1988). Critical incidents in counselor development: themes and patterns. *Journal of Counseling and Development, 67*, 131–132.

Cotton, A.H. (2001). Private thoughts in public spheres: issues in reflection and reflective practices in nursing. *Journal of Advanced Nursing, 36*(4), 512–519.

Cowan, J. (1998). *On becoming an innovative university teacher*. Milton Keynes: Society for Research into Higher Education and Open University Press.

Cox, M. (1992). Metaphor in psychotherapy supervision. In S. Jennings (ed.) *Dramatherapy: theory and practice 2*. London: Routledge.

Craster, E. (1975). The centipede. In J.M. Cohen (ed.) *A choice of comic and curious verse*. Harmondsworth: Penguin.

Crème, P. (2005). Should student learning journals be assessed? *Assessment and Evaluation in Higher Education, 30*(3), 287–296.

Csikszenthmihalyi, M. (1990). *Flow: the psychology of optimal experience*. New York: Harper Perennial.

Curtis, R., Weeden, P. and Winter, J. (2000). Measurement, judgement, criteria and expertise. In T. Atkinson and G. Claxton (eds) *The intuitive practitioner: on the value of not always knowing what one is doing*. Buckingham: Open University Press.

Cushway, D. and Knibbs, J. (2004). Trainees' and supervisors' perceptions of supervision. In I. Fleming and L. Steen (eds) *Supervision and clinical psychology: theory, practice and perspectives*. Hove: Brunner-Routledge.

Daniels, J. and Feltham, C. (2004). Reflective and therapeutic writing in counsellor training. In G. Bolton, S. Howlett, C. Lago and J.K. Wright (eds) *Writing cures: an introductory handbook of writing in counselling and therapy*. Hove: Brunner-Routledge.

DasGupta, S. and Charon, R. (2004). Personal illness narratives: using reflective writing to teach empathy. *Academic Medicine, 79*(4), 351–356.

Davidson, S. and Patel, N. (2009). Power and identity: considerations for personal and professional development. In J. Hughes and S. Youngson (eds) *Personal development and clinical psychology*. Chichester: BPS Blackwell.

Davison, G.C., Vogel, R.S. and Coffman, S.G. (1997). Think-aloud approaches to cognitive assessment and the articulated thoughts in simulated situations paradigm. *Journal of Consulting and Clinical Psychology, 65*(6), 950–958.

De Bono, E. (2000). *Six thinking hats*. London: Penguin.

Delpit, L. (1995). *Other people's children: cultural conflict in the classroom*. New York: New Press.

Deshler, D. (1990). Metaphor analysis: exorcising social ghosts. In J. Mezirow (ed.) *Fostering critical reflection in adulthood*. San Franciso, CA: Jossey-Bass.

Dewey, J. (1933). *How we think*. Boston, MA: J.C. Heath.

Disability Rights Commission (2002). *Interview with Mat Fraser*. Retrieved 31 December 2002 from: www.drc-gb.org/drc/default.asp

Dixon, N. (1998). Action learning: more than just a task force. *Performance Improvement Quarterly, 11*(1), 44–58.

Donati, M. and Watts, M. (2005). Personal development in counsellor training: towards a clarification of interrelated concepts. *British Journal of Guidance, 33*(4), 475–484.

Draper, S. (2008). *Electronic voting systems and interactive lectures: entrance lobby.* Retrieved 5 March 2009 from: www.psy.gla.ac.uk/~steve/ilig/

Drevdahl, D.J. and Dorcy, K.S. (2002). Using journals for community health students engaged in group work. *Nurse Educator, 27*(6), 255–259.

Driscoll, J. and O'Sullivan, J. (2007). The place of clinical supervision in modern healthcare. In J. Driscoll (ed.) *Practising clinical supervision*, 2nd edn. Philadelphia, PA: Baillière Tindall Elsevier.

Drury-Hudson, J. (1999). Decision making in child protection: the use of theoretical, empirical and procedural knowledge by novices and experts and implications for fieldwork placement. *British Journal of Social Work, 29*, 147–169.

Dufour, C. (1998). Mobilizing gay activists. In A.N. Costain and A.S. McFarland (eds) *Social movements and American political institutions*. Lanham, MD: Rowman & Littlefield.

Dugosh, K.L., Paulus, P.B., Roland, E.J. and Yang, H-C. (2000). Cognitive stimulation in brainstorming. *Journal of Personality and Social Psychology, 79*, 722–735.

Duke, S. (2004). When reflection becomes a cul-de-sac – strategies to find a focus and move on. In C. Bulman and S. Schutz (eds) *Reflective practice in nursing*, 3rd edn. Oxford: Blackwell.

Dumas, L. (2000). Improving the ability to learn from experience in clinical settings. In J. Spouse and L. Redfern (eds) *Successful supervision in health care practice*. Oxford: Blackwell.

Edelman, G.M. and Tononi, G. (2000). *Consciousness: how matter becomes imagination*. London: Penguin.

Edwards, D., Cooper, L., Burnard, P., Hanningan, B., Adams, J., Fothergill, A. and Coyle, D. (2005). Factors influencing the effectiveness of clinical supervision. *Journal of Psychiatric and Mental Health Nursing, 12*, 405–414.

Edwards, R.M. (1989). An experiment in student self-assessment. *British Journal of Educational Technology, 20*(1), 5–10.

Efstation, J.F., Patton, M.J. and Kardash, C.M. (1990). Measuring the working alliance in counselor supervision. *Journal of Counseling Psychology, 37*, 322–329.

Egan, G. (1994). *The skilled helper*, 5th edn. Monterey, CA: Brooks/Cole.

Ellis, M.V. and Ladany, N. (1997). Inferences concerning supervisees and clients in clinical supervision: an integrative review. In C.E. Watkins, Jr. (ed.) *Handbook of psychotherapy supervision*. New York: Wiley.

Ellis, M.V., Ladany, N., Krengel, M. and Schult, D. (1996). Clinical supervision research from 1981 to 1993: a methodological critique. *Journal of Counseling Psychology, 43*, 35–50.

El-Shamy, S. (2005). *Role play made easy*. San Francisco, CA: Wiley.

Epston, D. (1993). Internalised other questioning with couples: the New Zealand version. In S. Gilligan and R. Price (eds) *Therapeutic conversations*. New York: Norton.

Errek, H. and Randolph, D. (1982). Effects of discussion and role-playing activities in the acquisition of consultant interview skills. *Journal of Counseling Psychology, 29*, 304–308.

Evans, D. (1997). Reflective learning through practice-based assignments. Paper presented at the British Educational Research Association Annual Conference, University of York, 11–14 September. Retrieved 21 July 2009 from: www.leeds.ac.uk/educol/documents/000000468.htm

Everett, D.R. and Ahem, T.C. (1994). Computer-mediated communication as a teaching tool: a case study. *Journal of Research on Computing in Education, 26*, 336–357.

Fabry, J. (1988). *Guideposts to meaning: discovering what really matters.* Oakland, CA: New Harbinger.

Falender, C.A. and Shafranske, E.P. (2004). *Clinical supervision: a competency-based approach.* Washington, DC: American Psychological Association.

Falender, C.A. and Shafranske, E.P. (2007). Competence in competency-based supervision practice: construct and application. *Professional Psychology, Research and Practice, 38*(3), 232–240.

Fall, M. and Sutton, J.M., Jr. (2004). *Clinical supervision: a handbook for practitioners.* Boston, MA: Allyn & Bacon.

Farren, M. (2005). *How can I create a pedagogy of the unique through a web of betweenness?* Unpublished PhD thesis, University of Bath. Retrieved 19 September 2009 from: www.actionresearch.net/farren.shtml

Figley, C.R. (1995). *Compassion fatigue: coping with secondary traumatic stress disorder in those who treat the traumatized.* New York: Brunner-Mazel.

Figley, C.R. (ed.) (2002). *Treating compassion fatigue.* New York: Brunner-Routledge.

Fisher, A. (2001). *Critical thinking: an introduction.* Cambridge: Cambridge University Press.

Flanagan, B. (2008). Debriefing: theory and technique. In R.H. Riley (ed.) *Manual of simulation in health care.* New York: Oxford University Press.

Flanagan, J.C. (1954). The critical incident technique. *Psychological Bulletin, 51*(4), 327–358.

Flannery-Schroeder, E. (2005). Treatment integrity: implications for training. *Clinical Psychology: Science and Practice, 12*, 388–390.

Fleming, N.D. (1999). Biases in marking students' written work: quality? In S. Brown and A. Glasner (eds) *Assessment matters in higher education.* Buckingham: Society for Research into Higher Education and Open University Press.

Flynn, J.M. (1972). Evaluation and the fate of innovations. *Educational Technology,* April, 52–54.

Fook, J. (1999). Critical reflectivity in education and practice. In B. Pease and J. Fook (eds) *Transforming social work practice: postmodern critical perspectives.* London: Routledge.

Fordham, A.S., May, B., Boyle, M., Bentall, R.P. and Slade, P. (1990). Good and bad clinicians: supervisors' judgements of trainees' competence. *British Journal of Clinical Psychology, 29*, 113–114.

Frame, M.W. (2001). The spiritual genogram in training and supervision. *Family Journal, 9*, 109–115.

Francis, D. (1995). The reflective journal: a window to preservice teachers' practical knowledge. *Teaching and Teacher Education, 11*(3), 229–241.

Frawley O'Dea, M.G. and Sarnat, J. (2001). *The supervisory relationship: a contemporary psychodynamic approach.* New York: Guilford Press.

Freire, P. (1972). *Pedagogy of the oppressed.* Harmondsworth: Penguin.

French, T. and Wardle, T. (eds) (2007). *The problem-based learning workbook: medicine and surgery*. Abingdon, Oxon: Radcliffe.

Freshwater, D. (2007). Teaching and learning reflective practice. In T. Stickley and T. Basset (eds) *Teaching mental health*. Chichester: Wiley.

Friedman, S., Brecher, S. and Mittelmeier, C. (1995). Widening the lens, sharpening the focus: the reflecting process in managed care. In S. Friedman (ed.) *The reflecting team in action: collaborative practice in family therapy*. New York: Guilford Press.

Furr, S.R. and Carroll, J.J. (2003). Critical incidents in student counselor development. *Journal of Counseling and Development, 81*(4), 483–489.

Ghaye, T. (2007). Is reflective practice ethical? (The case of the reflective portfolio). *Reflective Practice, 8*(2), 151–162.

Ghaye, T. and Lillyman, S. (1997). *Learning journals and critical incidents: reflective practice for health care professionals*. Dinton, Wilts: Quay Books, Mark Allen.

Gibbs, G. (1988). *Learning by doing: a guide to teaching and learning methods*. Oxford: Further Education Unit, Oxford Brookes University.

Gibbs, G. (1999). Using assessment strategically to change the way students learn. In S. Brown and A. Glasner (eds) *Assessment matters in higher education*. Buckingham: Society for Research into Higher Education and Open University Press.

Gil, E. (2003). Family play therapy: the bear with short nails. In C.E. Schaefer (ed.) *Foundations of play therapy*. San Francisco, CA: Jossey-Bass.

Gilbert, M.C. and Evans, K. (2007). *Psychotherapy supervision: an integrative relational approach to psychotherapy supervision*. Buckingham: Open University Press.

Gilbert, P. (2009). *The compassionate mind*. London: Constable & Robinson.

Gilbert, T. (2001). Reflective practice and clinical supervision: meticulous rituals of the confessional. *Journal of Advanced Nursing, 36*(2), 199–205.

Gilbride, D., Breithaupt, B. and Hoehle, B. (1996). The use of the Internet to support both on and off-campus learners in rehabilitation education. *Rehabilitation Education, 10*(1), 47–62.

Gilmore, A. (1999). *Review of the United Kingdom Evaluative Literature on Clinical Supervision in Nursing and Health Visiting*. London: UKCC (United Kingdom Central Council for Nursing, Midwifery and Health Visiting).

Gitterman, A. (1988). Teaching students to connect theory and practice. *Social Work with Groups, 11*, 33–41.

Gladwell, M. (2005). *Blink: the power of thinking without thinking*. London: Penguin.

Goffman, E. (1968). *Asylums*. Harmondsworth: Penguin.

Goldberger, N., Tarule, J., Clinchy, B. and Belensky, M. (1996). *Knowledge, difference and power*. New York: Basic Books.

Goldratt, E.M. (1997). *Critical chain*. Aldershot: Avebury.

Goodman, J. (1984). Reflection in teacher education: a case study and theoretical analysis. *Interchange, 15*(3), 9–26.

Gordon, D.R. (2001). Research application: identifying the use and misuse of formal models in nursing practice. In P. Benner (ed.) *From novice to expert: excellence and power in clinical nursing practice*. Upper Saddle River, NJ: Prentice Hall Health.

Graf, N.M. and Stebnicki, M.A. (2002). Using e-mail for clinical supervision in practicum: a qualitative analysis – qualitative analysis of e-mail supervision [electronic version]. *Journal of Rehabilitation, 68*(3), 41–50.

Grant, B. (1999). Walking on a rackety bridge: mapping supervision. HERDSA

Annual International Conference, Melbourne. Retrieved 8 December 2008 from: www.herdsa.org.au/wp-content/uploads/conference/1999/pdf/grant.pdf

Gray, D.E. (2007). Facilitating management learning: developing critical reflection through reflective tools. *Management Learning, 38*, 495–517.

Green, D.R. (1998). *Investigating the core skills of clinical supervision: a qualitative analysis.* Unpublished D. Clin Psych. Dissertation, University of Leeds.

Greenwood, J. (1998). The role of reflection in single and double loop learning. *Journal of Advanced Nursing Practice, 27*(5), 1048–1053.

Guanaes, C. and Rasera, E.F. (2006). Therapy as social construction: an interview with Sheila McNamee. *Interamerican Journal of Psychology, 40*(1), 127–136. Retrieved 18 September 2009 from: www.psicorip.org/Resumos/PerP/RIP/RIP036a0/RIP04014.pdf

Guerrero, A. and Piasecki, M. (eds) (2008). *Problem-based behavioral science and psychiatry.* New York: Springer.

Guest, D.E. and Conway, N. (2002). *Pressure at work and the psychological contract.* London: Chartered Institute of Personnel and Development. Accessed 24 January 2007 from: www.cipd.co.uk/subjects/empreltns/psycntrct/psycontr.htm

Guiffrida, D.A., Jordan, R., Saiz, S. and Barnes, K.L. (2007). The use of metaphor in clinical supervision. *Journal of Counseling & Development, 85*(4), 393–400.

Gutheil, T.G. and Gabbard, G.O. (1993). The concept of boundaries in clinical practice: theoretical and risk-management dimensions. *American Journal of Psychiatry, 150*, 188–196.

Habermas, J. (1984). *Theory of communicative action.* Boston, MA: Beacon Press.

Hagstrom, D., Hubbard, R., Hurtig, C., Mortola, P., Owstrow, J. and White, V. (2000). Teaching is like. . . .? *Educational Leadership, 57*(8), 24–27.

Hahn, W.K. (2001). The experience of shame in supervision. *Psychotherapy, 38*, 272–282.

Halpert, S.C., Reinhardt, B. and Toohey, M.J. (2007). Affirmative clinical supervision. In K.J. Bieschke, R.M. Perez and K.A. DeBord (eds) *Handbook of counseling and psychotherapy with lesbian, gay and transgender clients*, 2nd edn. Washington, DC: American Psychological Association.

Handal, G. and Lauvås, P. (1987). *Promoting reflective teaching: supervision in action.* Milton Keynes: Open University Press.

Hargreaves, D.H. (1996). Teaching as a research-based profession: possibilities and prospects. Teacher Training Agency annual lecture. Retrieved 27 August 2009 from: www.bera.ac.uk/files/2008/12/hargreaves_1996.pdf

Hargreaves, J. (2004). So how do you feel about that? Assessing reflective practice. *Nurse Education Today, 24*, 196–201.

Harlen, W. (2003). How high stakes testing impacts on motivation for learning. *Science Teacher Education, 37*, 2–6.

Harlen, W. (2009). Assessment for learning: research that is convincing (Part 1). *Education in Science, 231*, 30–31.

Harley, T. (2008). *The psychology of language: from data to theory*, 3rd edn. Hove: Psychology Press.

Harris, M. (2008). Scaffolding reflective journal writing – negotiating power, play and position. *Nurse Education Today, 28*, 314–326.

Hattie, J.A.C. (2009). *Visible learning: a synthesis of over 800 meta-analyses relating to achievement.* London: Routledge.

Hawkins, P. and Shohet, R. (2006). *Supervision in the helping professions*, 3rd edn. Maidenhead: Open University Press.

Hays, J.M. (2004). Keeping a learning journal. *Australian National University, Management and Organisations, The Community Project*. Retrieved 31 March 2009 from: www.teaching.fec.anu.edu.au/MGMT7030/

Heath, H. (1998). Keeping a reflective practice diary: a practical guide. *Nurse Education Today, 18*, 592–598.

Hendrickson, S.M., McCarthy Veach, P. and LeRoy, B.S. (2002). A qualitative investigation of student and supervisor perceptions of live supervision in genetic counselling. *Journal of Genetic Counseling, 11*(1), 25–49.

Hensley, P.H. (2002). The value of supervision. *The Clinical Supervisor, 21*(1), 97–110.

Heppner, P.P. and Roehlke, H.J. (1984). Differences among supervisees at different levels of training: implications for a developmental model of supervision. *Journal of Counseling Psychology, 31*, 76–90.

Hillbrand, M., Hawkins, D., Howe, D.M. and Stayner, D. (2008). Through the eyes of another: improving the skills of forensic providers using a consumer-informed role-play procedure. *Psychiatric Rehabilitation Journal, 31*(3), 239–242.

Hobbs, N. (1948). The development of a code of ethical standards for psychology. *American Psychologist, 3*, 80–84.

Hobbs, V. (2007). Faking it or hating it: can reflective practice be forced? *Reflective Practice, 8*(3), 405–417.

Holloway, E.L. (1995). *Clinical supervision: a systems approach*. Thousand Oaks, CA: Sage.

Holloway, E.L. and Neufeldt, S.A. (1995). Supervision: its contribution to treatment efficacy. *Journal of Consulting and Clinical Psychology, 63*, 207–213.

Holt, J. (1969). *How children fail*. Harmondsworth: Penguin.

Hopfe, A. (1999). *New vision does blind culture*. Retrieved 24 October 2002 from: www.geocities.com/EnchantedForest/Meadow/8921/blindculture.html.

Hounsell, D. (2007). Towards more sustainable feedback to students. In D. Boud and N. Falchikov (eds) *Rethinking assessment in higher education: learning for the longer term*. London: Routledge.

Hughes, J. and Youngson, S.C. (2009). *Personal development and clinical psychology*. London: Blackwell.

Hunt, C. (2001). Shifting shadows: metaphors and maps for facilitating reflective practice. *Reflective Practice, 2*(3), 275–287.

Hunter, K.M. (1993). *Doctors' stories*. Princeton, NJ: Princeton University Press.

Huxley, A. (1952). *The doors of perception*. Retrieved 4 March 2009 from: www.huxley.net/doors-of-perception/aldoushuxley-thedoorsofperception.pdf

Inskipp, F. and Proctor, B. (1993). *The art, craft and tasks of counselling supervision. Part 1: making the most of supervision*. 4 Ducks Walk, Twickenham, Middlesex: Cascade.

Inskipp, F. and Proctor, B. (1995). *The art, craft and tasks of counselling supervision. Part 2: becoming a supervisor*. 4 Ducks Walk, Twickenham, Middlesex: Cascade.

Ishiyama, F.I. (1988). A model of visual case processing using metaphors and drawings. *Counselor Education and Supervision, 28*, 153–161.

Jampolsky, G.G. (2004). *Love is letting go of fear*. Berkeley, CA: Celestial Arts.

Jarvis, J., Dyson, J., Thomas, K., Graham, S., Iantaffi, A. and Burchell, H. (2004).

Learning through creating stories: developing student teachers' understanding of the experiences of pupils with special educational needs in mainstream classrooms. Paper presented at the British Educational Research Conference Annual Conference, University of Manchester, 16–18 September. Retrieved 21 July 2009 from: www.uhra.herts.ac.uk/dspace/bitstream/2299/1030/1/901184.pdf

Jasper, M. (2003). *Beginning reflective practice*. Cheltenham: Nelson Thornes.

Jasper, M. (2004). Using journals and diaries. In C. Bulman and S. Schutz (eds) *Reflective practice in nursing*, 3rd edn. Oxford: Blackwell.

Johns, C. (1999). Reflection as empowerment? *Nursing Inquiry, 6*(4), 241–249.

Johns, C. (2000). Working with Alice: a reflection. *Complementary Therapies in Nursing and Midwifery, 6*, 199–203.

Johns, C. (2004). *Becoming a reflective practitioner*, 2nd edn. Oxford: Blackwell.

Johnston, K., Needham, R. and Brook, A. (1990). *Children's Learning in Science Project: interactive teaching in science: workshops for training courses: workshop 1*. Norwich: HMSO.

Johnston, M. (1994). Contrasts and similarities in case studies of teacher reflection and change. *Curriculum Inquiry, 24*(1), 9–26.

Jones, M. (1986). Evaluation and assessment 11–16. In D. Boardman (ed.) *Handbook for geography teachers*. Sheffield: Geographical Association.

Kagan, N. (1984). Interpersonal Process Recall: basic methods and recent research. In D. Larson (ed.) *Teaching psychological skills*. Monterey, CA: Brooks/Cole.

Kagan, N. and Krathwohl, D.R. (1967). *Studies in human interaction: Interpersonal Process Recall stimulated by videotape*. East Lansing, MI: Michigan State University.

Kagan-Klein, H. and Kagan, N. (1997). Interpersonal Process Recall: influencing human interaction. In C.E. Watkins, Jr. (ed.) *Handbook of psychotherapy supervision*. New York: Wiley.

Kane, M. and Trochim, W. (2007). *Concept mapping for planning and evaluation*. Thousand Oaks, CA: Sage.

Kanz, J.E. (2001). Clinical-supervision.com: issues in the provision of online supervision. *Professional Psychology: Research and Practice, 32*, 415–420.

Karp, M., Holmes, P. and Bradshaw Tauvon, K. (1998). *The handbook of psychodrama*. New York: Routledge.

Kavanagh, M. (2000). The 'Messy Mirror': confronting personal issues in fieldwork placements. In J. Spouse and L. Redfern (eds) *Successful supervision in health care practice*. Oxford: Blackwell.

Kearney, P. and Rosen, G. (1999). Shaping routine. *Community Care, 26*, 32–33.

Kees, N.L. and Leech, N.L. (2002). Using group counselling techniques to clarify and deepen the focus of supervision groups. *Journal for Specialists in Group Work, 27*, 7–15.

Kellogg, S. (2004). Dialogical encounters: contemporary perspectives on 'chairwork' in psychotherapy. *Psychotherapy: Theory, Research, Practice, Training, 41*(3), 310–320.

Kelly, G.A. (1955). *The psychology of personal constructs*. New York: Norton. Reprinted by Routledge (London), 1991.

Kemp, S.J. (2008). *Conceptions of teaching and pedagogical actions: influences of professional development*. Unpublished Ph.D. dissertation, University of Sheffield.

Kerka, S. (1996). *Journal writing and adult learning*. ERIC digest 174.

Kidner, P. (2000). A management perspective. In H. Martin (ed.) *Developing reflective practice*. Bristol: Policy Press.

Kilminster, S.M. and Jolly, B.C. (2000). Effective supervision in clinical practice settings: a literature review. *Medical Education, 34*(10), 827–840.

Kingston, P. and Smith, D. (1983). Preparation for live consultation and live supervision when working without a one-way screen. *Journal of Family Therapy, 5,* 219–233.

Klitzke, M.J. and Lombardo, T.W. (1991). A 'bug-in-the-eye' can be better than a 'bug-in-the-ear'. *Behavior Modification, 15,* 113–117.

Kolb, D.A. (1984). *Experiential learning – experience as the source of learning and development*. Englewood Cliffs, NJ: Prentice Hall.

Kopp, R.R. (1995). *Metaphor therapy: using client-generated metaphors in psychotherapy*. Bristol, PA: Brunner-Mazel.

Kuhn, T.S. (1962). *The structure of scientific revolutions*. Chicago, IL: University of Chicago Press.

Kunak, D.V. (1989). The critical event technique in job analysis. In K. Landau and W. Rohmert (eds) *Recent developments in job analysis*. London: Taylor & Francis.

Ladany, N., Ellis, M.V. and Friedlander, M.L. (1999). The supervisory working alliance, trainee self-efficacy, and satisfaction. *Journal of Counseling and Development, 77*(4), 447–455.

Lahad, M. (2000). *Creative supervision: the use of expressive arts methods in supervision and self-supervision*. London: Jessica Kingsley.

Lally, V. and Scaife, J.A. (1995). Towards a collaborative approach to teacher empowerment. *British Educational Research Journal, 21*(3), 323–338.

Larsen, D., Flesaker, K. and Stege, R. (2008). Qualitative interviewing using Interpersonal Process Recall: investigating internal experiences during professional-client conversations. *International Journal of Qualitative Methods, 7*(1), 18–37.

Lawrence, D.H. (1994). *The works of D.H. Lawrence*. Wordsworth Poetry Library. Ware, Herts: Wordsworth Editions.

Lawson, D.M. (1989). Using family sculpting in groups to enrich current intimate relationships. *Journal of College Student Development, 30,* 171–172.

Lee, L. and Littlejohns, S. (2007). Deconstructing Agnes – externalisation in systemic supervision. *Journal of Family Therapy, 29,* 238–248.

Lee-Baldwin, J. (2005). Asynchronous discussion forums; a closer look at the structure, focus and group dynamics that facilitate reflective thinking. *Contemporary Issues in Technology and Teacher Education, 5,* 93–116.

Lenney, M.J. (2006). Inclusion, projections of difference and reflective practice: an interactionist perspective. *Reflective Practice, 7*(2), 181–192.

Leonard, M. and Davey, C. (2001). *Thoughts on the 11 plus*. Belfast: Save the Children Fund.

Lepore, S.J. and Smyth, J.M. (eds) (2002). *The writing cure: how expressive writing promotes health and emotional well-being*. Washington, DC: American Psychological Association.

Lesage-Higgins, S.A. (1999). Family sculpting in premarital counseling. *Family Therapy, 26,* 31–38.

Lewicki, P., Hill, T. and Czyzewska, M. (1992). Nonconscious acquisition of information. *American Psychologist, 47,* 796–801.

Liese, B.S. and Beck, J. (1997). Cognitive therapy supervision. In C.E. Watkins, Jr. (ed.) *Handbook of psychotherapy supervision*. New York: Wiley.

Lillis, T. (2001). *Student writing: access, regulation and desire*. London: Routledge.

Lipson, M.Y. (1983). The influence of religious affiliation on children's memory for text information. *Reading Research Quarterly, 18*, 448–457.

Lizzio, A., Stokes, L. and Wilson, K. (2005). Approaches to learning in professional supervision: supervisee perceptions of processes and outcome. *Studies in Continuing Education, 27*(3), 239–256.

Locke, L.D. and McCollum, E.E. (2001). Clients' views of live supervision and satisfaction with therapy. *Journal of Marital and Family Therapy, 27*(1), 129–135.

Long, G., Grandis, S. and Glasper, E.A. (1999). Investing in practice: enquiry and problem-based learning. *British Journal of Nursing, 8*(17), 1171–1174.

Loughran, J. (1996). *Developing reflective practice: learning about teaching and learning through modelling*. London: Falmer Press.

McDonald, R. and Harrison, S. (2004). Autonomy and modernisation: the management of change in an English primary care trust. *Health and Social Care in the Community*, 12, 194–201.

McDowell, L. and Sambell, K. (1999). The experience of innovative assessment: student perspectives. In S. Brown and A. Glasner (eds) *Assessment matters in higher education*. Buckingham: Society for Research into Higher Education and Open University Press.

McGill, I. and Brockbank, A. (2004). *The action learning handbook: powerful techniques for education, professional development and training*. London: Routledge Falmer.

McGregor, S.L.T. (2004). Transformative learning: we teach who we are. Kappa Omicron Nu FORUM, *14*(2) ISSN: 1546–2676. Retrieved 19 September 2009 from: www.kon.org/archives/forum/14-2/forum14-2_article4.html

MacKnight, C.B. (2000). Teaching critical thinking through online discussions. *Educause Quarterly, 23*(4), 38–41.

Mahoney, M.J. (1986). The tyranny of technique. *Counseling and Values, 30*, 169–174.

Mahoney, M.J. (2003). *Constructive psychotherapy: theory and practice*. New York: Guilford Press.

Mandinach, E.B. (2005). The development of effective evaluation methods for e-learning: a concept paper and action plan. *Teachers College Record, 107*(8), 1814–1835.

Mantzoukas, S. (2007). Reflection and problem/enquiry-based learning: confluences and contradictions. *Reflective Practice, 8*(2), 241–253.

Marchetti-Mercer, M.C. and Cleaver, G. (2000). Genograms and family sculpting: an aid to cross-cultural understanding in the training of psychology students in South Africa. *The Counseling Psychologist, 28*(1), 61–80.

Marquardt, M. (2004). *Optimizing the power of action learning*. Palo Alto, CA: Davies-Black.

Marrow, C.E., Hollyoake, K., Hamer, D. and Kenrick, C. (2002). Clinical supervision using video-conferencing technology: a reflective account. *Journal of Nursing Management, 10*(5), 275–282.

Marshall, P.A. and O'Keefe, J.P. (1995). Medical students' first-person narratives of a patient's story of AIDS. *Social Science and Medicine, 40*(1), 67–76.

Marsick, V.J. and O'Neil, J. (1999). The many faces of action learning. *Management Learning, 30*(2), 159–176.

Marton, F. and Booth, S. (1997). *Learning and awareness*. Hillsdale, NJ: Lawrence Erlbaum.

Mason, B. (1993). Towards positions of safe uncertainty. *Human Systems, 4*, 189–200.

Mattinson, J. and Sinclair, I. (1979). *Mate and stalemate*. Oxford: Blackwell.

Mearns, D. (1997). *Person-centred counselling training*. London: Sage.

Meredith, R. and Bradley, L. (1989). Differential supervision: roles, functions and activities. In L. Bradley (ed.) *Counselor supervision*. Muncie, IN: Accelerated Development.

Mezirow, J. (1981). A critical theory of adult learning and education. *Adult Education, 32*(1), 3–24.

Mezirow, J. (1997). Cognitive processes: contemporary paradigms of learning. In P. Sutherland (ed.) *Adult learning: a reader*. London: Kogan Page.

Mezirow, J. (2000). *Learning as transformation: critical perspectives on a theory in progress*. San Francisco, CA: Jossey-Bass.

Mezirow, J. and associates (1990). *Fostering critical reflection in adulthood: a guide to transformational and emancipatory practice*. San Francisco, CA: Jossey-Bass.

Middleman, R.R. and Rhodes, G.B. (1985). *Competent supervision: making imaginative judgments*. Englewood Cliffs, NJ: Prentice Hall.

Milne, D. (2007). An empirical definition of clinical supervision. *British Journal of Clinical Psychology, 46*(4), 449–459.

Milne, D. (2009). *Evidence-based clinical supervision*. Chichester: Wiley Blackwell.

Milne, D. and James, I.A. (2000). A systematic review of effective cognitive-behavioural supervision. *British Journal of Clinical Psychology (BJCP), 39*, 111–127.

Minghella, E. and Benson, A. (1995). Developing reflective practice in mental health nursing through critical incident analysis. *Journal of Advanced Nursing, 21*(2), 205–213.

Mollon, P. (1989). Anxiety, supervision and a space for thinking: some narcissistic perils for clinical psychologists in learning psychotherapy. *British Journal of Medical Psychology, 62*, 113–122.

Moon, J. (1999). *Reflection in learning and personal development*. London: Kogan Page.

Moon, J. (2001). *Short courses and workshops: improving the impact of learning and professional development*. London: Kogan Page.

Moon, J. (2004). *A handbook of reflective and experiential learning: theory and practice*. London: RoutledgeFalmer.

Moon, J. (2006). *Learning journals*, 2nd edn. London: Routledge.

Morales-Mann, E.T. and Kaitell, A.C. (2001). Problem-based learning in a new Canadian curriculum, *Journal of Advanced Nursing, 33*(1), 13–19.

Muijs, D. and Reynolds, D. (2006). *Effective teaching: research and practice*. London: Sage.

Mullen, J.A. and Luke, M. (2007). Supervision can be playful, too: play therapy techniques that enhance supervision. *International Journal of Play Therapy, 16*(1), 69–85.

Murphy, S. and Smith, M.A. (1991). *Writing portfolios: a bridge from teaching to assessment*. Markham, Ontario: Pippin.

Mutch, A. (2003). Exploring the practice of feedback to students. *Active Learning in Higher Education, 4*(1), 24–38.

Myers, D. and Wee, D. (2005). *Disaster mental health services: a primer for practitioners.* New York: Routledge.

Naleppa, M.J. and Reid, W.J. (1998). Task-centered case management for the elderly: developing a practice model. *Research on Social Work Practice, 8*, 63–85.

Napoli, M. (2006). *A family casebook: problem based learning and mindful self-reflection.* Boston, MA: Allyn & Bacon.

National Center on Education and the Economy (2006). *Tough choices or tough times: the report of the New Commission on the Skills of the American Workforce (Executive summary).* Washington, DC. Retrieved 21 July 2009 from: www.skillscommission.org/pdf/exec_sum/ToughChoices_EXECSUM.pdf

National Occupational Standards (undated). Various articles on 'Reflective practice'. In *Skills for Business.* Retrieved 31 March 2009 from: www.ukstandards.org.uk

Neden, J. and Burnham, J. (2007). Using relational reflexivity as a resource in teaching family therapy. *Journal of Family Therapy, 29*(4), 359–363.

Nelson, M.L., Barnes, K.L., Evans, A.L. and Triggiano, P.J. (2008). Working with conflict in clinical supervision: wise supervisors' perspectives. *Journal of Counseling Psychology, 55*(2), 172–184.

Neufeld, V. and Barrows, H. (1974). The McMaster philosophy: an approach to medical education. *Journal of Medical Education, 49*, 1040–1050.

Newton, R. (1996). Getting to grips with barriers to reflection. *SCUTREA Conference Papers* (electronic version). Retrieved 23 March 2009 from: www.leeds.ac.uk/educol/documents/00003059.htm

Norberg-Hodge, H. (1991). *Ancient futures: learning from Ladakh.* Shaftesbury: Element.

Norman, G.R. and Schmidt, H.G. (1992). The psychological basis of problem-based learning: a review of the evidence. *Academic Medicine, 67*(9), 557–565.

Norman, I.J., Redfern, S.J., Tomalin, D.A. and Oliver, S. (1992). Developing Flanagan's critical incident technique to elicit indicators of high and low quality nursing care from patients and their nurses. *Journal of Advanced Nursing, 17*(5), 590–600.

Norton, L., Richardson, J.T.E., Hartley, J., Newstead, S. and Mayes, J. (2005). Teachers' beliefs and intentions concerning teaching in higher education. *Higher Education, 50*, 537–571.

Novak, J.D. (2008). *Concept maps: what the heck is this?* Retrieved 19 July 2009 from: www.msu.edu/~luckie/ctools/

Novak, J.D. and Cañas, A.J. (2006). The theory underlying concept maps and how to construct and use them. *Institute for Human and Machine Cognition.* Retrieved 19 February 2009 from: www.cmap.ihmc.us/Publications/ResearchPapers/TheoryCmaps/TheoryUnderlyingConceptMaps.htm.

Oates, J. (producer/director) (2005a). *Terry* (DVD 00128). Milton Keynes: The Open University.

Oates, J. (producer/director) (2005b). *Susan* (DVD 00127). Milton Keynes: The Open University.

Obholzer, A. (1994). Managing social anxieties in public sector health organisations. In A. Obholzer and V. Zagier-Roberts (eds) *The unconscious at work: individual and organisational stress in human services.* London: Routledge.

O'Connell, B. (2005). Solution-focussed supervision. In B. O'Connell, *Solution-focussed therapy*, 2nd edn. London: Sage.

Ögren, M.L., Apelman, A. and Klawitter, M. (2001). The group in psychotherapy supervision. *The Clinical Supervisor, 20*, 147–175.

O'Hagan, M. (1996). Two accounts of mental distress. In J. Read and J. Reynolds (eds) *Speaking our minds*. London: Macmillan.

O'Hagan, M. (2009). *Making sense of madness from the inside*. Retrieved 22 September 2009 from: www.outoftheirminds.co.nz/?p=222

O'Hanlon, B. and Weiner-Davis, M. (2003). *In search of solutions: a new direction in psychotherapy*, 2nd edn. New York: Norton.

Olkin, R. (1999). *What psychotherapists should know about disability*. New York: Guilford Press.

O'Neil, J. (1999). *The role of the learning adviser in action learning*. Unpublished doctoral dissertation, Teachers College, Columbia University, New York.

Open University (2005). *Observation skills in psychology*. Milton Keynes: The Open University.

Osborn, A.F. (1963). *Applied imagination: principles and procedures of creative problem solving*, 3rd revised edn. New York: Scribner.

Osmond, J. and Darlington, Y. (2005). Reflective analysis: techniques for facilitating reflection. *Australian Social Work, 58*(1), 3–14.

Osterman, K.F. and Kottkamp, R.B. (1993). *Reflective practice for educators: improving schooling through professional development*. Newbury Park, CA: Corwin Press.

Osterman, K.F. and Kottkamp, R.B. (2004). *Reflective practice for educators: professional development to improve student learning*, 2nd edn. Thousand Oaks, CA: Corwin Press.

Ovens, P. (2003). A patchwork text approach to assessment in teacher education. *Teaching in Higher Education, 8*(4), 545–562.

Padesky, C.A. (1993). *Socratic questioning: changing minds or guided discovery*. Retrieved 1 July 2007 from: www.padesky.com/clinicalcorner/pdf/socquest.pdf

Page, S. and Wosket, V. (2001). *Supervising the counsellor: a cyclical model*, 2nd edn. London: Routledge.

Paré, D. (2001). Crossing the divide: the therapeutic use of internalized other interviewing. *Journal of Clinical Activities, Assignments and Handouts in Psychotherapy Practice, 1*(4), 21–28.

Paul, R.W. (1993). *Critical thinking: what every person needs to survive in a rapidly changing world*. Santa Rosa, CA: Foundation for Critical Thinking.

Paul, R.W. and Elder, L. (2006). *Critical thinking: tools for taking charge of your learning and your life*. Englewood Cliffs, NJ: Prentice Hall.

Paulus, P.B. and Brown, V.R. (2007). Toward more creative and innovative group idea generation: a cognitive-social-motivational perspective of brainstorming. *Social and Personality Psychology Compass, 1*(1), 248–265.

Paulus, P.B. and Yang, H.C. (2000). Idea generation in groups: a basis for creativity in organizations. *Organizational Behavior and Human Decision Processes, 82*, 76–87.

Pavlovich, K. (2007). The development of reflective practice through student journals. *Higher Education Research and Development, 26*(3), 281–295.

Pecheone, R.L., Pigg, M., Chung, R.R. and Souviney, R.J. (2005). Performance assessment and electronic portfolios: their effect on teacher learning and education. *The Clearing House, 78*(4), 164–176.

Pedder, J. (1986). Reflections on the theory and practice of supervision. *Psychoanalytic Psychotherapy, 1*, 1–12.

Perls, F.S. (1969). *Gestalt therapy verbatim*. Lafayette, CA: Real People Press.

Peters, T.J. and Waterman, R.H. (1982). *In search of excellence: lessons from America's best-run companies*. New York: Harper & Row.

Petticrew, M. and Roberts, H. (2006). *Systematic reviews in the social sciences*. Oxford: Blackwell.

Polkinghorne, D. (1988). *Narrative knowing and the human sciences*. Albany, NY: State University of New York Press.

Postman, N. and Weingartner, C. (1971). *Teaching as a subversive activity*. Harmonds-worth: Penguin.

Power, M. (1996). *The audit society: rituals of verification*. Oxford: Oxford University Press.

Presbury, J., Echterling, L.G. and McKee, J.E. (1999). Supervision for inner vision: solution-focused strategies. *Counselor Education and Supervision, 39*, 146–156.

Price, B. (2003). *Studying nursing using problem-based and enquiry-based learning*. Basingstoke: Palgrave Macmillan.

Prince, G. (1975). Creativity, self and power. In I.A. Taylor and J.W. Getzels (eds) *Perspectives in creativity*. Chicago, IL: Aldine.

Proctor, B. (2000). *Group supervision: a guide to creative practice*. London: Sage.

Proctor, B. and Inskipp, B. (2009). Group supervision. In J.M. Scaife (ed.) *Supervision in clinical practice*. Hove: Brunner-Routledge.

Progoff, I. (1992). *At a journal workshop*. New York: Tarcher/Putnam.

Quinn, M.F. (2000). *Principles and practice of nurse education*. Cheltenham: Stanley Thornes.

Race, P. (2001). A briefing on self, peer and group assessment. *LTSN Generic Centre*. Retrieved 19 July 2009 from: www.heacademy.ac.uk/resources/detail/SNAS/snas_901

Rai, L. (2006). Owning (up to) reflective writing in social work education. *Social Work Education, 25*(8), 785–797.

Rath, A. (2002) Action research as border crossing: stories from the classroom. In N. Lyons and V. Kubler LaBoskey (eds) *Narrative inquiry in practice: advancing the knowledge of teaching*. New York: Teachers College Press.

Reay, D. and Wiliam, D. (1999). 'I'll be a nothing': structure, agency and the construction of identity through assessment. *British Educational Research Journal, 25*(3), 343–354.

Redmond, B. (2006). *Reflection in action*. Aldershot: Ashgate.

Rees, E.C. (2004). The problem with outcomes-based curricula in medical education: insight from educational theory. *Medical Education, 38*, 593–598.

Rhine, S. and Bryant, J. (2007). Enhancing pre-service teachers' reflective practice with digital video-based dialogue. *Reflective Practice, 8*(3), 345–358.

Riley, R.H. (2008). *Manual of simulation in health care*. New York: Oxford University Press.

Rinpoche, R. (1992). *The Tibetan book of living and dying*. London: Rider.

Robbins, A. and Erismann, M. (1992). Developing therapeutic artistry: a joint counter-transference supervisory seminar/stone sculpting workshop. *The Arts in Psychotherapy, 19*, 367–377.

Roberts, J. (1998). *Language teacher education*. London: Arnold.

Roberts, M. (1989). Writing as reflection. In F. Slater (ed.) *Language and learning in the teaching of geography*. London: Routledge.

Rolfe, G. and Gardner, L. (2006). Do not ask who I am: confession, emancipation and (self-)management through reflection. *Journal of Nursing Management, 14*(8), 593–600.

Rolfe, G., Freshwater, D. and Jasper, M. (2001). *Critical reflection for nursing and the helping professions: a user's guide*. Basingstoke: Palgrave.

Ronen, T. and Rosenbaum, M. (1998). Beyond direct verbal instructions in cognitive behavioral supervision. *Cognitive and Behavioral Practice, 5*, 7–23.

Rosen, V. (1993). Black students in higher education. In M. Thorpe, R. Edwards and A. Hanson (eds) *Culture and processes of adult learning*. London: Routledge.

Rosenbaum, M. and Ronen, T. (1998). Clinical supervision from the standpoint of cognitive-behaviour therapy. *Psychotherapy, 35*, 220–230.

Rosenblatt, A. and Mayer, J.E. (1975). Objectionable supervisory styles: students' views. *Social Work, 20*(3), 184–189.

Roth, S. and Epston, D. (1995). *Framework for a White/Epston type interview*. Retrieved 27 July 2009 from: www.narrativeapproaches.com/narrative%20 papers%20folder/white_interview.htm

Rothschild, B. and Rand, M. (2006). *Help for the helper: the psychophysiology of compassion fatigue and vicarious trauma*. New York: Norton.

Rowland, S. (2000). *The enquiring university teacher*. Milton Keynes: Society for Research into Higher Education and Open University Press.

Rubin, N.J., Bebeau, M., Leigh, I.W., Lichtenberg, J.W., Nelson, P.D., Portnoy, S., Smith, I.L. and Kaslow, N.J. (2007). The competency movement within psychology: an historical perspective. *Professional Psychology: Research and Practice, 38*(5), 452–462.

Ruiz, J.G., Mintzer, M.G. and Leipzig, R. (2006) The impact of e-learning in medical education. *Academic Medicine, 81*(3), 207–212.

Ryle, A. (2004). Writing by patients and therapists in cognitive analytic therapy. In G. Bolton, S. Howlett, C. Lago and J.K. Wright (eds) *Writing cures: an introductory handbook of writing in counselling and therapy*. Hove: Brunner-Routledge.

Saiz, S.G. and Guiffrida, D.A. (2001). The use of metaphor in the supervision of counselor education students. Paper presented at the North Atlantic region of the Association for Counselor Education and Supervision annual meeting, University of Massachusetts-Amherst.

Salzberger-Wittenberg, I. (1983). Part 1: beginnings. In I. Salzberger-Wittenberg, G. Henry and E. Osborne (eds) *The emotional experience of teaching and learning*. London: Routledge & Kegan Paul.

Santoro, N. and Allard, A. (2008). Scenarios as springboards for reflection on practice: stimulating discussion. *Reflective Practice, 9*(2), 167–176.

Savin-Baden, M. (2003). *Facilitating problem-based learning: illuminating perspectives*. Maidenhead: Society for Research into Higher Education and Open University Press.

Sawicki, J. (1991). *Disciplining Foucault: feminism, power and the body*. New York: Routledge.

Sayers, J. and Franklin, T. (2008). Culture shock! Cultural issues in a tertiary course using reflective techniques. *Reflective Practice, 9*(1), 79–88.

Scaife, J.A. and Scaife, J.M. (1996). A General Supervision Framework: applications in teacher education. In J. Trafford (ed.) *Learning to teach: aspects of initial teacher education.* Sheffield: USDE Papers in Education.

Scaife, J.A. and Wellington, J.J. (2008). A case-study investigating university teachers' and students' ideas about assessment of student learning. Paper presented at the Frontiers in Higher Education: Proceedings of the Fifth International Conference on Teaching and Learning in Higher Education, Singapore, 3–5 December.

Scaife, J.M. (1993a). Application of a general supervision framework: creating a context of cooperation. *Educational and Child Psychology, 10*(2), 61–72.

Scaife, J.M. (1993b). Setting the scene for supervision: the application of a systems framework to an initial placement consultation. *Human Systems, 4*, 161–173.

Scaife, J.M. (1995). *Training to help: a survival guide.* Sheffield: Riding Press.

Scaife, J.M. (2001). *Supervision in the mental health professions.* London: Brunner-Routledge.

Scaife, J.M. (2009). *Supervision in clinical practice.* Hove: Brunner-Routledge.

Schein, E.H. (1996). Kurt Lewin's change theory in the field and in the classroom. *Organizational Dynamics, 9*(2): 27–47.

Schluter, J., Seaton, P. and Chaboyer, W. (2008). Critical incident technique: a user's guide for nurse researchers. *Journal of Advanced Nursing, 61*(1), 107–114.

Schön, D.A. (1983). *The reflective practitioner: how professionals think in action.* New York: Basic Books.

Schön, D.A. (1987). *Educating the reflective practitioner.* San Francisco, CA: Jossey-Bass.

Schutz, S., Angove, C. and Sharp, P. (2004). Assessing and evaluating reflection. In C. Bulmer and S. Schutz (eds) *Reflective practice in nursing*, 4th edn. Oxford: Blackwell.

Scott, F.R. (1966). Examiner. *Selected poems.* Toronto: McClelland & Stewart.

Sebba, J., Deakin Crick, R., Yu, G., Lawson, H., Harlen, W. and the Evidence for Policy and Practice Information and Co-ordinating Centre (EPPI-Centre) (2008). *Impact of self and peer assessment on students in secondary schools: a systematic review of the literature.* Retrieved 18 July 2009 from: www.dcsf.gov.uk/research/programmeofresearch/index.cfm?type=5&keywordlist1=0&keywordlist2=0&keywordlist3=0&andor=or&keyword=self+assessment&x=0&y=0

Senge, P., Cambron-McCabe, N., Lucas, T., Smith, B., Dutton, J. and Kleiner, A. (2000). *Schools that learn: a fifth discipline fieldbook for educators, parents, and everyone who cares about education.* New York: Doubleday-Currency.

Shaw, B.F. and Dobson, K.S. (1989). Competency judgements in the training and evaluation of psychotherapists. *Journal of Consulting and Clinical Psychology, 56*, 666–672.

Sheikh, A.I., Milne, D.B. and MacGregor, V.L. (2007). A model of personal professional development in the systematic training of clinical psychologists. *Clinical Psychology and Psychotherapy, 14*, 278–287.

Shulman, L.S. (1986). Those who understand: knowledge growth in teaching. *Educational Researcher, 15*(2), 4–14.

Simons, L. (2008). Peer supervision where everyone has a voice. *Clinical Psychology Forum, 191*, 52–53.

Sinclair-Penwarden, A. (2006) Listen up: we should not be made to disclose our personal feelings in reflection assignments. *Nursing Times, 102*(37), 12.

Skovholt, T.M. and McCarthy, P.R. (1988). Critical incidents: catalysts for counselor development. *Journal of Counseling and Development, 67*, 69–72.

Sloan, G. (2007). Psychological approaches to the clinical supervision encounter. In J. Driscoll (ed.) *Practising clinical supervision*, 2nd edn. Philadelphia, PA: Baillière Tindall Elsevier.

Smith, A. and Russell, J. (1991). Using critical learning incidents in nurse education. *Nurse Education Today, 11*, 284–291.

Smith, A. and Russell, J. (1993). Critical incident technique. In J. Reed and S. Proctor (eds) *Nurse education: a reflective approach*. London: Edward Arnold.

Smith, D. and Fitzpatrick, M. (1995). Patient-therapist boundary issues: an integrative review of theory and research. *Professional Psychology: Research and Practice, 26*(5), 499–506.

Smith, D. and Kingston, P. (1980). Live supervision without a one-way screen. *Journal of Family Therapy, 2*, 379–387.

Smith, K. and Lev-Ari, L. (2005). The place of the practicum in pre-service teacher education: the voice of the students. *Asia-Pacific Journal of Teacher Education, 33*(3), 289–302.

Smith, L.B. (2002). *Unsent letters: writing to resolve and renew*. Cincinnati, OH: Writer's Digest Books.

Smith, P.A.C. (2001). Action learning and reflective practice in project environments that are related to leadership development. *Management Learning, 32*(1), 31–48.

Smyth, J. (1991). *Teachers as collaborative learners*. Milton Keynes: Open University Press.

Snadden, D., Thomas, M.L., Griffin, E.M. and Hudson, H. (1996). Portfolio-based learning and general practice vocational training. *Medical Education, 30*, 148–152.

Sommer, C.A. and Cox, J.A. (2003). Using Greek mythology as a metaphor to enhance supervision. *Counselor Education and Supervision, 42*, 326–335.

Spalding, E. and Wilson, A. (2002). Demystifying reflection: a study of pedagogical strategies that encourage reflective journal writing. *Teachers College Record, 104*(7), 1393–1421.

Spall, B., Read, S. and Chantry, D. (2001). Metaphor: exploring its origins and therapeutic use in death, dying and bereavement. *International Journal of Palliative Nursing, 7*(7), 345–353.

Stalker, J. (1996). Sharing the secrets of perspectives. In D. Boud and N. Miller (eds) *Working with experience: animating learning*. London: Routledge.

Stark, S. (2006). Using action learning for professional development. *Educational Action Research, 14*(1), 23–43.

Stebnicki, M.A. and Glover, N.M. (2001). E-supervision as a complementary approach to traditional face-to-face clinical supervision in rehabilitation counseling: problems and solutions. *Rehabilitation Education, 15*, 283–293.

Steffensen, M.S., Joag-dev, C. and Anderson, R.C. (1979). A cross-cultural perspective on reading comprehension. *Reading Research Quarterly, 15*, 10–29.

Steinbeck, J. (2000). *The log from the sea of Cortez*. London: Penguin Classics.

Steinberg, D. (2004). From archetype to impressions: the magic of words. In G. Bolton, S. Howlett, C. Lago and J.K. Wright (eds) *Writing cures: an introductory handbook of writing in counselling and therapy*. Hove: Brunner-Routledge.

Stevens, E.G. (2007). *Our non-directed support organization*. Retrieved 15 February 2010 from: www.frontrangeeducators.com/non-directed.htm

Stevens, E.G. (2008). *Confidence quotes*. Retrieved 20 November 2008 from: www.quotations.about.com/cs/inspirationquotes/a/Confidence3.htm

Stewart, S. and Richardson, B. (2000). Reflection and its place in the curriculum: should it be assessed? *Assessment and Evaluation in Higher Education, 25*(4), 369–380.

Stiler, G.M. and Philleo, T. (2003). Blogging and blogspots: an alternative format for encouraging reflective practice among preservice teachers. *Education, 123*(4), 789–797.

Stoltenberg, C.D. and McNeill, B.W. (2009). *IDM supervision: an integrated developmental model for supervising counselors and therapists*. San Francisco, CA: Jossey-Bass.

Stoltenberg, C.D., McNeill, B.W. and Crethar, H.C. (1994). Changes in supervision as counselors and therapists gain experience: a review. *Professional Psychology Research and Practice, 25*, 416–449.

Strathern, M. (2000). The tyranny of transparency. *British Educational Research Journal*, 26, 309–321.

Strosahl, K. and Jacobson, N. (1986). Training and supervision of behaviour therapists. *The Clinical Supervisor, 4*, 183–206.

Suhre, M.J.C. and Harskamp, G.E. (2001). Teaching planning and reflection in nurse education. *Nurse Education Today, 21*, 373–381.

Svartberg, M. and Stiles, T.C. (1992). Predicting patient change from therapist competence and patient–therapist complementarity in short-term anxiety-provoking psychotherapy: a pilot study. *Journal of Consulting and Clinical Psychology, 60*, 304–307.

Swann, W.B., Jr., Guiliano, T. and Wegner, D.M. (1982). Where leading questions can lead: the power of conjecture in social interaction. *Journal of Personality and Social Psychology, 42*, 1025–1035.

Sweeney, G., Webley, P. and Treacher, A. (2001). Supervision in occupational therapy. Part 1: the supervisor's anxieties. *British Journal of Occupational Therapy Special Issue, 64*(7), 337–345.

Taggart, G.L. and Wilson, A.P. (2005). *Promoting reflective thinking in teachers: 50 action strategies*, 2nd edn. Thousand Oaks, CA: Corwin Press.

Talbot, M. (2002). Reflective practice: new insights or more-of-the-same? Thoughts on an autobiographical critical incident analysis. *Reflective Practice, 3*(2), 225–229.

Taylor, C. (1985). Theories of meaning. In C. Taylor, *Human agency and language: philosophical papers 1*. Cambridge: Cambridge University Press.

Taylor, F.W. ([1911] 1998) *Principles of scientific management*. Norcross, GA: Engineering and Management Press.

Thobaben, M. and Cherry, P. (2005). Role reversal: from nurse to patient. An eye-opening experience. *Home Health Care Management Practice, 16*, 222–224.

Tomm, K. (1987). Interventive interviewing. Part II: reflexive questioning as a means to enable self-healing. *Family Process, 26*, 167–183.

Tomm, K. (1988). Interventive interviewing. Part III: intending to ask lineal, circular, strategic or reflexive questions. *Family Process, 27*, 1–15.

Torosyan, R. (2001). Motivating students: evoking transformative learning and growth. *Etc, 58*(3), 311–328.

Tracey, T.J., Ellickson, J.L. and Sherry, P. (1989). Reactance in relation to different supervisory environments and counselor development. *Journal of Counseling Psychology, 365*, 336–344.

Trilling, L. (1979). *Of this time, of that place, and other stories*. New York: Harcourt Brace Jovanovich.

Tripp, D. (1993). *Critical incidents in teaching*. London: Routledge.

Trollope, A. (1953). *Barchester Towers*. Oxford: Oxford University Press.

Troster, A.I., Paolo, A.M., Glatt, S.L., Hubble, J.P. and Koller, W.C. (1995). Interactive video conferencing in the provision of neuro-psychological services in rural areas. *Journal of Community Psychology, 23*, 85–88.

Tsui, M.S., Ho, W.S. and Lam, C.M. (2005). The use of supervisory authority in Chinese cultural context. *Administration in Social Work, 29*(4), 51–68.

Tudor, K. and Worrall, M. (2004). Person-centred philosophy and the theory in the practice of supervision. In K. Tudor and M. Worrall (eds) *Freedom to practise: person-centred approaches to supervision*. Ross-on-Wye, Herefordshire: PCCS Books.

UK Centre for Legal Education (2008). *What is reflective practice?* Retrieved 19 July 2009 from: www.ukcle.ac.uk/resources/reflection/what.html

University of Manchester (2008). *What is enquiry-based learning (EBL)?* Centre for Excellence in Enquiry-Based Learning. Retrieved 2 March 2009 from: www.campus.manchester.ac.uk/ceebl/ebl/

University of Toronto Libraries (2000). *Introduction to EBM: what is EBM?* (online). Toronto: University of Toronto Libraries. Retrieved 16 September 2002 from: www.cebm.utoronto.ca/intro/whatis/.htm

Valadez, A.A. and Garcia, J.L. (1998). In a different light: an environmental metaphor of counselor supervision. *Texas Counseling Association Journal, 26*, 92–106.

Van Knippenberg, D. and Schippers, M.C. (2007). Work group diversity. *Annual Review of Psychology, 58*, 514–541.

Van Manen, M. (1990). *Researching lived experience: human science for an action sensitive pedagogy*. Albany, NY: State University of New York Press.

Van Ments, M. (1999). *The effective use of role play: practical techniques for improving learning*, 2nd edn. London: Kogan Page.

Varner, D. and Peck, S. (2003). Learning from learning journals: the benefits and challenges of using learning journal assignments. *Journal of Management Education, 27*(1), 52–77.

Visintainer, M. (1986). The nature of knowledge and theory in nursing. *Image: The Journal of Nursing Scholarship, 18*, 32–38.

Visser, C. and Norman, H. (2004). *The solution focussed reflecting management team*. Retrieved 22 February 2009 from: www.solutionsology.co.uk/trainingpages/SFRT.htm

Von Foerster, H. (1981). *Observing systems*. Seaside, CA: Intersystems.

Von Foerster, H. (1991). Through the eyes of the other. In F. Steier (ed.) *Research and reflexivity*. London: Sage.

Vygotsky, L.S. (1962). *Thought and language*. Cambridge, MA: The MIT Press.

Walker, D. (1985). Writing and reflection. In D. Boud, R. Keogh and D. Walker (eds) *Reflection: turning experience into learning*. London: Kogan Page.

Wallcraft, J. and Michaelson, J. (2001). Developing a survivor discourse to replace the 'psychopathology' of breakdown and crisis. In C. Newnes, G. Holmes and

C. Dunn (eds) *This is madness too: critical perspectives on mental health services.* Ross-on-Wye, Herefordshire: PCCS Books.

Waller, R. (2000). A view from the trenches. *Children and Young People's Health Directorate Newsletter*, March.

Wannan, G. and York, A. (2005). Using video and role play to introduce medical students to family therapy: is watching better than appearing? *Journal of Family Therapy, 27*, 263–271.

Watkins, C.E., Jr. (ed.) (1997). *The handbook of psychotherapy supervision.* New York: Wiley.

Weiner, E. (2008). *The geography of bliss.* New York: Hachette.

Weinert, F.E. (2001). Concept of competence: a conceptual clarification. In D.S. Rychen and L.H. Salganik (eds) *Defining and selecting key competencies.* Seattle, WA: Hogrefe & Huber.

Wellington, J. and Szczerbinski, M. (2007). *Research methods for the social sciences.* London: Continuum.

West, J.D. (1984). Utilizing simulated families and live supervision to stimulate skill development of family therapists. *Counselor Education and Supervision, 24*, 17–27.

Westbrook, D., Kennerley, H. and Kirk, J. (2007). *An introduction to cognitive behaviour therapy.* London: Sage.

Wheeler, J. (2007). Solution-focused supervision. In T.S. Nelson and F.N. Thomas (eds) *Handbook of solution-focused brief therapy: clinical applications.* Binghamton, NY: Haworth Press.

Wheeler, M.A., Stuss, D.T. and Tulving, E. (1997). Towards a theory of episodic memory: the frontal lobes and autonoetic consciousness. *Psychological Bulletin, 121*, 331–354.

Wheeler, S. and Richards, K. (2007). The impact of clinical supervision on counsellors and therapists, their practice and their clients: a systematic review of the literature. *Counselling and Psychotherapy Research, 7*(1), 54–65.

Whipp, J. (2003). Scaffolding critical reflection in online discussions: helping prospective teachers think deeply about field experiences in urban schools. *Journal of Teacher Education, 54*(4), 321–333.

Whitaker, C.A. and Bumberry, W.M. (1988). *Dancing with the family: a symbolic-experiential approach.* Levittown, PA: Brunner-Mazel.

White, M. (1993). Deconstruction and therapy. In S.G. Gilligan and R.E. Price (eds) *Therapeutic conversations.* New York: Norton.

White, M. (2000). Reflecting teamwork as definitional ceremony revisited. In M. White (ed.) *Reflections on narrative practice: essays and interviews.* Adelaide: Dulwich Centre.

White, M. and Epston, D. (1990). *Narrative means to therapeutic ends.* New York: Norton.

Wilbur, M.P., Roberts-Wilbur, J., Hart, G.M., Morris, J.R. and Betz, R.L. (1994). Structured group supervision (SGS): a pilot study. *Counselor Education and Supervision, 33*, 262–279.

Wilkie, K. and Burns, I. (2003). *Problem-based learning: a handbook for nurses.* Basingstoke: Palgrave Macmillan.

Williams, A. (1988). Action methods in supervision. *Clinical Supervisor, 6*, 13–27.

Williams, A. (1995). *Visual and active supervision.* New York: Norton.

Williams, M. (1996). *The velveteen rabbit.* London: Bodley Head.

Wilson, T.D. (2002). *Strangers to ourselves: discovering the adaptive unconscious*. Cambridge, MA: Harvard University Press.

Winefield, H., Murrell, T. and Clifford, J. (1994). Sources of occupational stress for Australian GPs, and their implications for postgraduate training. *Family Practice, 11*, 413–417.

Winter, M. and Holloway, E.L. (1991). Relation of trainee experience, conceptual level, and supervisor approach to selection of audiotaped counseling passages. *Clinical Supervisor, 9*, 87–103.

Winter, R., Buck, A. and Sobiechowska, P. (1999). *Professional experience and the investigative imagination: the art of reflective writing*. London: Routledge.

Wood, J.A.V., Miller, T.W. and Hargrove, D.S. (2005). Clinical supervision in rural settings: a telehealth model. *Professional Psychology: Research and Practice, 36*, 173–179.

Woodward, H. (1998). Reflective journals and portfolios: learning through assessment. *Assessment and Evaluation in Higher Education, 23*, 415–423.

Worthen, V.E. and McNeill, B.W. (1996). A phenomenological investigation of 'good' supervision events. *Journal of Counseling Psychology, 43*, 25–34.

Worthen, V.E. and McNeill, B.W. (2001). What is effective supervision? A national survey of supervision experts. *Educational Resources Information Centre*. Retrieved 31 January 2008 from: www.eric.ed.gov/ERICDocs/data/ericdocs2sql/content_storage_01/0000019b/80/19/20/57.pdf

Worthington, E.L., Jr. and Roehlke, H. (1979). Effective supervision as perceived by beginning counselors in training. *Journal of Counseling Psychology, 26*, 64–73.

Wosket, V. (1999). *The therapeutic use of self: counselling practice, research and supervision*. London: Routledge.

Wright, J.K. (2005). A discussion with myself on paper: counselling and psychotherapy masters student perceptions of keeping a learning log. *Reflective Practice, 6*(4), 507–521.

Yaphe, J. and Street, S. (2003). How do examiners decide? A qualitative study of the process of decision making in the oral examination component of the MRCGP examination. *Medical Education, 37*, 764–771.

York-Barr, J., Sommers, W.A., Ghere, G.S. and Montie, J. (2006). *Reflective practice to improve schools: an action guide for educators*, 2nd edn. Thousand Oaks, CA: Corwin Press.

Yorke, M. (2003). Formative assessment in higher education: moves towards theory and the enhancement of pedagogic practice. *Higher Education, 45*, 477–501.

Young, P. (2000). 'I might as well give up': self esteem and mature students' feelings about feedback on assignments. *Journal of Further and Higher Education, 24*(3), 409–418.

Youngson, S.C. (2009). Personal development in clinical psychology: a context. In J. Hughes and S.C. Youngson (eds) *Personal development in clinical psychology*. London: Blackwell.

Author index

Subject index